MW01115441

TALKING THROUGH DEATH

Talking Through Death examines communication at the end of life from several different communication perspectives: interpersonal (patient, provider, family), mediated, and cultural. By studying interpersonal and family communication, cultural media, funeral related rituals, religious and cultural practices, medical settings, and legal issues surrounding advance directives, readers gain insight into the ways symbolic communication constructs the experience of death and dying, and the way meaning is infused into the process of death and dying. The book looks at the communication-related health and social issues facing people and their loved ones as they transition through the end of life experience. It reports on research recently conducted by the authors and others to create a conversational, narrative text that helps students, patients, and medical providers understand the symbolism and construction of meaning inherent in end of life communication.

Dr. Christine S. Davis is a Professor in the Communication Studies Department at the University of North Carolina at Charlotte. She received her BA degree from Virginia Polytechnic Institute and State University; her MA from the University of North Carolina at Greensboro; and her PhD from the University of South Florida, all in the field of communication studies. She publishes regularly on topics such as children's health, end of life communication, disability, and qualitative research methods.

Dr. Deborah C. Breede is a Professor of Communication and teaches communication, women's and gender studies, and graduate courses at Coastal Carolina University (CCU) in Conway, South Carolina. Her primary research, teaching, and service interests focus on the formation, development, maintenance, and challenges of community within a variety of contexts – including interpersonal and familial relationships; educational, cultural, and community collaborations; and during end of life experiences.

TALKING THROUGH DEATH

Communicating About Death in Interpersonal, Mediated, and Cultural Contexts

Christine S. Davis and Deborah C. Breede

Routledge
Taylor & Francis Group

NEW YORK AND LONDON

First published 2019
by Routledge
711 Third Avenue, New York, NY 10017

and by Routledge
2 Park Square, Milton Park, Abingdon, Oxon OX14 4RN

Routledge is an imprint of the Taylor & Francis Group, an informa business

© 2019 Taylor & Francis

The right of Christine S. Davis and Deborah C. Breede to be identified as the authors of this work has been asserted by them in accordance with sections 77 and 78 of the Copyright, Designs and Patents Act 1988.

Trademark notice: Product or corporate names may be trademarks or registered trademarks, and are used only for identification and explanation without intent to infringe.

Library of Congress Cataloging-in-Publication Data
A catalog record has been requested for this book.

ISBN: 978-1-138-23169-6 (hbk)
ISBN: 978-1-138-23170-2 (pbk)
ISBN: 978-0-429-50659-8 (ebk)

Typeset in Bembo
by Apex CoVantage, LLC
Printed and bound by CPI Group (UK) Ltd, Croydon, CR0 4YY

This book is dedicated to mothers and daughters, memories of loved ones, and all those who have loved and lost.

Christine Salkin Davis dedicates this book to her husband Jerry Davis, without whose support this book would not have been written, and to the memory of her parents, Margaret M. Salkin and Arthur J. Salkin, the memory of her grandson John Kumako, and to her grandson Jonah Kumako who represents all that is innocent and good for our collective futures. Deborah Breede dedicates this book to her husband Lenny Breede, without whose support this book would not have been written, and, to her "little Italian yankee southern belle," Marguerite Maria Carmelita Ferlauto Cunningham, aka "Mom."

CONTENTS

ACKNOWLEDGEMENTS

Christine Davis wishes to acknowledge, first of all, my co-author Deborah Breede, who has been a dear friend, colleague, and co-author for more years than it seems. From the day we said, "we should write something together!" she embraced this project, kept us on task, deepened and expanded the writing and made the book better and better; thank you for "playing" with me; it has been a delightful experience. From Florida to Myrtle Beach to Georgetown and Charleston, and to Newland, thank you for all the acres and miles of plantation ruins and graveyards, cemeteries, and museums we have walked together, time spent writing together in the mountains and at the beach and the wine sipped over warm girlfriend conversations and much laughter. Thank you to graduate research assistants Brittany Pailthorpe, Elizabeth Medlin, Robin Cavin, Rachael Thomas, and Emily Tamilin who materially assisted in the scope of this research and provided valuable research assistance and suggestions. For our work on Chapter 9, "Communicating about Death in Cemeteries and Burials," we would like to acknowledge and thank Rose Young and Friends of Old Westview Cemetery, Inc., for providing us with the necessary access and data to complete this project, for letting us enter this sacred space, and for their support of this project. Thank you also to the family members of people buried at Old Westview Cemetery for letting us hear their stories. Finally, thanks to Regina Young for her helpful feedback to an early draft, India Solomon and Dr. Akin Agundiran for their work at the cemetery and assistance with our early research on the cemetery, and especially to Dr. Jonathan Crane for his insightful contributions to the direction of the project. For Chapter 3, "Communicating about Death in Ghostly Lore," thank you to Sarah Pitzer for introducing me to ghost stories and the haunted wine shop, and to my sister Kelli for going ghost hunting with me so I wouldn't have to go alone. Thank you too for the many people we interviewed and observed in the course of this research. I also acknowledge the many mentors who have encouraged and supported my interest in end of life communication, including Buddy Goodall, Carolyn Ellis, Art Bochner, Ken Cissna, and Stacy Holman-Jones, among many others. I also want to acknowledge my colleague and friend Jon Crane who has nurtured my intellectual interest in cultural and film studies and end of life scholarship and has taught me greatly about writing and thinking deeply and thoughtfully, among other important things. I also acknowledge Jon Crane, Maggie Quinlan, Debbie Baker, and Jan Warren-Findlow for their support, partnership, and friendship and whose work in collaboration with me was represented in this book and was instrumental in moving this body of research forward. I want to thank other friends and colleagues who also continue to offer me support and encouragement and useful scholarly suggestions – Dan Grano, Jason Black, Ashli Stokes, Rachel Plotnick, Jaime Bochantin, Shawn Long, and Erin Basinger; and friends and family Barbara Eudy, Leslie Griffin, Sue Herberg, Glenn and Doris Simmons, Betty Russell, Kathy Salkin, and Kelli Salkin for their love and support. Finally, I want to thank my husband Jerry and daughter Robin for their ongoing love and support, and patience with phone calls not answered, things not done around the house, and multiple death-themed vacation trips.

Deborah Breede wishes to acknowledge, also first of all, my co-author Cris Davis. We began as graduate school cohorts at University of South Florida, became dear friends and colleagues, and now co-authors. We have shared more than we can remember: from being co-recipients of the Arthur P. Bochner Award for Outstanding Achievement in Doctoral Studies, 2003–2004, all the way to sharing a Top Faculty Paper Award, 2017; to sharing our homes with each other in the Carolinas; to sharing conference and paper presentations; we've shared bottles of wine over late night gossip sessions; and we've celebrated and consoled each other through joys and sorrows, births and deaths; laughter and grief. Thank you for sharing more with me than I can share here. I echo Cris's acknowledgement of our friend and colleague, Jan Warren-Findlow, who spent two years traveling and researching with us, and whose contributions to this work in thought and deed cannot be understated. We also must acknowledge George Chastain and Lee Brockington, the executive director and senior interpreter, respectively, at Hobcaw Barony, Georgetown, South Carolina. We could neither have completed this book nor much of this research without your kind assistance, valuable information, and steady support throughout these years. Thank you to undergraduate research assistants Ashley McCulley, Janae Drayton, Kelci Pike, and Louise "Bessie" Wilson, who also assisted in the scope of this research. I, too, acknowledge the many scholars and mentors who have encouraged and supported my interests, including Davis Houck, Michael Budd, Jane Jorgensen, Jennifer Erdely Mahato, and David Purnell, among many others. These scholars have both listened and spoken, generously and thoughtfully. I, too, want to gratefully acknowledge family members, many of whom are introduced within this book: my Mom and Dad, whose pride in my accomplishments has always been my greatest inspiration; my "Aunties:" Honey, Margaret, Joan, Marcia, Pat, and Violet; my cousin Carole; my brothers; my nephews; my uncles and grandfathers; and especially, my grandmothers, who never went to college, and always dreamed that I would. Finally, to my best friend and husband, Lenny, with whom all things are possible.

PREFACE

Genesis: Communicating about Death

Everyone dies, some far later than they wish, some far earlier than we wish, some long after they comprehend and some long before they understand.

Yet, you don't feel death – really feel it – until it comes home to you – until it is the death of someone you know and love.

I am grieving the loss of my grandson, the loss of holding him in my arms, feeding him, changing his diapers, playing with him. I am grieving the loss of my dreams of being there at the delivery, seeing him born, cutting the umbilical cord, holding him. I am grieving the opportunity to hold two babies, one in each arm, and overflow with infant love. I am grieving the sadness of his parents and the loss of the pure joy – untainted with sorrow – they waited months – years – to arrive. And I am grieving their inability to take their other newborn son home yet, having to wait hours to see either of their babies after they were born, and having to wait a day to hold them.

I am grieving the narrative breach. It wasn't supposed to happen this way.

Cris and Deb meander up the brick walkway to the iron gate leading into the Kingston Presbyterian Church Cemetery in Conway, South Carolina. The morning sun shimmers through the Spanish moss hanging from the huge oak trees. Cris studies the tan gravestones from across the fence, some crumbling, some shaded by the trees and the moss, the dappled shadows casting browns and grays on the stone faces.

"Spanish moss always reminds me of visiting my grandmother in Savannah," she says. "I would like my burial place to have Spanish moss!"

"I thought you wanted to be buried in that cemetery on the Ireland coast!" Deb says.

"That, too!" Cris says, laughing. "Good thing I plan to be cremated so I don't have to make a decision on a grave site."

"Then you'll just have to decide what you want Jerry to do with your ashes!" Deb says.

"If I'm dead, will it matter?" Cris asks.

"I think everyone's death matters," Deb says, turning somber. "To quote John Donne's famous line, 'any [one's] death diminishes me, because I am involved in [human]kind. Therefore never send to know for whom the bells tolls; it tolls for thee' (Donne/Alford, 1839, para. 3). Everyone's death matters because everyone's life matters."

Cris nods, and they walk silently for a minute. They peer over the wrought iron posts surrounding the cemetery and admire the lacy, ghostly foliage inside the cemetery. The sandy grass and sand-covered walkways are beautifully shaded by the large trees.

"What a perfectly appropriate place to visit on Halloween!" Cris says to Deb as she wanders toward the entrance sign.

"We should be here dressed as ghosts or zombies today," Deb says, laughing.

Cris walks through the gates and reads the entrance sign. "'Founded 1858,'" she reads aloud.

"'No dogs,'" Deb reads the next line.

"Too bad," Cris says, "I'd want my dog to visit my grave."

Cris heads to the first set of graves. She reads the two-foot-high head stone:

In memory of Henry B. Holmes born June 29, 1838; died October 9, 1841. His stay upon earth was transient, his residence in heaven eternal.

Next to this stone is another that says:

Henry the adopted son of Thomas H. and S. Jane Holmes died 29th October 1854 age 18 months and 1 day.

The foot stone on this grave reads:

Henry 1854.

"Oh, how sad," says Cris. "Graves of babies."

"Yeah," says Deb. "They are beautiful." She pauses. "Is this hard for you to see?"

"You mean because of John?" Cris asks. "I guess it makes me think of him, and Robin and Jonah, but I think of them all the time anyway."

Cris's twin grandsons John and Jonah were born a few months earlier, and John died at birth. Cris helped her daughter Robin make the arrangements with the funeral home and deal with the immediate emotional turmoil. "John was cremated," she says, even though she knows Deb has heard this story before. It's helpful to talk about it. "We got a beautiful heart-shaped urn, covered in tiny silver doves, to put his ashes in."

Cris pauses as she looks up at an eight-foot stone obelisk. "Husband and wife," she says as she reads the inscription.

"How is Jonah doing?" Deb asks.

"Good," Cris says. The twins were born six weeks early and Jonah, her second twin grandson, spent three weeks in the Neonatal Intensive Care Unit. "He's home now, feeding successfully, and gaining weight. He's healthy. And adorable of course. Robin and her husband are grieving appropriately," she adds. "How are you doing? I know this has been a tough year for you, with your mom and two aunts dying within ten months of each other."

"Yeah," Deb responds. "It's been the worst year of my life."

"Are you okay talking about it?" Cris asks.

Deb nods. "Yeah, some. I have some distance now, especially from my mom's death." She stops and faces Cris. "You know, after my mom was diagnosed with Alzheimer's in 2005, and then, deteriorated so quickly, I really thought the eleven years prior to her death would have prepared me better for her death."

Cris reaches out to rub Deb's arm. "I know that at one point during those years you prayed for her to die, and then at other times, you were so happy that you could visit her, touch her, smell her."

Deb looks around at the ornately carved marble tombstones and monuments surrounding them. She nods. "I really thought I was ready." Tears well up in her eyes and begin to spill down her cheeks, and she wipes at them angrily. "I don't think we're ever ready to lose someone we love as much as I loved my mom. Accepting the deaths of our loved ones is so hard."

"Yeah," Cris says. "Accepting our own death is hard, too. I think that generally people are so unprepared for death. We should talk about it more. Death is part of life; philosophers say our death is what makes our lives worthwhile."

Deb walks over to an elaborate black iron fence surrounded by magnolia and oak trees framing a family plot. Under the Spanish moss are two-foottall gravestones, white marble with a marble rose carved on top. Deb reads the inscription:

> Sacred to the memory of Norman Gurganus, son of William D. and Lucy A. Gurganus. Born May 10, 1867, died August 13, 1867. Of such is the kingdom of heaven.

"Three months old," Cris says.

Deb moves over to the second grave stone and reads:

"'William.' This is the dad. 'Born in Williamston, North Carolina July 18, 1836 died May 10th, 1870.' He died at 34 years old,"

Deb says, doing the math in her head.

"When his son Norman had been dead for three years," Cris notes.

Deb continues reading: "'He lived respected and died lamented by all who knew him.'"

"It's too bad they don't put epitaphs on gravestones anymore," says Cris. "It's such a beautiful way to memorialize the life of a loved one."

"Here are some more," Deb says, moving to another fenced in area of graves surrounded by more moss covered oak trees. "'Mary F. Pulidge,'" she reads from the white stone. "'86 years.' Next to her is 'William Heely, July 19th, 1831 – May 29th, 1900. At rest.'"

Cris reads from another stone close by:

> Our beloved mother Sarah Jordan, born in Green county, North Carolina. October 3rd, 1810 died June 8th, 1869. Age 59 years 8 months and 5 days. For many years a devoted Christian, she has gone to that home prepared for such as do as repent of their sins. Dearest mother thou has loved us and thy loss was deeply feel but tis God who has breathed us, he can have all our sorrows healed.

"Here's more virtues epitaphs," says Cris. "Gravestones that list gendered virtues – beauty for women, accomplishments for men. What does this one say?"

"'Raised in duty and affection,'" Deb reads. "'The early grave of Wife of William Durrant.'" She pauses; a break in the tombstone making deciphering it difficult. "'Exchanged time for eternity on the 8th October 1831.'"

"'Wife of,'" Cris says. "She didn't get her name on her own gravestone?"

They move along as they read.

> A.R., wife of J.H. Grant, MD. Born August 28th, 1813, died February 18th, 1881 in death as in life she was humble. She was triumphant.

"Hmph!" Cris says. "Another unnamed woman!"

"She was 'triumphant,' though," Deb says wryly.

"Triumphant," Cris repeats. "She may have been triumphant but she didn't even get her own name on her grave."

"She's dead and nameless," Deb says.

They move to an area resplendent with shade trees. The graves in this section are dated in the late 1800s. Some are knocked over, some are illegible. Based on the names, they seem to be related to each other.

"It starts as 'Anderson' and marries into 'Floyd,'" Deb reads.

"Then that's 'Anderson' again," says Cris.

"Here's 'M. Anderson' and 'Emory Floyd,'" Deb says.

"'Infant son of Emma Anderson and Emory Floyd. August 7th, 1900 – September 18th, 1900,'" Cris reads. "He lived to be a little over a month old."

They continue on, struggling to make out the words from the worn carvings.

> Mrs. Anna R. Burton, died September 4th, 1852, age 23 years 5 months and 9 days. Cold in the dust this perished heart may lie, but that which warmed it once shall never die.
>
> In memory of Samuel Thomas Burton who was born the 11th June 1815 and died 3rd October 1852. Sleep my son beneath this tomb til God shall bid you rise, then with angels, wing your way to him above the skies.

"They sure were poetic."

"They've got a whole theological treatise going on right there."

Like all cemeteries, Kingston Presbyterian Church Cemetery serves both functional and emotional purposes. As we will discuss in Chapter 9, cemeteries combine the sacred and the human, the religious and the mortal; they transcend space and time. They are also places of memory; spaces to remember emotional connections, relationships, lives lived, and loves lost. Cemeteries remind us that, beneath these gravestones, behind these names and dates carved into the headstones, were people who once had friends and hobbies, got angry and lusted, fought boredom and dangers. The dead were once us. They are our ancestors; they birthed us, raised us, and one day we will be them.

End of life practices and customs – the ways we memorialize the dead, remember them, and talk about them, are all related to individual and cultural identity. The way we die reflects history, culture, and traditions. Remembering the dead strengthens social, cultural, and personal identity; preserves relationships; validates our basic humanity; and creates communal legacies. Our practices and rituals socially construct a shared past and provide tangible ways to deal with the terrifying awareness of our mortal natures.

Understanding death has intrigued scholars, artists, writers, philosophers, and mere mortals throughout time. Death has inspired innumerable great works of art and literature, songs and poetry, conventional pastimes and leisure pursuits, interpersonal relationships, and professional services. In this book, we examine communication at end of life through cultural practices and rituals – material culture, popular culture, and religious communication; through mediated communication – news, television, film, and communication online; and through interpersonal communication – legal communication, family communication, and medical communication. We consider cemeteries and burials; monuments and memorials; thanatourism and horror films; elegies and laments; news stories about death and dying; breaking bad news and saying goodbye; and obituaries, eulogies, and funerals, as sites to examine the myriad of ways we communicate about end of life.

Communication at end of life matters because it shapes the quality of life before and after death for the dying and the survivors. Studying communication at end of life matters because a good death and a good life go hand in hand. Developing a relationship with death will help you deepen your relationship with yourself – who you are, where you come from, what road you are taking as you wander the pathways and detours of your life – your one life – as you live out your day-to-day existence from your date of birth to your date of death. Join us in this book as we each consider our mortality.

This book represents six years of fieldwork and writing, building on two decades of our own research on end of life communication and a lifetime of our personal experiences with the death and dying of loved ones. The information in this book is part empirical, part experiential, part a synthesis of the existing knowledge base. Working on this project, we utilized personal experience, participant observation, and in-depth interviews. We participated in ghost hunting activities and conducted in-depth interviews with paranormal investigators. We visited many different cemeteries, monuments, memorials, and museums. We watched horror films, war films, and other films about death and dying; read a myriad of poetry and literature, and listened to multiple songs about death and dying. We pored over news stories and obituaries, eulogies and epitaphs. We attended funerals and burials and memorial services. We talked to people who have had loved ones die; healthcare providers, patients, and family members; advocates for green burials and the home funeral movement; religious clergy and religious leaders; news professionals; and descendants of people buried in historic cemeteries. In this book, we discuss our previous research on end of life communication as well as new knowledge. Sadly, we've experienced many deaths of friends, family, and loved ones, and we incorporated our personal experiences into this book. We've also taught hundreds of graduate and undergraduate students in End of Life Communication classes.

This project is close to our hearts. When we discuss visiting a grave, you can be sure that we know what it feels like to sit at a grave and remember a loved one buried there, what it's like to watch a loved one die over weeks, months, and years. We have gotten the phone calls late at night and early in the morning, that call that tells us a loved one is dead, and we've rushed to the death, trying to still time as we raced. We know what it's like to enforce a DNR (Do Not Resuscitate Order) for a loved one, make the decision to discontinue life-prolonging treatments, and to watch an undertaker carry a loved one's body out of our home. We've picked out burial attire and cremation urns; we've made funeral and burial arrangements. We've cried and grieved and held others in their tears and grief. And, perhaps most importantly, we are well aware that – like you – we are mortal. Our own deaths loom large; we know that the actuarial tables tell us that we have more days behind us than ahead of us. You may be younger than we are, but your days, too, are numbered.

Much of this book is written as a narrative. As we discuss in Chapter 2, humans are story-tellers; we make sense of our lives through stories. Our lives have narrative trajectories, our story arcs have beginnings and turning points, plot twist and endings. Scholars tell us that one of the developmental tasks of our lives is to make sense of our personal narratives. Finding meaning in our deaths helps us find meanings in our lives.

When Cris's father died after an 18-month long, painful battle with prostate cancer, the point of life felt so futile to her. There is nothing that makes you face your own mortality like being forced to acknowledge that someone you love is permanently, intractably, forever, gone. Like many people before us, Cris asked why we are even born if our end is to be so painful, undignified, and seemingly pointless. Hanging around graveyards will teach you that, even for people who were seemingly important, who did significant things in their lives, it doesn't take long for most of us to be forgotten soon after we die. As we point out in this book, death interrupts our stories. It is part of being human that we have to write our stories without knowing how they will end – except that we do know they will end.

We are part of the march of humanity; people who have come before us influence the world in ways that affect everything about our lives. We, in turn, influence the world for our descendants, the people who will come after us. Our lives are our legacies. Living well translates into dying well. In this book, we take you through this mortal march from the point of view of our shared humanity. Chapters 1, 2, and 3 ponder the ways in which play, pastimes, and leisure activities about death (literally, playing with death) construct ideas about life and death. In Chapter 1, we take you through child's play and introduce you to the significance of our lives in the face of our deaths. In Chapter 2, we examine cultural artifacts about death and dying – mediated tales, poetry, novels, and songs about death and dying – to understand how these cultural narratives construct our joint ideas about our ends. We investigate ghost stories and ghost hunting in Chapter 3 and analyze how these after-death stories help us understand ourselves and our world.

In Chapters 4, 5, and 6, we probe death in the real world. We look at ways in which news stories construct and reflect ideas about death and dying in Chapter 4. In Chapter 5, we scrutinize interpersonal communication between patients, families, and healthcare providers. Chapter 6 considers what death looks like within the family. In Chapters 7 through 11, we analyze the ways in which we make meaning around both loved one's and stranger's deaths. In Chapter 7, we rhetorically analyze the stories we tell about a person's life in obituaries, our final life stories. Chapter 8 delves into the public performances of retrospective sensemaking, ritually bringing closure to a person's life in funerals and eulogies. In Chapter 9, we dissect material culture as we explore ways in which cemeteries construct ideas about our lives personally and communally. We examine epitaphs in Chapter 10, those short personal and public memorial statements about a person's life carved on tombstones. In Chapter 11, we consider what happens when death becomes public, when memory moves to the communal level within which meaning in death constructs ideas of nationalist identity.

When you finish this book, you should understand the macro and the micro contexts within which we all live and die. You should have a greater understanding of what it means to be mortal and a greater appreciation for our cultural reactions to our collective demise. You will become aware of the pervasive influence of death in our mediated, familial, social, and cultural worlds. We hope you will not only understand death in new ways, but we also hope that you will begin to embrace your life in new ways as well.

Reference

Donne, J./Alford, H. (Ed.). (1839). *The works of John Donne, vol. III*. London, U.K.: John W. Parker. Retrieved from: http://www.luminarium.org/sevenlit/donne/meditation17.php

1

TRICK OR TREAT: COMMUNICATING ABOUT DEATH IN CULTURE AND PLAY

"This is the last of it," Cris says as she dumps a bag of miniature Snickers candies into the orange bucket Deb is holding out. Cris peers into the almost full bucket. "Do you think this will be enough?" She takes a candy out as Deb takes the bucket out of her hands.

"I'm sure it will," Deb says with a confident air. "There's not that many kids in this neighborhood anymore." Deb lights the candle in the Jack-o'-Lantern in the window and dims the overhead light.

"Your decorations are awesome!" Cris says as she peeks out the window at the spider webs hanging from the front porch and the ghosts hanging from the trees.

"Thanks," Deb says. "Lenny loves to decorate, especially since his family's religious beliefs prevented him from going trick-or-treating when he was a kid. And our neighbors always do a lot of decorating for Halloween."

"That's funny," Cris says. "I was just reading that holiday decorating is strongly associated with neighborhood attachment. The more cohesive a neighborhood is, the more likely they are to decorate their homes and yards for holidays (Brown & Werner, 1985)." Cris nibbles on the candy as she settles in the couch to wait for the first trick-or-treater.

The doorbell rings. "Our first customer!" Cris says as they both jump up and head for the door. Deb grabs the bucket of candy as Cris opens the door.

"Trick or treat!" a chorus of children's voices calls out.

"How cute!" Deb and Cris say, exclaiming over the gaggle of miniature superheroes, brides, animals, and firefighters. "Here you go!"

A second group of kids arrive, this time three adorable little girls in coordinating princess costumes.

"You're such a beautiful princess!" Cris says as she puts handfuls of candy in their princess-themed bags.

"Halloween costumes are so gendered!" Cris exclaims as the girls move out of ear shot. "I've noticed that more of the costumes are of heroes than anything else but the heroes depicted are very gendered (Nelson, 2000). Policemen and warriors for boys, beauty queens and princesses for girls, and boys are more likely to dress up as symbols of death than are girls (Lennon et al., 2016; Nelson, 2000). And women's costumes are so hypersexualized (Lennon et al., 2016)!"

"Yes," Deb says. "My students dressed up for Halloween in class yesterday. You wouldn't believe how sexy some of the costumes were."

"Seven out of ten college students dress up for Halloween (Lennon et al., 2016)." Cris says. "I was reading recently that Halloween costumes are one of the main occasions in which women's clothes are most revealing, and the more revealing the costume, the more sexually objectified the woman (Lennon et al., 2016). Even elementary school costumes are sexualized (Boas, 2016)!"

"Halloween is such an interesting cultural event!" Deb says. "It's one of the few in which children play a central role. And while it's just play to them, their playful activities serve as ritualistic explorations of spirituality, death, and fantasy (Davis & Edwards, 1998; Skal, 2002). And of sex (Boas, 2016)! But their fantasies are rooted in reality; traditional race, class, and gender roles; and cultural symbols (Boas, 2016). For instance, girls' costumes are more likely to reflect passivity while boys' costumes are more likely to reflect agency. In this way, Halloween costumes reinforce gendered stereotypes (Nelson, 2000). Halloween also reinforces consumer culture (Boas, 2016; Skal, 2002), with so much money spent on decorations, costumes, and candy."

"Yes, it's so commercialized! Even the commercialization of Halloween is ritualized (Davis & Edwards, 1998; Nelson, 2000)!" Cris adds. "It's not Halloween if it doesn't include specific ritualistic symbols and activities – pumpkins, witches, ghosts, gravestones, skeletons, broomsticks, vampires, black cats, zombies, and trick-or-treating (Davis & Edwards, 1998). It's a co-mingling of the spiritual and the economic (Davis & Edwards, 1998); even spending money on the holiday has ritualistic elements."

"Yes," Deb says, grimacing. "I probably spent $50 at least just for candy!"

"And of course, it can only be certain kinds of candy. And how much do you suppose those princess costumes cost?" Cris asks.

Deb grabs her phone. She looks up a minute later. "Here's a Disney one for $44.49," she says. Her eyes widen. "Oh my gosh, here it says that in the U.S. in 2015, $2.53 billion was spent on Halloween costumes! Halloween is second only to Christmas in the amount of consumer spending – $950 million on costumes for kids! $350 million on costumes for pets (Lennon et al., 2016; Rogers, 2002)!"

"I can see you dressing up Wiley in a princess costume!" Cris says, laughing, as she looks over at Deb's large German Shepherd sleeping on the floor.

Deb laughs.

"Halloween is an interesting way that kids can play with identity and different social roles, with the idea of being somebody other than who they are (Davis & Edwards, 1998; Lennon et al., 2016; Skal, 2002)," Cris says thoughtfully. "And many of the costumes are of things that are supernatural, scary, forbidden, and ominous. They can pretend to be monsters or devils; they dress up as people or things they could never consider being in real life (Davis & Edwards, 1998). And, even though we think of small kids trick-or-treating when we think of Halloween, participating in Halloween is as much an adult pastime – 65% of American adults partake in Halloween festivities (Rogers, 2002)."

Deb nods, excited at the conversation. "Halloween is all about being masked and disguised (Davis & Edwards, 1998). And crossing boundaries, opportunities to cross the lines between life and death, human and non-human, good and evil, light and dark, feast and famine, and childhood and adulthood (Davis & Edwards, 1998). Halloween is also a subversive holiday. It's a subversion of authority; most of the activities take place after dark and 'trick-or-treating' is such a socialist activity!" Deb says. "And extortionist! Give me candy or I will play a trick on you (Davis & Edwards, 1998)!"

"Halloween has an interesting history," Cris says, looking down at her phone. "It's a type of Carnival, but in this one, the focus has been switched from adults to children. It has both a Christian and a pre-Christian tradition. The supernatural association came from Celtic folklore in which children's misbehavior on Halloween was blamed on fairies and ghosts. The Celtic festival of Samhain was a day to remember the dead and was a day in which evil spirits reportedly walked among mortals (Rogers, 2002; Skal, 2002). Wearing costumes comes from the customs of Druids who dressed up in costumes to hide their mortality from mischievous ghosts (Davis & Edwards, 1998; Nelson, 2000). And the holiday also has origins from the celebration of All Souls Day in which the souls of the dead were allowed to join the living, and in which a person would offer to pray for someone's soul in exchange for food or money (Davis & Edwards, 1998; Skal, 2002). In the 17th century, Halloween was noted for considerable masquerade celebrations (Skal, 2002). And isn't it related to Mexico's Day of the Dead celebration – *El Día De Los Muertos*?" Cris asks.

"Well, they're similar," Deb says. "Mexico's celebration is an All Soul's Day celebration also, but today it's still much more about memorializing specific loved ones than Halloween. They have food and flowers and some people do dress up, but it's more about remembering specific people, where with Halloween in the U.S., death is a more abstract concept. In the U.S. southwest, though, the two celebrations have become intertwined in practice. Day of the Dead celebrations include altars – called ofrenda – which are artistic exhibits with personal, political, and cultural meanings. The Day of the Dead remembrance is a responsibility people have to their deceased ancestors (Davis & Edwards, 1998; Santino, 1994)."

They are interrupted by the doorbell and spend the next 30 minutes handing out candy and admiring the children. When the costumed guests start getting bigger and taller and less frequent, they have time to catch their breath.

"Well," Cris says as they settle back down in their chairs between doorbells and munch on chocolate candy, "You can't escape death. We all will die someday. No matter who you are, your background, whether you take care of your body or not, some sooner and some later, we all will die."

Causes and Types of Death

We all will die. The most common causes of death include heart attack; old age; Alzheimer's disease; murder; accidents, suicide, and euthanasia; AIDS; viruses; and cancer (Nuland, 1993). Coronary heart disease is America's biggest killer – 1.5 million Americans suffer a myocardial infarction each year (Nuland, 1993). Among teenagers and young adults, death is more likely to occur from accidents, suicide, and homicide (Nuland, 1993). Life expectancy is affected by lifestyle issues such as smoking, frequency of visiting physicians, exposure to industrial pollutants and hazards, stress, and social support, as well as loneliness, diet, alcohol consumption, smoking, and exercise. The higher education level you have, the longer you are projected to live. Life expectancy of minorities is affected by environmental factors such as poorer health care, inadequate nutrition, inadequate housing and poorer living conditions. Life expectancy of people of lower SES (socio-economic-status) is affected by differential treatment by medical personnel and inadequate diagnosis (Nuland, 1993).

The death of a person does not occur all at once. Throughout our lives, cells die and are replaced with new cells, until you reach an old enough age when that doesn't happen as effectively or frequently. There are many different types of death (Aiken, 2001). Biological death is defined as either circulatory death: cessation of respiration – respiratory failure – the body's inability to get oxygen to the lungs and irreversible loss of function of the heart; or brain death (Aiken 2001). The Uniform Determination of Death Act says that you are dead when either of the following occurs:

1 irreversible cessation of circulatory and respiratory functions, or
2 irreversible cessation of all functions of the entire brain, including the brain stem (Sade, 2012, pp. 146–147).

This distinction is important in the case of organ donation in which a person might be brain dead but whose lungs and heart might still be working (and thus able to be used for transplantation) (Aiken, 2001; Sade, 2012). The diagnosis of death is usually made after a clinical examination by a physician to look for evidence of brain stem reflexes and respiratory function (Goila & Pawar, 2009).

When you die, your brain cells die first. Skin, nail, and hair cells and bone cells may remain viable for some time (Aiken, 2001). Social death is the term for when others act as if a person is already dead, prior to the actual death. If a person has a terminal illness, this frequently happens when people quit coming to visit because they can't bear to see a dying friend or loved one (Aiken, 2001). Legal death is a judgment by a legal authority that a person is dead, such as with people who are war MIAs (missing in action) and are declared legally dead after a period of time (Aiken, 2001).

Common folklore tells us that it used to be difficult to determine if someone was actually dead, and there were reports in the 16th through 19th centuries of people being accidentally buried alive. This is how the ritual developed of having a body lay in the parlor for three days, to be sure their loved one wouldn't wake up. And that's where the term "wake" came from; the loved ones would gather around to watch to see if their loved one woke up. Fortunately, today, with medical advances, it is quite unlikely that anyone would be accidentally buried alive.

Social Construction of Death and Dying

It bears repeating – we all will die. Despite that fact, what death *means* to us differs from person to person and culture to culture because the meaning of death is a social construction. The theory of social constructionism says that we construct ideas about how things are, about our reality, through communication – interpersonal, mediated, and cultural communication. In today's western culture, death is sensationalized (horror films), desensitized (reporting of war dead), and mystified (today, only 20% of Americans die at home) (Aiken, 2001). Of course, even though we try to ignore death, we are still exposed to many deaths in our lifetimes, and the ways in which death is presented to us affects the way we think of death. The graphic depictions of death on TV, fiction, and the news, and movies desensitizes us to violence (Aiken, 2001). War deaths have been so negatively portrayed in the past two or three generations that war deaths are seen as less heroic then they used to be (Davis & Crane, in press). Because our ideas about the nature of reality are socially constructed, the reality of death is experienced differently for various people. You probably know many people with diverse ideas about death. So, for example, some of us believe in an afterlife which might give us hope that death is not permanent. Some of us see death as a welcome release, or a passage to a better place. Some see death as a natural part of life. Others see death as an interruption, or deviation, from life. Many people imagine death as something mysterious or unknown. Others are sure they know what death will be like, despite the fact that no scientific evidence has proven someone has actually died and reported back. Attitudes toward death range from thinking of death as the enemy to accepting death, or even welcoming death. Most people are somewhere in the middle (Aiken, 2001). We tend to view death as something that happens to someone else but not to us. Some people are terrified of the thought of the inevitable deaths of themselves and their loved ones and see death as a "grim adversary to be overcome" (Nuland, 1993, p. 10). In fact, modern death practices attempt to "transform death into hope … [and] 'kill' death" (Seale, 1998, p. 3). Most of us avoid thinking about death so we can maintain an illusion of invulnerability. Despite the fact that modern western society has embraced an elaborate social organization for death (practices, rituals, beliefs), many of which we discuss in this book, today death is still removed and hidden from everyday life (Seale, 1998).

Denial and Fear of Death

Terror Management Theory (TMT) is based on Becker's (1973) book *Denial of Death*, in which he talks about human's universal fear of death. Becker says: "to see the world as it really is, is devastating and terrifying … it makes routine, automatic, secure, self-confident activity impossible. It makes thoughtless living in the world of [humans] an impossibility. It places a trembling animal at the mercy of the entire cosmos" (p. 60).

In trying to overcome death, or maintain amnesia about our own mortality, we pretend we are in control of our lives and our deaths. Sadly, in trying to prevent death, we make both our lives and our deaths more horrible, says Becker (1973). Because we try to manage our deaths, we don't allow ourselves to enjoy life. Becker suggests, "We repress our bodies to purchase a soul that time cannot destroy; we sacrifice pleasure to buy immortality; we encapsulate ourselves to avoid death. And life escapes us while we huddle within the defended fortress of character" (p. xiii). This fight against death enslaves us, fences us in, and prevents us from reaching our full potential. We create a life for ourselves that we consider to be manageable. We keep busy through frantic activity. We map out every inch of our lives. Beliefs in the afterlife give us hope that death is not permanent, and because of this, some people welcome death and see it as a passage to a more blissful state of being (Becker, 1973).

From time immemorial, humans have tried to overcome death. The first known tale of human's Search for Immortality is the Sumerian tale the *Epic of Gilgamesh* (Anonymous/Sandars, 1972), which was written on

clay tablets about 2100 BC. This story is about Gilgamesh who was a Mes-
opotamian king. Gilgamesh was a demigod – two-thirds God, one-third
human. Gilgamesh became anxious about his mortality and told his father,

> *Here in the city man dies oppressed at heart, man perishes with despair in his
> heart … I see … that will be my lot also ….Whoever is tallest among men can-
> not reach the heavens, and the greatest cannot encompass the earth ….*
> *Anonymous/Sandars, 1972, p. 72.*

> *I am afraid of death …. [My brother's] fate lies heavy upon me. How can I be
> silent; how can I rest? He is dust and I too shall die.*
> *p. 103.*

His father told Gilgamesh to accept his fate and enjoy life while he could:

> *Gilgamesh, fill your belly with good things day and night, night and day, dance
> and be merry, feast and rejoice. Let your clothes be fresh, bathe yourself in water,
> cherish the little child that holds your hand, and make your wife happy in your
> embrace, for this too is the lot of man.*
> *p. 102.*

Gilgamesh ignored his father's advice and went off in search of the land of
immortality. The rest of the Epic is the story of his journeys to the Land of
Living. He fought gods and men, crossed oceans and mountains. He finally
found a Garden of Life and after fighting with and convincing the gods guard-
ing the Land of Living, he was allowed inside. He was told the story of the
immortality of the gods and although he was told that mortals cannot avoid
death, he was given a plant that would grant him immortality. Unfortunately,
a serpent stole the plant and Gilgamesh was instead pursued by the Angel of
Death (Anonymous/Sandars, 1972; Sitchin, 1995).

Perhaps in some ways, we do control our death. Hospice workers frequently tell stories of people timing their deaths to wait for a certain date, or
a certain visitor, or for when they are alone (Davis, 2010). Demographics tell
us that people can postpone dying until occasions of great personal significance, birthdays, for example, are over (Aiken, 2001). Of course, we cannot
ultimately prevent dying, but we sometimes do have at least some measure of
control over how and when we die. Perhaps this is why some of us study end
of life issues, to try to develop a sense of control over our deaths. At least, if we
have to die, we can make it a "good death."

Paradoxically, death is terrifying to us but we are drawn to it. Our main
mission in life, suggests Becker (1973), is to transcend death, through projects
that seek to make us symbolically immortal. The irony is that, even though
we are symbolic creatures, able to temporarily forget and transcend death,

ultimately, we still will die. Sometimes, in the midst of closing our eyes to our mortality, things happen to make us remember that we will die, such as a loved one dying, or reading a book like this one. We use interpersonal, cultural, and mediated communication and discourse to construct and manage our fears, hopes, and desires about death and dying. We create culture and cultural rituals, suggests Becker (1973), to give us a sense of safety and security.

Terror Management Theory (TMT) (Rosenblatt et al., 1989) suggests that we are motivated by the desire to overcome our fear of death by constructing meaning and significance in our lives in various ways. A social psychology theory, TMT has been used to explain cultural worldviews, human cognition, and motivation in the face of mortality salience, or awareness of death. The secularization of death contributes to the cultural fascination with death and dying, suggest Stone and Sharpley (2008). As Becker and other terror management theorists argue, most modern societies have been separated from death. Once the purview of the home and church, death now is corporatized, commodified and hidden from view. We know it's there, always waiting for us; its presence is assured, yet our participation in it is lessened and/or absent. This "absent/present paradox" (p. 585) insures that we lack mechanisms to cope with our own assured mortalities, and thus, seek to cope through activities such as play, tourism, art and literature. Stone and Sharpley argue that "the more diverse (and reflexive) the approaches to death in contemporary societies, the more difficult it becomes to contain death within social frameworks and thus limit existential anxiety and the level of ontological security it potentially offers to the individual" (p. 583). The medicalization of death, and the resulting institutionalization of death, creates anxiety around death, and, as this book will discuss, we alleviate this fear through various activities by reconstructing the ideas of death and dying as something more enjoyable and less terrifying, providing us with an opportunity to deal with our own mortality in socially safe ways.

We play with death; dress up as death; create works of art, literature, and music in an attempt to understand and "tame" death (Becker, 1973, p. 238), to create a legacy, something of us that will remain long after we are gone. It is the way we live our lives, suggests Nuland, that gives meaning to our deaths: "the greatest dignity to be found in death is the dignity of the life that proceeded it …. Hope resides in the meaning of what our lives have been" (Nuland, 1993, p. 242).

The Significance of Death

Death is ubiquitous – whether we are willing to face the knowledge or not, the fact that we all will die permeates our entire lives. As Seale (1998) suggests, "our bodies give to us both our lives and our deaths so that social and cultural life can, in the last analysis, be considered as a human construction in the face of death" (p. 8).

Death is both personal and communal – when you are thinking of your own death, it's intensely personal, but when you're thinking of the death of a loved one, it is intensely relational. Death not only has the power to end an individual life, but it also disrupts relationships, families, cultures, social order itself (Seale, 1998). Death is also relational, suggests Davis (2010) in that it's important to develop a relationship with death itself that approaches a dialogic relationship – a relationship that deeply accepts, embraces, and understands death, so that you become comfortable with it, because it is inevitable that you will be touched by death many times over in your lifetime. To enter into a dialogic relationship with death requires approaching the idea of death with openness and curiosity, in order to face death directly and courageously (Davis, 2010).

Humans are the only creatures with the knowledge of our own death, and thus, we have the unique opportunity to seek to understand our own eventual demise. We suggest that studying death is important to bring into the open something that has traditionally been taboo. We think being open to understanding death is a healthy way to approach what will affect us all, as we have said. We also like to study death as a site of communication because death makes all forms of communication more poignant. Death infuses all forms of communication with heightened symbolism and significance. Death also makes life itself more significant. Death gives life meaning. The inevitability of death brings value to life, says Popper: "if there was no end to life, life would have no value. It is the ever-present danger of losing it which helps to bring home the value of life" (Popper, 1977, p. 148).

Visibility of Death

In the early 19th century, most people in the U.S. died at home. Now, most Americans die in hospitals, clinics, medical centers, and nursing homes (Aiken, 2001). In the Middle Ages and the Renaissance, death and dying were more visible. Public executions, mortal fights, and mass epidemics were common and made death quite visible. For instance, the Black Plague killed 25% of the population of Europe during the 14th century and death was an everyday occurrence (Aiken, 2001). Dying people used to hold death rituals in their own bedrooms. Family members, physicians, priests, and legal representatives gathered around the beside and these rituals might last for days. People were able to say goodbye and this was believed to let the dying person die in peace (Aiken, 2001). Today, this ritual has evolved into funerals, and these are pretty quick and minimal, even the more formal ones, compared to the days-long rituals of the past.

Nowadays, as we've said, we rarely witness death and this makes us hide it, deny it, and pretend it won't happen to us. The more experience we have with death, the less we are afraid of it (Aiken, 2001). Today, 80% of Americans die in a hospital, so few of us actually witness the death of a loved one. Most people agree that an ideal death would also be a death with dignity and without suffering or pain. Ironically, most of our deaths frequently aren't dignified because of the dramatic treatments we inflict upon dying patients in our attempts to delay death (Nuland, 1993). Modern dying takes place in a hospital where we think we can overcome death. In speaking of death in the hospital, Nuland (1993) suggests that "the quest to achieve true dignity fails when our bodies fail" (p. xvii). Modern efforts to control death represent efforts to interfere with death's normal progression by trying to control what we consider to be premature death, resisting deliberately imposed death (through prohibiting it as "murder" for example) and relieving the physical suffering of dying. Unfortunately, in attempting to control death, we actually increase its uncertainty, which then leads to the appearance of death as something that is unnatural and to be feared (Seale, 1998).

Philosophies About Death and Dying

Death and dying raise many ultimately unanswerable existential questions. An awareness of mortality makes people concerned with the significance of their lives, and philosophers throughout the ages have pondered the concepts of living and dying, mortality and immortality.

For instance, in considering the importance of the dead body, many philosophers, poets, and writers throughout time have argued for the value of the human body, reasoning that the body matters because it is, simply, a body – once alive, once human, once us, as poet Thomas Traherne wrote, "eyes, hands, and feet they had like mine" (qtd. in Laqueur, 2015, p. 55).

Many other scholars, however, have suggested that once we are dead, we will have no awareness of our death, and concern about our deaths was considered, to scholars such as Freud, Wittgenstein, and Lucretius, to be, as Laqueur (2015) said, "an act of projection: attributing our own thoughts and emotions into nature, a case of acting as if there were someone there when we know there is not" (p. 57). Diogenes believed that the body does not matter after we are dead (Laqueur, 2015), and Epicurus (341–270 BC) said that death is simply the end of existence (Aiken, 2001). Similarly, 17th century philosophers Hobbes, Milton, Locke, and Newton believed in no existence after death (Laqueur, 2015).

Other philosophers, writers, and thinkers imagined different forms of an afterlife – some with maintenance of family and relational bonds (Laqueur, 2015). Socrates (469–399 BC) and Aristotle (384–322 BC) believed in the existence of a soul, and 18th century philosopher Georg Hegel (1770–1831) said death is the reconciliation of the spirit with itself; a reuniting of the individual with cosmic matter (Aiken, 2001).

Philosophers have also tackled the question of how one can live with the knowledge of one's own mortality. Epicurus (341–270 BC) said that we should focus on enjoying life as it lasts. Socrates (469–399 BC) and Plato (427–347 BC) both said that we should be cheerful in the face of death since death is preferable to life. Aristotle (384–322 BC) said that it is easy to be courageous in death if it is a noble death, and 19th century philosopher Ludwig Feuerbach (1804–1872) said life must be lived fully in spite of death. Martin Heidegger (1889–1976) said that a person's life becomes more purposeful when s/he faces his/her own death, and Jean-Paul Sartre (1905–1980) said that the constant awareness of death intensifies the sense of life – faced with the inevitability of a personal ending, we try to live a life that will have some social significance (Aiken, 2001).

Simmel (2007) said that life and death are two sides of the same coin and rely on each other for definition. In other words, life has no meaning without knowledge of our death. Life and death, in fact, intersect because death gives boundaries to life. Therefore, death forms our life, just as our lives give shape to our deaths. Death hovers over us all the time but rarely actually affects us, and for most of us, life reaches a high point before we begin our decline toward death. Of course, said Simmel (2007), we are continually dying – death is an ever-present reality. Death makes us stronger. It continually colors and influences each aspect, each moment of our lives. In order to live, we must die. We can't have one without the other. Because of this, death makes life more meaningful. While, says Simmel (2007), most of us don't spend every moment thinking about our deaths, we do live every moment as mortal beings.

Hyde and McSpiritt (2007) suggest that it is our language (rhetoric) of perfection that motivates our aversion to thinking about death. They suggest that, compared to the perfection of God, we are imperfect people – insignificant, incomplete, and unstable. Yet, we are always striving to be perfect. Illness, aging, disabilities, and death proves we are imperfect. This causes us to feel despairing and helpless. Hyde and McSpiritt (2007) suggest that our wish to make something of ourselves – to be significant, beautiful, pure, and perfect – is a reaction to our mortality. The concepts of a good death, and a good life, stem from our desire for perfection. Of course, we do understand at some level that we are not perfect until we die. Throughout our lives, we strive for perfection as we strive to be the best person we can be. These scholars suggest that perfection is a God term, associated with God. Yet, if God is associated with eternal life, then is death imperfect, they ask. Or is death a means to achieve perfection? When a loved one dies, or we receive a serious diagnosis ourselves, we face a disruption, "a moment of truth" (p. 156). The distinction between life and death (or varying degrees of both) can be based on an individual and/or cultural definition of perfection (Hyde & McSpiritt, 2007).

Playing with Death

Our inevitable deaths, say scholars, are so out of our control that the only way we can rob death of its sting is by choosing our reactions to it. Humor, play, laughing, or joking – "creative illusion[s]" to Becker (1973, p. 190) – are possible ways to maintain the pretense of control over our mortality. Playful activities, then, let us "try on" death without actually having to deal with its reality (Davis & Crane, in press). Play is a type of activity with specific cultural meaning (Bateson, 1956; Goffman, 1986). Play is how children make sense of their world (Becker, 1973). We play with our bodies, our environments, our behaviors, to test things out in non-threatening arenas. Play mimics real-life activities, but, of course, it is not the same thing as those real-life activities. For instance, baby animals play-fight with each other, but they don't actually bite each other. Human children do the same thing, and in case the person with whom we're playing isn't sure what side of the reality/play divide we're on, we assure her, "I'm just playing!" Bateson (1956) calls these frames, or keys, referring to the bracketed behaviors that fall under specified, socially expected, behaviors. Play falls under the frame or category of make-believe, in which we mimic serious behaviors but don't actually engage in them. Play requires what we call metacommunication – communication about communication – the overarching understanding that what I'm doing now is "just playing." We communicate when play starts and stops through various verbal and nonverbal signals or cues.

We test out death through play as well, and, of course, Halloween and its accompanying costuming, candy eating, decorating, partying, and trick-or-treating are forms of play. We play with death throughout our childhood, and our cultural death play starts as early as when our babies are newborn. Lullabies and nursery rhymes, the most innocent and gentle sounding of songs and poems, paint grim stories of political espionage, kidnapping, and torture. *Rock-a-Bye Baby*, for example, reportedly represents the accusation that the son of King James II of England was an illegitimate heir and a thinly veiled threat to the to the monarchy line (Listverse staff, 2009).

> Rock-a-bye baby, in the treetop
> When the wind blows, the cradle will rock
> When the bough breaks, the cradle will fall
> And down will come baby, cradle and all

London Bridge ("is falling down") is reported to be about children being entombed alive in the London Bridge as sacrifices to keep the bridge safe (Listverse staff, 2009). *Three Blind Mice* ("she cut off their tails with a carving knife") is said to tell the story of three men who plotted against Queen Mary I and were subsequently burned at the stake (Kidd, 2010). *Humpty Dumpty* ("had a great fall") is speculated to be about the downfall of either King

Richard III of England or Cardinal Wolsey at the hand of King Henry VIII (Listverse staff, 2009). *Mary Mary Quite Contrary* ("how does your garden grow?") is about Queen Mary I, her instruments of torture, and a graveyard (Kidd, 2010; Listverse staff, 2009).

Other childhood pastimes – storybooks and games, for example – offer opportunities to play with death, and in the process, offer some advice for the living. Western childhoods are full of death play: séances, Ouija Boards, and sitting around the campfire telling ghost stories. Many families have spent countless hours playing the murder mystery board game *Clue*. The childhood staple *Little Red Riding Hood* ("all the better to eat you with, my dear!") tells the tale of a little girl attacked by a wolf who had first eaten the girl's invalid grandmother. This story offers a caution for young ladies to steer clear of wolves of all kinds. The simple game of Hangman is a word game won by constructing a dead man hanging from a gallows. The popular children's game, Cowboys and Indians, or the myriad of war games children play, are ways to – literally – play *with* death. Children playing war are not simply playing *about* death. Think of what happens when a child is play-killed in a game. They literally play dead. They clutch their chest, stagger across the yard, make choking sounds, and dramatically die.

Video games represent another way we offer death play to youth. The average U.S. male adolescent spends over 40 minutes a day playing video games. The game *Grand Theft Auto* was famously sued after two teens reported that their fatal shooting spree was inspired by the game (ABC News, 2003), and video game violence has been accused of contributing to societal violence (Smith et al., 2003). Violence is a key ingredient in 68% of interactive video games, and according to Smith et al., (2003), "those who select games rated [Teen or Mature] may witness over 180 incidents of aggression per day or 5,400 incidents per month" (Smith et al., 2003, p. 70).

In all of these instances of play we've mentioned, the play is predicated on the basis that the object of our activity – play death – is not authentic. However, another type of play – thanatourism – that vacation pastime in which tourists visit graveyards, ghost haunts, monuments and memorials, and sites of death and destruction – is centered on the opposite notion. The attraction to thanatourists is that they are indeed exploring actual locations on which can be found historical, spiritual, material, and cultural evidence of death and dying. For most of us, playing with the authenticity of death is only palatable because it is real for another, not ourselves.

All of this playing with death lets us practice death and dying in a non-threatening way. These games give us an opportunity to better know death, and thus, fear it less. These types of death play represent resistance play – using the frame of playing in order to fight against things we are not supposed to fight against – power, cultural rules, social roles, and – even death. In this sense, they are resistance against many types of death:

social death, legal death, and physical death. These stories, games, songs, warn us to stick close to our cultural expectations, and they communicate beliefs and superstitions about death, the afterlife, about one's place in society, about power, about strangers, about justice, just to name a few. Death play conquers our fear of death by controlling it. You may be playing Cowboys and Indians, and perhaps today you are an Indian who gets play-killed by a cowboy, but you remain in control of your death; you die the way you wanted to die, and tomorrow you'll get to be the cowboy and do the killing.

Conclusion

As we have made clear in this chapter, we will all die, and this certainty is terrifying for most of us. In fact, we suggest our mortality is the most significant feature of our lives. Regardless of what you might believe about a possible afterlife, or the amount of fear you have about death, or your level of awareness of your own death, your looming death affects every facet of your life. In this chapter, we discuss how life and death – like reality and play – are two sides of the same coin, each side helping us understand the other, each side enhancing the significance of the other. From ringing doorbells dressed as Zombies and Sleeping Beauty; to *Ring Around the Rosie* sung by children during London's plague to explain the horrors they saw around them; to *London Bridge is Falling Down* to explain the consequences of such social disorder; to the word game Hangman; children's games, stories, and make-believe are full of death-defying activities. We play games with death as children, use death as a rite of passage as adolescents, and visit death as adults. We eat dinner with death at "murder mystery tours" and "bear witness" at sites such as Auschwitz, Buchenwald, and a Shanksville, Pennsylvania field. We masquerade as death at cultural celebrations such as *El Día De Los Muertos*, and we plan vacations around opportunities to visit historic cemeteries, places of death. Making death our friend, we suggest, avoids making an enemy of death. And should at any time that precarious balance fail, we have an even greater need to get close to death. We are drawn to these depictions of death, yet we are simultaneously repulsed by them. Although tourists flock to murder mysteries, cemetery tours, *El Día De Los Muertos* celebrations, archeological digs, and other such locations of death, there are no dark tourism sites on the Top 25 worldwide tourist destinations (Stein, 2015). Terror Management theorists suggest that we play with death in order to understand death, and we have also shown that we play with death in order to understand life. We try to control death through fighting it, ignoring it, overcoming it, understanding it, and finding meaning and significance in it. Life, and death – each enhances the poignancy of the other.

References

ABC News. (2003 September 6). Did video game drive teens to shootings? Retrieved from: http://abcnews.go.com/GMA/story?id=124797

Aiken, L. R. (2001). Dying, death, and bereavement. Mahwah, New Jersey: Lawrence Erlbaum.

Anonymous/Sandars, N. K. (1972). The epic of Gilgamesh. London, England: Penguin.

Bateson, G. (1956). The message "this is play". In Schaffner, B. (Ed.), Group processes: Transactions of the second conference. pp. 145–242. New York: Josiah Macy, Jr. Foundation.

Becker, E. (1973). The denial of death. New York: Free Press.

Boas, E. M. (2016). Education in disguise: Sanctioning sexuality in elementary school Halloween celebrations. Sex Education, 16(1), 91–104.

Brown, B. B., & Werner, C. M. (1985). Social cohesiveness, territoriality, and holiday decorations: The influence of cul-de-sacs. Environment and Behavior, 17(5), 539–565.

Davis, C. S. (2010). Death: The beginning of a relationship. Cresskill, NJ: Hampton Press.

Davis, C. S., & Crane, J. L. (in press). Crossing over: Media and mortality in the Dead Zone. New York, NY: Routledge.

Davis, R. A., & Edwards, L. D. (1998). Children and spirituality in the context of a traditional festival: Halloween. International Journal of Children's Spirituality, 3(1), 9–34.

Goffman, I. (1986). Frame analysis: an essay on the organization of experience. Boston, MA: Northeastern University Press.

Goila, A. K., & Pawar, M. (2009). The diagnosis of brain death. Indian Journal of Critical Care Medicine, 13(1), 7–11.

Hyde, M. J., & McSpiritt, S. (2007) Coming to terms with perfection: The case of Terri Schiavo. Quarterly Journal of Speech, 93(2), 150–178.

Kidd, N. (2010). The hidden history of nursery rhymes. Education.com. Retrieved from https://www.education.com/magazine/article/hidden_history_of_nursery_rhymes/

Laqueur, T. W. (2015). The work of the dead: A cultural history of mortal remains. Princeton, NJ: Princeton University Press.

Lennon, S. J., Zheng, Z., & Fatnassi, A. (2016). Womens' revealing Halloween costumes: Other-objectification and sexualization. Fashion & Textiles, 3(21). 1–19. doi: 10.1186/s40691–40016–0073-x

Listverse staff. (2009). 10 nursery rhymes and their origins. Retrieved from: http://listverse.com/2009/08/19/10-nursery-rhymes-and-their-origins/

Nelson, A. (2000). The pink dragon is female: Halloween costumes and gender markers. Psychology of Women Quarterly, 24, 137–144.

Nuland, S. B. (1993). How we die: Reflections on life's final chapter. New York, NY: Vintage.

Popper, K. R. (1977). How I see philosophy. In Mercier, A., & Silvar, M. (Eds), Philosophers on Their Own Work, Vol. III. p. 148. Peter Lang: Bern, Switzerland.

Rogers, N. (2002). Halloween: From pagan ritual to party night. New York, NY: Oxford University Press.

Rosenblatt, A., Greenberg, J., Solomon, S., Pyszczynski, T., & Lyon, D. (1989). Evidence for terror management theory I: The effects of mortality salience on reactions to those who violate or uphold cultural values. Journal of Personality and Social Psychology, 57, 681–690.

Sade, R. M. (2012). Brain death, cardiac death, and the dead donor rule. Journal of the South Carolina Medical Association, 107(4), 146–149.

Santino, J. (1994). Halloween: And other festivals of death and life. Knoxville, TN: University of Tennessee Press.

Seale, C. (1998). Constructing death: The sociology of dying and bereavement. Cambridge, UK: Cambridge University Press.

Simmel, G. (2007). The metaphysics of death. Theory, Culture, & Society, 24(7–8). 72–77.

Sitchin, Z. (1995). Divine encounters: A guide to visions, angels, and other emissaries. New York, NY: Avon.

Skal, D. J. (2002). Death makes a holiday: A cultural history of Halloween. New York, NY: Bloomsbury.

Smith, S. L., Lachlan, K. A., & Tamborini, R. (2003). Popular video games: Quantifying the presentation of violence and its context. Journal of Broadcasting and Electronic Media, 47, 58–76.

Stein, A. (2015). Attracting attention: Promotion and marketing for tourism management. New York, NY: Peter Lang.

Stone, P., & Sharpley, R. (2008). Consuming dark tourism: A thanatological perspective. Journal of Tourism Research, 35(2). 574–595. doi: 10.1016/j.annals.2008.02.003

2

SHOW AND TELL: COMMUNICATING ABOUT DEATH IN FICTIONAL NARRATIVES

The doorbell has not rung for 15 minutes.

"Maybe it's dying down now," Cris says. "That was quite a rush for a while!"

Deb nods. "That was a lot of trick-or-treaters for around here! I didn't realize we had so many neighbors with small kids. You ready for the movie?"

Cris nods and grins in anticipation. *The Shining* (Kubrick, 1980) is one of her favorite horror films. The Stanley Kubrick classic is based on the Stephen King novel about supernatural forces at a remote Colorado hotel. *The Guardian* (Billson, 2010) named it as one of the top five best horror films of all time.

"Best horror book of all time, too!" Deb says as they settle down in their seats to watch the story of a father Jack, mother Wendy, and young son Danny facing down ghosts, alcohol, and insanity at the almost-empty Overland Hotel.

The film opens with foreboding horn music in the background and they are traveling down a river, scene shaky at first, then they are flying, an island coming closer, then fading to a long shot of a car driving down a forest road, up a long mountain road, heading toward snow covered mountains.

"That is some creepy music," Cris says.

"That music is called 'Dies Irae,' 'The Day of Wrath,' from Berlioz' *Symphony Fantastique*," says Deb. "It was played in the Catholic requiem mass. It was also played in *Fasut*, with its storyline of despair, condemnation, and self-destruction" (Kearns, nd-a).

The music turns even more eerie as percussion, strings, and shakers join the horns and the scene turns desolate; there is a long shot of the Volkswagen driving along cliff edges, prisms of light playing with the focus as the opening credits roll.

About 30 minutes into the movie, inside the cavernous Overlook Hotel, Danny rides his Big Wheel down the service hallway, the kitchen everywhere around him, then he rides down the lobby, then the lounge, the camera at wheel height as he rides round and round the hotel; Wendy, wearing her blue, yellow, and pink bathrobe, wheels a silver service breakfast cart down the service hallway, into the guest hallway, bringing juice, coffee, eggs, and bacon to Jack in bed. A scene later, Jack types on his Adler manual typewriter, with a lit Marlboro in the ashtray next to him. Another scene later, Jack bounces a ball against the wall (Kearns, nd-b).

"I will never be able to walk down another carpeted hotel hallway without seeing this film in my mind!" Cris says. She anticipates the impending plot, "… and I don't know whether to be more afraid of the ghosts or of the caretaker, Jack!"

Deb nods. "It's so interesting how Jack is at the hotel to keep it safe and clean and in order, but it's his own weaknesses – his alcoholism and anger – that adds to the chaos and the evil."

"Second best horror book, I think, is the sequel to *The Shining, Doctor Sleep* (King, 2013)", Cris says as they take a break to refresh their drinks. "I love that book. Danny Torrence, the little boy in *The Shining*, is grown. He's an alcoholic and is haunted by the ghosts from the Overlook Hotel. His possession of the 'shining,' the psychic energy he had as a child in *The Shining*, is strong enough that he is able to use it to comfort people who are dying. My favorite line is, 'we're all dying. The world's just a hospice with fresh air' (King, 2013, p. 66)."

Deb nods and quotes, "'The only way through is to embrace death' (King, 2013, p. 30). It's about a group of people – The True Knot – who are immortal by feasting on the psychic energy of children who have the shining. Danny has to embrace his gift to use telepathic communication and astral projection to rescue a friend from this group (Stephen King Wiki, nd)."

Cris nods. "My other favorite classic horror film is George Romero's (1968) *Night of the Living Dead*," she says, as Deb hits "play." "The 1968 landmark film is about a group of people who take refuge in an abandoned house to escape a horde of zombies. It started the zombie craze that is still popular today. It's also a great sociological examination of a group under stress and trauma."

"It's really interesting how these popular cultural artifacts convey what our culture values and believes about life and death," Deb says.

"Yes!" Cris says. "For instance, according to *Night of the Living Dead*, death is scary, bleak, and gruesome. I love how the female lead Barbara keeps asking, 'what's happening?' She never gets an answer. Death is unknown."

Deb and Cris watch the television in silence. In the next scene:

> *Jack … storms around the hotel, making his way to the Gold Ballroom. Sinking defeatedly into a stool at an empty bar, his head in his hands, Jack declares that he would sell his soul for one drink. When he looks up he discovers a bartender …, who serves him a drink. Jack is nonplussed by the sudden appearance of the*

bartender and even addresses him by his name, Lloyd. In the course of telling his troubles to Lloyd, Jack reveals that he unintentionally dislocated Danny's shoulder, the same accident Wendy mentioned to Danny's pediatrician earlier. Notably, Jack states that the injury happened three years ago, while in explaining the same story to the pediatrician, Wendy said that Jack, who vowed to quit drinking immediately following the accident, has currently been sober for only five months.

A frantic Wendy enters, finding Jack seemingly alone at the bar; she pleads with him to investigate Danny's claim that a "crazy woman" attacked him in the bathtub of Room 237. Jack, who acts a bit tipsy, grudgingly agrees to go have a look.

As Jack approaches the door to Room 237, Danny appears to be having a seizure in his own room. Dick, [one of the seasonal workers whom we've met in a previous scene, who is back at his home in Florida,] stares wide-eyed as he picks up on a signal Danny is sending.

Jack cautiously enters Room 237. The bedroom is empty and he proceeds to the bathroom. He watches lustfully as a young, beautiful, naked woman … pulls back the shower curtain and steps slowly out of the bathtub. The two approach each other and embrace in a passionate kiss. Jack catches a glimpse of their reflection in the mirror and sees the woman is actually a rotting corpse. He recoils in horror – the young lady standing before him has transformed into an elderly woman … ; a walking corpse with rotten, sagging skin. She cackles madly while reaching for him with outstretched arms. Stunned, Jack staggers out of the room, locking the door after him.

When he reports back to Wendy, Jack … becomes irate, … he storms out, returning to the Gold Room, which is now the scene of an extravagant party with guests dressed in 1920's fashion. Lloyd serves him a drink and Jack strolls through the crowd.

IMDb The Shining *Plot, para 13–17.*

"I've always been a fan of the ghoulish," Cris says. "I loved Edgar Allan Poe when I was young. Still do. 'The Tell-Tale Heart' (Poe, 2006a) and 'The Cask of Amontillado' (Poe, 2006b) were my favorites. In 'The Tell-Tale Heart,' the narrator kills an old man because he hates the man's eye, cuts up the body and buries it under the floor. He confesses the perfect murder to the police because he is convinced he hears the man's heart beating underneath them. In 'The Cask of Amontillado,' the narrator revenge-kills a man by luring him deep into an underground crypt where he chains him to the wall and then bricks up the opening. Another perfect murder."

"Poe wrote stories with strong symbolic meaning about death," says Deb. "In Poe's world, some people deserve to die. Also, in Poe's stories, people who commit murder are insane, yet we sympathize with them and are horrified by them at the same time. In many of Poe's works, death comes at night. Midnight is the hour of death."

They turn back to the movie. Havoc has broken loose. Jack has an axe and is trying to kill Wendy and Danny. He manages to kill Dick Halloran, the Overlook Hotel employee who is alerted of the danger through his shining power and has returned back from vacation to try to save Danny and Wendy. Cris and Deb sit at the edge of their seats as Danny runs outside in the swirling snowstorm, Wendy fights ghosts to follow Danny, and Jack chases Danny into the tall hedge maze outside. Danny emerges from the maze as Jack gets increasingly lost deep in the maze. Danny and Wendy escape as Jack freezes to death, hopelessly lost in the maze.

Cris turns to Deb. "Danny embraces his supernatural abilities to overcome the evil at the hotel. An awareness of our death requires a conscious choice to abide in the face of terror. Once we accept death, we overcome it."

The cultural ramifications for death as both a taboo subject yet also an entertainment topic are many. Our mediated communication about death and dying, through films, books, television shows, performances, and music serve as a macro-level backdrop to constructions of both our cultural ideas about death and dying as well as our culturally approved and constrained behaviors at end of life (Seale, 1998). Death in the media is a social and cultural activity which frames death as something to fear at the same time as it serves as a coping mechanism by allowing audience members an opportunity to practice the idea of dying and to detach themselves from death (Davis & Crane, 2015, Davis & Crane, in press; DeSpelder & Strickland, 1999; Durkin, 2003; Leming and Dickinson, 2002; Schultz and Huet, 2000; Seale, 1998).

The Creative Impulse

The realization that our days are numbered and that death may be waiting just around the corner has challenged people since antiquity to make the most of their lives and leave their mark upon the world. Death, mysterious since the dawn of civilization, has always moved humans to create poetic and emotional accounts. Cultural rituals and practices reified superstitious beliefs and were captured in material and creative works of art (Ariès, 1981) The creative impulse – Eros – is the opposite of death, destruction, and personal extinction. Related to creation is procreation – the continuation of ourselves through our offspring, again, the opposite of death. We create – and procreate – through art and love, and art about love, as a response to the fact we will die someday (Aiken, 2001; Becker, 1973; Crane & Davis, 2016, Davis & Crane, in press).

Themes of life and death have been represented in religious and commemorative purposes, in painting, sculpture, architecture, music, memorials and monuments, gravestones, coffins, cemeteries, and death announcements. These works of art reveal something about the artist and his/her historical time, especially fears of annihilation and punishment, hopes for an afterlife, and a desire to understand and represent the human condition. Deathbed scenes in works of art and ancient narratives – tales of the *Knights of the Round Table* and *Tristan and Isolde*, for instance, convey accounts of loss, grief, fear, aversion to death, regret, and acceptance. Marchant's 15th century woodcut taken from the French mural featuring realistic representations of decaying bodies and accompanying poetry depicting death called *Danse Macabre* states, "Many long for death. Not I" (Ariès, 1981, p. 15), and a character in the 17th century French literature *Fables* says "O death, leave me alone" (Ariès, 1981, p. 15). Similar is the 16th century *Triumph of Death*, a large painting depicting the end of the world with skeletal remains attacking the living, representing "the collective power of death" (Ariès, 1981, p. 18).

Many sculptured scenes on tombs and caskets have been commemorative, designed to keep alive the memory of the dead in the minds of the living. Memento mori tombs in late Middle Ages, for instance, were decorated with an effigy of a naked decaying corpse below a picture of the deceased as he/ she appeared in life. The purpose of this double image was to illustrate the corruption of death and its egalitarian nature (Aiken, 2001).

Of course, throughout time, religious artwork, literature, and iconography has depicted the beliefs of the day surrounding death and the afterlife. For instance, the 15th century Last Judgment fresco in Albi, France, has pictures of the saved and the damned naked souls (Ariès, 1981). The 15th century *artes moriendi*, "treatises on the art of dying well" (Ariès, 1981, p. 105), depicts one's book of good deeds weighed against one's book of evil.

Today, you might see death personified, depicted, or symbolized in films and other popular culture as an angel of death, a rider on a pale horse, the Grim Reaper, twin brothers of sleep, coffins, cemeteries, amputated limbs, deathbeds, skulls, bones, vultures, an inverted torch, a clock set at the hour of death (midnight to 1 a.m.), a skeletal figure with an hourglass, Father Time with scythe, winter landscapes, ruins, leafless trees, trees struck by lightning, dead birds, gray skies, rain, thunder in graveyards, burial scenes, birds, butterflies, or beetles (Aiken, 2001). Death and dying are such personal, confusing, mysterious, painful, and mystical experiences, sometimes poetry and artwork, literature, and mediated stories are the only ways we can communicate about it.

Of course, when you consider mediated depictions of death and dying, you have to consider that – as in life – almost all feature films have death as part of either a plot line or backstory. But there are many genres of mediated fiction that foreground death as a key part of the story. Davis and Crane (in press) divide films with death foregrounded into several categories: horror films; dark comedies; war films; action-adventure and disaster movies; and romantic movies.

Films About Death and Dying

The horror genre – be it mediated through cinema, television, short story, or novel – is one of the genres most connected with death and dying, in which death as a central character entertains the imagination (Davis & Crane, 2015). Of course, scholars recognize that horror fiction does not have one uniform goal and much of the genre seeks to represent other goals than simply familiarizing us with death – horror fiction is also read as a metaphor for war, corruption, and political, social, and economic anxiety; and many of the horror works are centered around themes of anti-science, gender, rebellion, and forbidden desire, among others (Bishop, 2009; Crane, 1994; Davis & Crane, 2015; do Vale, 2010; Keisner, 2008; Trencansky, 2001). Still, horror fiction plays on both our fear of and fascination with death and dying and provides a safe space in which to give in to our basest instincts to kill self and other, and to look closely at the other side of the life-death dialectic (Davis & Crane, 2015).

Humans are universally afraid of death, especially of unexpected or violent death (Becker, 1973). One of the things we are most afraid of at end of life is being out of control (Davis & Crane, in press). Horror fiction (films and novels) exploit this fear to evoke a sense of terror in the audience. They use suspense and gore to create a terror beyond that which we experience in our everyday lives (Crane, 1994), to communicate that there is a fate worse than death, and it is fear. The horror genre, identified as such by the evocation of a visceral fear-based reaction or revulsion, lets us feel something, whether it be terror, grief, or defensiveness, and particularly a fear that we too could face the same fate as the horror victim (Crane, 1994; Davis & Crane, 2015; Kinal, 2000). Horror fiction takes advantage of our fears to remind us that real life is scary – that potentially around every corner harm awaits (Crane, 1994).

Horror fiction – featuring monsters of all sorts, including vampires, werewolves, zombies, ghosts, human–animal hybrids, science experiments gone awry, and other scary humans, animals, and beings – is exemplified by classic movies such as the aforementioned Romero's 1968 zombie narrative *Night of the Living Dead* (Romero, 1968) and numerous sequels, and Kubrick's supernatural *The Shining* (Kubrick, 1980) based on King's book. Other famous works of horror include Mary Shelley's *Frankenstein* (Shelley, 1818/1922) about a scientist's monstrous creation; 2013's zombie story *World War Z* (Forster, 2013) about a zombie world takeover; the vampire movie *Interview with the Vampire* (Jordan, 1994) the personal story of a vampire; the 2001 supernatural thriller film *The Others* (Amenábar, 2001) about a woman and her children who live in a house in which the world of the dead and the world of the living are intertwined; and the many iterations of *The Fly* (Cronenberg, 1986) about a scientist who turns into a human fly. The 1950s and 1960s films starring Vincent Price are classic horror, such as his scary *House on Haunted Hill* (Castle & Horvath, 1959), about a group of friends who spend the night in a haunted house; and 1953's *House of Wax* (DeToth, 1953) about a wax museum populated with wax-covered corpses; among many others. Other novels by author Stephen King – and the movies made from his novels – are also classic examples of terror fiction. King's 1974 *Carrie*, about a teenage girl with telekinetic powers, and *Misery* (1987), a psychological thriller about a writer whose insane fan captures and tortures him are two of the scariest books and movies ever produced. Of course, no discussion of fictional horror, terror, thriller, or the supernatural is complete without mentioning films by director Alfred Hitchcock (e.g., *Psycho* (1960) about a woman terrorized in a secluded motel – the famous shower-slashing scene is responsible for many a nightmare; and *The Birds* (1963) about a woman attacked by thousands of birds). Horror fiction has frequently permeated the television screen also. *Dark Shadows* (Curtis, 1966–1971) was a daytime serial about a vampire and his family – its episodes go back and forth in time and tell the story about the cursed family living in a castle supernaturally imbued in Maine. The more recent highly rated television show *The Walking Dead* (Darabont, 2010), is about a post-zombie apocalypse world.

In horror fiction, suggest Davis and Crane (2015), the undead – whether vampires, zombies, or ghosts – represent a third space in which the living and the dead come together, and provide a way to bring the viewer closer to death in order to develop an acceptance and familiarity with the idea of our own mortality. Horror, then, is an avenue through which to play with death, examine it, try it out, and experience it, without actually going through with it (Davis & Crane, 2015). Horror tales are allegories for life and death, depicting what Simmel (2007) suggested is an "organic conceptualization" of death as "a shaping moment of the continual course of life from its beginning" (p. 75). Davis and Crane (2015) propose these stories suggest an alternative reaction to death – a dialogic one, in which the viewer embraces death for the release it provides from the pain of life and for the completion it gives to our lives.

Undead monsters in horror fiction define both the living and the dead in terms of their difference from each other, and – in the same way – define human and non-human. The undead have some significant differences and similarities among their ranks as well. Whether vampires, zombies, or ghosts, all are undead, all stuck at the point of death, in a liminal space, suspended, unable to move to it or away from it. They are neither alive nor dead because they are instead both alive and dead. All were once alive, and still exist in some sort of superhuman existence – all either will not or cannot entirely cease to exist. All remain undead by feeding off their victims and they infect their victims by consuming them (zombies consume the flesh, vampires the blood, and ghosts the mind), consigning their victims to the same liminal fate, maintaining the status quo for all eternity. In this way, the undead remind us that all of us are subject in a moment's change to be one of them (Davis & Crane, 2015).

In many ways, the undead still hold vestiges of being human and in other ways they are supra-human. Zombies lumber, vampires fly, and ghosts appear and disappear seemingly at will. Zombies, vampires, and ghosts are stronger, faster, and better than us. They've shed their elements of humanity which weaken us, and added elements of un-humanity that strengthen them – absence of conscience, emotion, pain, fear, self-consciousness, repulsion, remorse. They have superhuman strength, they don't get tired, and they don't age. They have superhuman sensory ability. They are human but not fully human. They are dead but not fully dead (Davis & Crane, 2015). Their liminal undeadness leads us to examine the question of what does it mean to be fully human, fully alive, fully yourself. The "undead" remind us that, even as we are half mortal and half immortal beings (Becker, 1973), with one foot in the grave, so to speak, we are still fully human because we are not monsters (Davis & Crane, 2015). The monsters in horror films – human flies, birds, and insane fans, are too, in a liminal space – not quite human, not quite monster, not quite civilized; they turn our expectations of life upside down.

In horror films, any of us could be the next victim. Regardless of rank, socio-economic status, education level, personality, or physical beauty, we are all subject to attack from the grim reaper of the moment. Horror films equalize death – no matter the youth, beauty, power, or wealth of the horror victim, all will ultimately die, and they remind us that death always comes, unexpectedly, in a life full of dreams and plans; death always interrupts a life in the midst of being lived (Davis & Crane, 2015). Death brings diverse people together. Horror stories remind us that in this world are people who are dead before they die; people who are socially dead, cut off from society and unable to function.

Horror films also teach us to resist death and, say Davis and Crane (2015), give us a visible enemy, something tangible we can fight – the monster, the vampire, the zombie, the attacking animals, the ghost, represent the cancer, brain damage, organ failure, poverty that threatens us. In this way, also, horror films personify the agonizing decision whether or not to discontinue life-prolonging treatment for a dying loved one. Watching one's seriously ill child or spouse or parent being kept alive through artificial means is, truly, a horror, and horror films let us articulate that, and they convey the idea that there are things enormously worse than death. Thus, in personifying the horror of death, these horror stories represent our epic struggle between life and death, forces of light and dark; they are metaphors for the minute by minute decisions and actions in hospitals, doctor's offices, and hospices (Davis & Crane, 2015). Horror films represent our attempts to live and to die on our own terms, to have some control in the midst of being out of control (Davis & Crane, 2015). They teach us that, ultimately, the key to overcoming death is to understand and accept its inevitability (Davis & Crane, 2015) and they teach us how to interact with full knowledge of our own death.

Of course, horror is not the only medium or genre that embraces death. For instance, there are many comedies in which death is a central part of the plot. Known as black humor, gallows humor, or dark humor, humor about the macabre, tragedy, or suffering is also a coping mechanism, a way to express an emotion about death other than fear or horror. Humor is a method of controlling our reactions to negative situations. This type of humor, says Davis and Crane (in press), is a farcical reaction to a meaningless situation. *The Adams Family* (Levy, 1964–1966), for instance, a popular television show in the mid-1960s and the story of a macabre family with supernatural powers, was a spoof on monster films. The 1983 *National Lampoon's Vacation* (Ramis, 1983) is about a family's cross-country vacation in which Aunt Edna and her dog Dinky both die and the trip continues with Aunt Edna strapped to the roof of their station wagon. *Throw Momma from the Train* (DeVito, 1987) is a 1980s comedy that plays off of the Hitchcock film *Strangers on a Train* to materialize a double murder. *Beetlejuice* (Burton, 1988) is a satire of ghost stories in which a couple die and haunt their home to rid themselves of the new owners. As we are writing this, we note that none of these plots sound funny as we describe them. Yet, they are laugh-out-loud funny to watch. As Davis and Crane (in press) claim, black humor lets us use humor to inject hope into an otherwise hopeless, sad situation. Black humor repels the horror of death because death is relegated to the backseat while we laugh together at the temporary suspension of reality (Davis & Crane, in press). In black humor, people who are powerless, put upon, taken advantage of, momentarily rule the day and we laugh as the bully gets his/her due (Davis & Crane, in press).

War films, action-adventure and disaster movies, and murder mysteries necessarily heavily involve death in the plot line. *Saving Private Ryan* (Spielberg, 1998) is a World War II drama about the reality of war and the human resilience to overcome hardship. *Apocalypse Now* (Coppola, 1979) is a drama about the horrors of the Vietnam War.

The film *Wonder Woman* (Jenkins, 2017), *Captain America* (Johnson, 2011), and a myriad of others of the same genre are based on comic book superheroes who save the world from annihilation and destruction. *Raiders of the Lost Ark* (Spielberg, 1981) is an action-adventure film about an archeologist who fights Nazis, others, and supernatural forces to recover the Ark of the Covenant.

Murder on the Orient Express (Branagh, 2017) is a recent remake of a suspenseful who-done-it film based on the 1934 Agatha Christie novel of the same name. Detective Poirot spends the film solving a murder on an Istanbul to London train and in the process, illustrates the way in which one's death – and life – intertwines with and affects so many others. *Basic Instinct* (Verhoeven, 1992) is a murder drama and erotic thriller in which a detective becomes involved with a murder suspect in a case he is investigating.

In these genres, the plot centers around, literally, fighting death as well as fighting-with-death – death as a tool of battle (Davis & Crane, in press). Like the material monuments of war (see Chapter 11), films about war either valorize or critique the institutionalized killing in a war zone. Regardless of the side taken, these films, like their action-adventure or mystery counterparts, carve heroes out of the fight against death. The death in these films is a menacing evil, but – unlike in horror fiction or the real life "war on cancer" – the good guys usually come out ahead in these battles. In war films, our heroes fight death with grit, determination, and weaponry; in action-adventure films, with courage supplemented with superhuman strength or powers; and in mysteries, with intelligence (Davis & Crane, in press). In all of these genres, it is death itself that is the enemy and the heroic protagonist conquers it in the end. Death is dehumanizing – it threatens to take away the basic humanity from those whose path it crosses. The hero's aim, therefore, is to maintain humanity, to draw upon the resilience of the human spirit, to fight to the end. Even if the hero dies, the basic building blocks of humanity – valor, courage, strength – ultimately cannot be killed (Davis & Crane, in press).

There are movies that romanticize death, that tell stories about death and grief, in which the key plot line is the death of a main character. *Love Story* (Hiller, 1970) is a film about a pair of mismatched lovers and a tragic death, a modern-day *Romeo and Juliet*, that interrogates love, family, and the way in which death forges bonds. *Terms of Endearment* (Brooks, 1983), a 1983 film, is about a woman, her mother and her cheating husband, and how her death reconciles them all. These are love stories in which farewells are merely turning points and love endures, even after death – especially after death. *Ghost* (Zucker, 1990) is a film about the ghost of a murdered man that solves his crime and loves his grieving widow from beyond the grave. This film crosses genres – it romanticizes death, it is a murder mystery, and it is a ghost story. Romantic stories such as these utilize death and love as opposing plot points in which they battle over the protagonists and ultimately call a draw – with both love and death surviving the end (Davis & Crane, in press). The death-bed scenes in these films are reminiscent of the deathbed scenes in ceremonial deaths through the Middle Ages – dramatic, poetic, erotic, and emotional (Ariès, 1981).

Poems and Literature About Death

From Milton's *Paradise Lost* (1667/2012) about human's fall and death as the consequence of sin (Daniel, 1994), to the poetry of Walt Whitman and Emily Dickinson which embrace death, to the elegies and laments of poets like Dylan Thomas and A. E. Housman, poetry is another art form in which we utilize creativity to come to terms with our eventual demise. As a case in point, poet Walt Whitman's (1855/2016) *Leaves of Grass* can be read as Whitman's fascination with mortality (Aspiz, 2004). Whitman was well acquainted with death, having lost numerous family and friends throughout his life, but his treatment of death was open and imaginative, sensitive and celebratory, respectful albeit uncertain (Aspiz, 2004). Whitman's poetry was regarded as particularly insightful and brave about death. To Whitman, death was both a tragic loss and a passage into an afterlife, and Whitman embraced both mortality and the spiritual soul. In his poem "Song of Myself," in which Whitman stands in a graveyard, praises the dead, and embraces mortality (Aspiz, 2004), Whitman writes, "It is not chaos or death — it is form, union, plan — it is eternal life — it is Happiness" (qtd. in Aspiz, 2004, p. 6). In "Tomb Blossoms," an early poem of Whitman's, Whitman writes of the grave as "a kind friend" who is responsible for "the weary spirit shall no more be weary, and aching head and aching heart will be strangers to pain, and the soul that has fretted and sorrowed away its little life on earth will sorrow not any more" (qtd. in Aspiz, 2004, p. 15).

Emily Dickinson's vast number of poems about death are, as Cooney (1998), states, invitations into the light of death, a recognition that we cannot understand our lives without understanding our deaths, or "affirm[ation of] our own souls and [a] stand [that is] 'adequate, erect' toward life" (p. 248). Cooney gives as examples Dickinson's famous "Because I could not stop for Death — He kindly stopped for me — " (Dickinson, 1958a, p. 86) and "I felt a Funeral, in my Brain, And Mourners to and fro … " (Dickinson, 1958b, p. 86). Dickinson's embrace of death can be seen in this poem, says Cooney (1998, p. 247):

> Of Death I try to think like this
> The Well in which they lay us
> Is but the Likeness of the Brook
> That menaced not to slay us,
> But to invite by that Dismay
> Which is the Zest of sweetness
> To the same Flower Hesperian,
> Decoying but to greet us.

Irish poet Dylan Thomas wrote many poems about death, including his "A Refusal to Mourn the Death by Fire of a Child in London" (1945) about World War II. Despite his frequent dark themes, Thomas's poems were said to be as joyful as they were sad (Brown, 2009).

Contrasted with Whitman's embrace of death, Dickinson's appreciation for death, and Thomas's appreciation for life in the face of death, is the 19th century consolation literature, written frequently by women for loved ones and children who died. One such poem of this genre is quoted in Ariès:

> His soul did from this cold world fly,
> By falling down a well.
> They got him out and emptied him;
> Alas it was too late.
> *Ariès, 1981, p. 452.*

Elegies are laments written to mourn someone's death. Perhaps one of the most famous elegies is Dylan Thomas's (1952) emotional lament over his father's death, "Do Not Go Gentle into That Good Night":

> Do not go gentle into that good night,
> Old age should burn and rave at close of day;
> Rage, rage against the dying of the light.
> Though wise men at their end know dark is right,
> Because their words had forked no lightning they
> Do not go gentle into that good night.
> Good men, the last wave by, crying how bright
> Their frail deeds might have danced in a green bay,
> Rage, rage against the dying of the light.
> Wild men who caught and sang the sun in flight,
> And learn, too late, they grieved it on its way,
> Do not go gentle into that good night.
> Grave men, near death, who see with blinding sight
> Blind eyes could blaze like meteors and be gay,
> Rage, rage against the dying of the light.
> And you, my father, there on the sad height,
> Curse, bless, me now with your fierce tears, I pray,
> Do not go gentle into that good night.
> Rage, rage against the dying of the light.
>
> *p. 239.*

Whitman's "Oh Captain! My Captain!" is a classic lament, reportedly in response to the death of Abraham Lincoln, that closes with these lines:

> My captain does not answer, his lips are pale and still,
> My father does not feel my arm, he has no pulse nor will.
> The ship is anchor'd safe and sound, its voyage closed and done,
> From fearful trip the factor ship comes in with object won;
> Exult O shores, and ring O bells!
> Walk the deck my Captain lies,
> Fallen cold and dead.
>
> *Whitman, 1958, p. 30.*

A. E. Housman's poem "To an Athlete Dying Young" is an elegy written for a funeral of a young man. It laments the tragedy of young death.

> The time you won your town the race
> We chaired you through the market-place;
> Man and boy stood cheering by,

And home we brought you shoulder-high.
Today, the road all runners come,
Shoulder-high we bring you home,
And set you at your threshold down,
Townsman of a stiller town.
Smart lad, to slip betimes away
From fields where glory does not stay,
And early though the laurel grows
It withers quicker than the rose.
Eyes the shady night has shut
Cannot see the record cut,
And silence sounds no worse than cheers
After earth has stopped the ears.
Now you will not swell the rout
Of lads that wore their honours out,
Runners whom renown outran
And the name died before the man.
So set, before its echoes fade,
The fleet foot on the sill of shade,
And hold to the low lintel up
The still-defended challenge-cup.
And round that early-laurelled head
Will flock to gaze the strengthless dead,
And find unwithered on its curls
The garland briefer than a girl's.
Housman, 1958, p. 162.

Songs About Death

Oh where, oh where can my baby be?
The Lord took her away from me.
She's gone to heaven, so I've got to be good,
So I can see my baby when I leave this world.
from Last Kiss, *Tarver, 1999,*
multiple releases.

The pop song *Last Kiss* (Tarver, 1999), recorded by numerous singers over the years, most recently a hit song in 1999 by Pearl Jam, is a song about a fatal auto accident and offers the oft-repeated storyline of a passionate love story interrupted by death and the resurrection of the relationship after death in the strength of their love (Crane & Davis, 2016).

Teenage death songs about tragic teen deaths proliferated in the 1960s and ushered in a genre known as "splatter platter" which continues to this day. Another of this genre is 1964's *Leader of the Pack* (Morton et al., 1964) recorded by the Shangri-las. This song tells a story about a teenage girl whose parents made her break up with her bad boy boyfriend. In his grief over the breakup, the boyfriend ("the leader of the pack") was in a fatal car wreck (the song features the shouted line "Look out! Look out! Look out!" and the sounds of squealing tires and crashing metal) (Crane & Davis, 2016).

> He sort of smiled and kissed me good bye
> The tears were beginning to show
> As he drove away on that rainy night,
> I begged him to go slow, whether he heard,
> I'll never know. Look out! Look out! Look out!
> I felt so helpless, what could I do
> Remembering all the things we'd been through?
> In school they all stop and stare
> I can't hide the tears, but I don't care
> I'll never forget him, the leader of the pack
> Ooh, the leader of the pack now he's gone
> the leader of the pack now he's gone
> the leader of the pack now he's gone.

1952 Vincent Black Lightning (Thompson, 1991), released by Richard Thompson, is about a bad boy, a tragic death, and a motorcycle, and also features a final kiss (Crane & Davis, 2016):

> And I don't mind dying, but for the love of you
> And if fate should break my stride
> Then I'll give you my Vincent to ride
> Come down, come down, Red Molly, called Sergeant McRae
> For they've taken young James Adie for armed robbery
> Shotgun blast hit his chest, left nothing inside
> Oh, come down, Red Molly to his dying bedside
> When she came to the hospital, there wasn't much left
> He was running out of road, he was running out of breath
> But he smiled to see her cry
> And said I'll give you my Vincent to ride
> Says James, in my opinion, there's nothing in this world
> Beats a 52 Vincent and a red headed girl
> Now Nortons and Indians and Greeveses won't do
> They don't have a soul like a Vincent 52
> He reached for her hand and he slipped her the keys
> He said I've got no further use for these
> I see angels on Ariels in leather and chrome

Swooping down from heaven to carry me home
And he gave her one last kiss and died.

Teen Angel (Surry, 1959), released by Mark Dinning in 1959, tells the story of a teenage girl killed by a train in another car wreck scenario. This song ends with a haunting spoken line, "Answer me, please?" (Crane & Davis, 2016).

Just sweet sixteen and now you're gone
They've taken you away
I'll never kiss your lips again
They buried you today
Teen angel, can you hear me?
Teen angel, can you see me?
Are you somewhere up above?
And I am still your own true love.

These songs – and a plethora of others of the death ballad genre – tell stories of tragic, uncontrollable, fatal circumstances from the point of view of surviving friends and loved ones, or – in some cases – from the viewpoint of the deceased teen. Every bit as poignant as Shakespeare's *Romeo and Juliet*, Housman's lament, or Whitman's elegy, these songs set to music heartbreak and grief, and plotlines of heroism, passion, and "the magnetic allure of endless, inexhaustible love" (Crane & Davis, 2016, p. 807). Erotic love, suggest Crane and Davis (2016) is a counteraction to our grief over death and loss, creation being the antithesis of annihilation (Becker, 1973). These songs suggest that love conquers death, that death in fact is the culmination of a deep and abiding love, that love is fulfilled through a tragic death.

Conclusion

Whether through tears forming in the corners of our eyes, goose bumps raising on our arms, hair standing up on the back of our necks, or belly laughs until our sides hurt, death in fiction – films, television, literature, or poetry – gives us an opportunity to use our bodies – literally – to come to terms with our mortality. Love and death, say Crane and Davis (2016), "make us feel truly alive" (p. 817). So, too, we suggest, does fear and laughter. Storytelling, engrossment in someone else's life, fictionalized accounts of tragedy, sustains us, comforts us, provides an escape from our own fears and suggests ways we might cope with our own losses. Stories help us understand our own experiences (Coles, 1989; Frank, 1995) and fiction lets us try out new characters, emotions, and approaches to difficult experiences in safe spaces (Davis & Warren-Findlow, 2011). We live our lives as stories, suggest Burke (1973) and Fisher (1987), and storytelling is a universal way we work through all the difficulties of our lives (Davis & Warren-Findlow, 2011). Whether sunk into a cushiony chair reading a novel, lying on the grass with a book of poetry, or on the edge of our seat at a horror film, absorbing ourselves in a story about death brings us face to face with the mortality of humanity and reminds us, we are all just passing through.

References

Aiken, L. R. (2001). Dying, death, and bereavement. Mahwah, New Jersey: Lawrence Erlbaum.

Amenábar, A. (2001). The others. [film]. United States: Cruise/Wagner Productions.

Ariès, P. (1981). The hour of our death: The classic history of Western attitudes toward death over the last one thousand years. New York, NY: Vintage.

Aspiz, H. (2004). So long! Walt Whitman's poetry of death. Tuscaloosa: The University of Alabama Press.

Becker, E. (1973). The denial of death. New York, NY: Simon & Schuster.

Billson, A. (22 October 2010). The Shining: No 5 best horror film of all time. The Guardian. Retrieved from: https://www.theguardian.com/film/2010/oct/22/shining-kubrick-horror

Bishop, K. (2009). Dead man still walking. Journal of Popular Film and Television, 37(1), 16–25.

Branagh, K. (2017). Murder on the Orient Express. [film]. United States: Twentieth Century Fox.

Brooks, J. L. (1983). Terms of endearment. [film]. United States: Paramount.

Brown, T. (2009). The Irish Dylan Thomas: versions and influences. Irish Studies Review, 17(1). Retrieved from: http://www.tandfonline.com/doi/full/10.1080/09670880802658133?scroll=top&needAccess=true

Burke, K. (1973). The philosophy of literary form. Berkeley, CA: University of California Press.

Burton, T. (1988). Beetlejuice. [film]. United States: Geffen.

Castle, W., & Horvath, R. (1959). House on Haunted Hill. [film]. United States: William Castle Productions.

Coles, R. (1989). The call of stories: Teaching and the moral imagination. Boston, MA: Houghton Mifflin.

Cooney, W. (1998). The death poetry of Emily Dickinson. Omega, 37(3), 241–249.

Coppola, F. F. (1979). Apocalypse Now. [film]. United States: Zoetrope Studios.

Crane J. L. (1994). Terror and everyday life: Singular moments in the history of the horror film. Los Angeles, CA: Sage.

Crane, J. L., & Davis, C. S. (2016). Baby, let me follow you down: The love-death dialectic in story and song. Qualitative Inquiry. 807–817.

Cronenberg, D. (1986). The fly. [film]. United States: SLM Production Group.

Curtis, D. (Producer). (1966–1971). Dark Shadows. [television series]. United States: ABC.

Daniel, C. (1994). Death in Milton's poetry. Lewisburg, PA: Bucknell University Press.

Darabont, F. (2010–). The Walking Dead. [television series]. United States: AMC.

Davis, C. S., & Crane, J. L. (2015). A dialogue with (un)death: Horror films as a discursive attempt to construct a relationship with the dead, Journal of Loss and Trauma, 20(5), 417–429. doi: 10.1080/15325024.2014.935215

Davis, C. S., & Crane, J. L. (in press). Crossing over: Media and mortality in the Dead Zone. New York, NY: Routledge.

Davis, C. S., & Warren-Findlow, J. (2011). Coping with trauma through fictional narrative ethnography: A primer. Journal of Loss and Trauma, 16, 563–572.

DeSpelder, L. A., & Strickland, A. L. (1999). The last dance: Encountering death and dying. Mountain View, CA: Mayfield.

DeToth, A. (1953). House of Wax. [film]. United States: Warner Brothers.

DeVito, D. (1987). Throw Momma from the Train. [film]. United States: Orion.

Dickinson, E. (1958a). Because I could not stop for death. In Williams, O. (Ed.), A pocketbook of modern verse: English and American poetry of the last 100 years. p. 86. New York, NY: Simon & Schuster.

Dickinson, E. (1958b). I felt a funeral in my brain. In Williams, O. (Ed.), A pocketbook of modern verse: English and American poetry of the last 100 years. p. 86. New York, NY: Simon & Schuster.

do Vale, S. (2010). Trash mob: Zombie walks and the positivity of monsters in western popular culture. At the Interface/Probing the Boundaries, 70, 191–202.

Durkin, K. (2003). Death, dying, and the dead in popular culture. In Bryant, C. D., & Peck, D. L. (Eds.), Handbook of Death and Dying. pp. 43–49. Thousand Oaks, CA: Sage.

Fisher, W. R. (1987). Human communication as narration: Toward a philosophy of reason, value, and action. South Carolina: University of South Carolina Press.

Forster, M. (2013). World War Z. [film]. United States: Paramount.

Frank, A. (1995). The wounded storyteller: Body, illness, and ethics. Chicago, IL: University of Chicago Press.

Hiller, A. (1970). Love story. [film]. United States: Paramount.

Hitchcock, A. (1960). Psycho [film]. United States: Paramount.

Hitchcock, A. (1963). The birds. [film]. United States: Universal.

Housman, A. E. (1958). To an athlete dying young. In Williams, O. (Ed.), A pocketbook of modern verse: English and American poetry of the last 100 years. p. 162. New York, NY: Simon & Schuster.

IMDb. (nd). The Shining Plot. Retrieved from: http://www.imdb.com/title /tt0081505/plotsummary

Jenkins, P. (2017). Wonder Woman [film]. United States: Warner Bros.

Johnson, J. (2011). Captain America. [film]. United States: Paramount.

Jordan, N. (1994). Interview with the vampire: The vampire chronicles. [film]. United States: Geffen.

Kearns, J. (nd-a). Film – Kubrick's "The Shining". Idyllopus Press: Retrieved from http://idylloppuspress.com/idyllopus/film/shining_opening.htm

Kearns, J. (nd-b). Film – Kubrick's "The Shining". Idyllopus Press: Retrieved from http://idylloppuspress.com/idyllopus/film/shining_toc.htm

Keisner, J. (2008). Do you want to watch? A study of the visual rhetoric of the postmodern horror film. Women's Studies, 37, 411–427.

Kinal, J. (2000). Boo? An exploration of the horror genre. Australian Screen Education, 23, 70–76.

King, S. (1974). Carrie. New York, NY: Pocket Books.

King, S. (1987). Misery. New York, NY: Scribner.

King, S. (2013). Dr Sleep. New York, NY: Simon & Schuster.

Kubrick, S. (1980). The Shining. (1980). [film] United States: Warner Brothers.

Leming, M. R., & Dickinson, G. E. (2002). Understanding death, dying, and bereavement. New York, NY: Harcourt.

Levy, D. (1964–1966). The Adams Family. [television series]. United States: MGM.

Milton, J. (1667/2012). Paradise lost. Danielson, D. (Ed.). New York, NY: Broadview.

Morton, G., Greenwich, E., & Barry, J. (1964). Leader of the pack [Recorded by The Shangri-Las]. On Leader of the pack [Album]. New York, NY: Red Bird.

Poe, E. A. (2006a). The tell-tale heart. In Poe, E. A., The best of Poe. pp. 81–86. Clayton, DE: Prestwick House.

Poe, E. A. (2006b). The cask of amontillado. In Poe, E. A., The best of Poe. pp. 161–166. Clayton, DE: Prestwick House.

Ramis, H. (1983). National Lampoon's Vacation. [film]. United States: Warner Brothers.

Romero, G. A. (1968). Night of the living dead. [film]. United States: Image Ten Production.

Schultz, N. W., & Huet, L. M. (2000). Sensational! Violent! Popular! Death in American movies. Omega – Journal of Death and Dying, 42(2), 137–149.

Seale, C. (1998). Constructing death: The sociology of dying and bereavement. Cambridge, UK: Cambridge University Press.

Shelley, M. W. (1818/1922). Frankenstein: Or, the modern Prometheus. Boston, MA: Cornhill.

Simmel, G. (2007). The metaphysics of death. (Trans. from 1910 by Teucher, U., & Kemple, T. M.). Theory, Culture, & Society, 2(7–8), 72–77.

Spielberg, S. (1981). Raiders of the Lost Ark. [film]. United States: Paramount.

Spielberg, S. (1998). Saving Private Ryan. [film]. United States: Dreamworks.

Stephen King Wiki (nd). Doctor Sleep. Retrieved from: http://stephenking.wikia.com/wiki/Doctor_Sleep

Surry, J. (1959). Teen angel [Recorded by Dinning, M.]. On Teen angel [Single]. Los Angeles, CA: MGM.

Tarver, J. L. (1999). Last kiss [Recorded by Jam, P.]. On Last kiss [CD Single]. Washington, D.C.: Epic.

Thomas, D. (1945). A refusal to mourn the death by fire of a child in London. The New Republic. Retrieved from https://www.youtube.com/watch?v=dnBrQ3euUxE

Thomas, D. (1952). The poems of Dylan Thomas. New York, NY: New Directions.

Thompson, R. (1991). 1952 Vincent black lightening [Recorded by Thompson, R.]. On Rumor and sigh [Album]. Los Angeles: CA: Capitol.

Trencansky, S. (2001). Final girls and terrible youth: Transgression in 1980s slasher horror. Journal of Popular Film and Television, 29(2), 63–73.

Verhoeven, P. (1992). Basic Instinct. [film]. United States: Carolco.

Whitman, W. (1855/2016). Leaves of grass. Sweden: Wisehouse Classics.

Whitman, W. (1958). O captain! My captain! In Williams, O. (Ed.), A pocketbook of modern verse: English and American poetry of the last 100 years. New York, NY: Simon & Schuster.

Zucker, J. (1990). Ghost. [film]. United States: Paramount.

3

HAUNTS AND HUNTS: COMMUNICATING ABOUT DEATH IN GHOSTLY LORE[1]

"Have you ever seen a ghost?" Deb asks Cris as they take a break from giving out Halloween treats to the goblins, ghosts, and superheroes ringing the doorbell. Deb opens a bottle of Riesling and pours as Cris ponders the question.

Cris thinks of the time she and her dog Oatie were hanging out with a friend in her very old, presumably haunted, farmhouse. Oatie suddenly raised up, his back hunched and his hair bristled, as he growled at an empty spot in the middle of the room. He circled the spot, growling and barking for 10 minutes. Cris never saw a thing.

Cris's mom used to tell an old family story about her Aunt Bess. Bess had nursed her husband Bob for years through serious, chronic, illnesses. Bob was so ill he slept in a hospital bed in their extra bedroom. On one occasion, when Bob was in the hospital quite ill, Bess was awakened in the middle of the night by Bob's voice calling her. She glanced at the time – 3:08 a.m. – and rushed down the hall to see what he needed, forgetting momentarily he wasn't there. Halfway to his room, she remembered, returned to bed and went back to sleep. The next morning, she received a phone call from the hospital telling her Bob had died during the night. His time of death: 3:08 a.m.

Cris thinks of her mom, who died precisely at 12:03 a.m. on 12/3, Cris's birthday, December 3.

Cris remembers the first Father's Day after her father died when he came into Cris's mind and the light on the table next to her spontaneously turned off. Then back on.

When Cris was searching for a name for her new dog she had the idea to name her after her mother. "Mom, let me know if that would be okay with you," she asked silently. A colleague suggested she do a search for "Dog Names" on the internet, and her search immediately found a web page which yielded only one suggestion – "Maggie" – Cris's mom's name. She has never been able to find that same web page again.

"No," she answers. "I've never *seen* a ghost. Have you?"

Deb looks away. "Sort of. In the 1970s," she says in a serious tone of voice, "several friends and I rented a large old farmhouse on a sprawling 12 acres. The house was built in the late 1800s and had been more recently purchased by our landlord, a veterinarian who lived in a loft above his veterinary clinic elsewhere on the property. In the early 1900s, indoor plumbing was installed in the farmhouse by adding a bathroom onto the side of the house. Nearby, later in the century, a modern kitchen was built. While it was remote, expensive for our budgets, and lacking air-conditioning and central heating, I loved living in the country." She pauses and raises her eyebrows.

"Unfortunately, we immediately began noticing oddnesses. We initially explained them away. For example, when we turned on or off the kitchen or bathroom lights, they often wouldn't function, but they would flicker or turn on or off randomly when we hadn't touched the switch. In the bathroom, the same thing happened with the water. We'd turn it on, and it would either flow then stop inexplicably, or not flow at all. These were very minor inconveniences, and we rationalized them because of the age of the house – old plumbing, old wiring, old fixtures. The house had very identifiable cold spots which we thought was because of the lack of central heat or air. Sometimes, we'd get the feeling that someone was behind us, but when we'd turn around expecting to see one of our roommates, the room would be empty. Rocking chairs rocked inexplicably; doors swung open or shut randomly, but again, poor grading, uneven flooring, and warping of old wood always satisfied as explanations."

"It sounds like a pretty spooky house," Cris says.

Deb shrugs. "It didn't matter, anyway; I loved living there. I converted a small closet off my bedroom into my office, and happily banged away on my old typewriter almost every morning, with the sun's bright beams streaming through the small window near my desk."

"But," Deb's voice slows dramatically, "one day, I decided to take a shower. I walked in the bathroom and turned on the light switch. No light. I silently cursed in exasperation, and repeatedly flicked the switch off and on until the light came on. I drew back the shower curtain and turned the water on. This time, I cursed aloud – no water. I turned the knobs impatiently; the water finally flowed. I stepped into the tub, turned the spigot, and enjoyed a hot and lovely shower. The water spigots stopped dispensing water as soon as I turned them off. I happily stepped over the tub's rim, dried my hair vigorously, and wrapped a white towel around it while I dried off. I wrapped another towel around my body, tucked one edge in, took the towel off of my head, and began brushing my long brown hair out. All of a sudden, I got that by now very familiar feeling that I was not alone. I put the hairbrush down on the vanity housing the sink, and rubbed the steam off of the mirror above it. No one was behind me. I even turned around to make sure. No one was behind me. I shrugged, shook my head, silently wondered why this house was so crazy, and extended my hand to lift the hairbrush to resume brushing my hair."

Deb pauses for dramatic effect. "My hand stopped in midair. I watched, first fascinated, then terrified, as the hairbrush *without me ever touching it* began to tremble ever so slightly. It then began shaking quite noticeably; I withdrew my hand, but I was otherwise frozen. I stared at the hairbrush as it began shimmying around the vanity like an overexcited Ouija guide, and then, at first imperceptibly, then rather quickly, it slid across the vanity and fell on the floor with a loud bang, amplified by the small bathroom. I began screaming, and the next thing I knew I was in my front yard, clad only in a towel, screaming and shaking and crying. My roommate Mike drove up from work right at that minute, put his arms around me, and guided me into the house. I was hysterical. I moved out less than a month later."

"Oh my gosh," Cris responds. "I would have been terrified. I wouldn't have lasted another day in that house."

Deb nods as she finishes her story. "As time went on, and I told other people this story, I realized that the house was rather famous for being haunted. Apparently, the house originally had a small, old, family graveyard on the side of it, but the modern bathroom and kitchen had been built upon it, without moving the graves. Unable to retain tenants, the landlord continued to try to rent it after my friends and I moved out, but he finally tore the house down, sold that portion of the land, and moved on."

Belief in Ghosts

Ghosts as subjects and objects of narrative, experience, or entertainment have a long and stormy history. "Most people have a ghost story," claim Bader, Mencken, and Baker (2010, p. 23), who note that everyone has one, "if not more than one: an aunt, uncle, parent, grandparent, or other relative who claims a ghost sighting as a child, or a best friend who insists his home was haunted. Some of us have seen a ghost ourselves" (Bader et al., 2010, p. 23). Various studies report population estimates of beliefs in the existence of ghosts ranging from 38% to 75% and personal experiences with a ghostly phenomenon from 13% to 20% (Bader et al., 2010; Fitch, 2013; Wiseman et al., 2003). In addition, a sizable number of Americans – approximately one-third – report having the ability to communicate with ghosts (Bader et al., 2010). Despite environmental and other non-paranormal explanations for ghostly sightings (including drafts, light levels, magnetic fields, and sound waves), reports on spectral experiences remains high (Wiseman, et al., 2003). In addition, over the thousands of years in which stories about ghostly sightings have been told, shared, and recorded, the story lines themselves remain consistently similar and play off of, suggest

Bader and colleagues (2010), "timeless human concerns" (p. 23). Research into ghost sightings and other paranormal experiences has long been dismissed as illegitimate and unscientific. In their research on paranormal and related investigations, Bader and colleagues (2010) note that Americans "are simultaneously fascinated and repulsed, intrigued and dismissive" of the paranormal (p. 5) and are suspicious of people who engage in paranormal investigations.

Ghost Hunting and Thanatourism

Ghost hunting as entertainment has been ubiquitous for decades. In fact, a quick internet search yields a list of well over 200 ghost hunting television shows from places as diverse as the U.S., U.K., Canada, Asia, Australia, Norway, Pakistan and Portugal, and from as early as 1949 to today (Hill, 2011). Television shows about ghost hunting and other paranormal experiences reportedly yield high ratings (Fitch, 2013), and some claim over two million viewers per episode (Seidman, 2009). The fictional and reality television shows with paranormal subject matter are entertainment mediums that feed beliefs about paranormal phenomena and reinforce certain religious ideas about the supernatural (Bader et al., 2010).

Beyond watching the people on television shows search for ghostly activity, ghost hunting – or paranormal investigating – is a popular pastime for average people. Thanatourism – also called "dark tourism" – refers to tourist visits to sites associated with death. Thanatourist sites include ghost tours and also visits to burial places with historic or cultural significance, including visits to shrines, cemeteries, dungeons, and genocide camps (Stone, 2006).

There are hundreds of haunted or ghost tours across the United States. You can go on a Colonial Lantern Tour in Plymouth Massachusetts or travel on a haunted bus on Salt Lake City's Grimm Ghost Tour. Ghosts represent "pseudo-history" (Hanks, 2015, p. 21), a subversion of history. For some of these ghostly sites, tours allow visitors to investigate and envision alternative histories that critique canonical versions of heritage narratives. Many thanatourist sites have a long history and date back to at least the medieval period (Stone, 2006; Stone & Sharpley, 2008). Other ghostly sites are less formally visited but also contribute to a culture's mythic histories, folklore, and legends, providing both identity narratives and rites of passage for adolescents and young adults (Bird, 2002). These adolescent rituals frequently include tests of bravery, storytelling to evoke terror, and forbidden activities such as alcohol or drug use, sexual experimentation, and vandalism (Bird, 2002).

There are also over 1,000 amateur paranormal research groups throughout the U.S. who investigate reports of ghostly activities as a leisure activity (Hill, 2012). In the course of this research, Cris attended a "call" at a local sandwich shop for new investigators to join a paranormal investigation group in a large southern city. Well over 100 interested people attended, and Hill (2012) notes that "ghost hunting is incredibly popular and trendy" (l. 85).

Paranormal Movements

Paranormal is defined as "that which cannot be explained by any known scientific explanation and is outside the realm of normal experience" (Fitch, 2013, p. 3). Disdained by scholars as "scientific fringe theories" and "anomalies" (Westrum, 1977, p. 271), the study of ghostly specters has thus been grouped with the inquiry into other phenomena such as UFOs, monsters, and the "occult" (p. 271). The local ghost hunters visited as part of this research described the interest in the paranormal as a perpetual human "fascination with the unexplained, … not just ghosts but UFOs, astrology; we would consider all of those paranormal" (Personal Interview). In North Carolina alone, there are reportedly 170 paranormal investigation groups listed in their industry directory. An examination of the website of one of these groups, for instance, reveals the following ancillary services: UFO investigations, Cryptozoology (investigations of lake monsters such as Bigfoot), investigations of ancient mysteries (e.g., stone carvings, Stonehenge), and investigation of space mysteries (e.g., examination of NASA moon images for previously unseen evidence) (LEMUR Paranormal Investigations, n.d.). What Fitch (2013) calls "the American paranormal experience" (p. 7) includes the Salem Witch Trials, stories such as Washington Irving's *The Legend of Sleepy Hollow*, holidays such as Halloween, movements such as Spiritualism, belief in flying saucers and Bigfoot, and horror films.

Spiritualism

Willingness to report sightings of anomaly phenomena typically requires social acceptance and frequently follows social contagion (Westrum, 1977), and there have been periods of time in which both were in greater supply than in other times. Today's paranormal investigations have similarities with the 19th century Spiritualist, or Spiritualism, movement. Spiritualists conducted séances using both eyewitness reports and pseudo-scientific instruments (such as Ouija boards) and claimed the ability to communicate with spirits, levitate, and ooze "ectoplasm" (Fitch, 2013, p. 14) from their bodies.

The Spiritualism movement was popular for over a century, and was most popular during the Civil War and World War I – both times in which the population experienced massive numbers of deaths of loved ones, and at a time in which – following publication of Darwin's *On the Origin of Species*, for instance – people were struggling with their beliefs about the meaning of life (Fitch, 2013). Even today, despite debunking of the Spiritualist movement, there are still Spiritualist churches in the US in which people receive psychic readings (Fitch, 2013).

Both the Spiritualist movement of the past and today's paranormal investigations are populist movements reaching a mass audience. Both serve the dual purposes of entertainment and belief construction – both involve public displays and both reify a belief in life after death. Both involve communication between "spirits" and people who are alive. Both involve a person who serves as a "bridge" between "the two worlds" – in the Spiritualism movement, it was a medium who conducted séances. In the paranormal investigation movement, the investigator is the bridge. Both rely on a combination of personal narrative and mechanical instrumentation for legitimation and proof. Both fight against a proliferation of deception and dishonesty within the ranks. Finally, both evoke dialectical tensions of rationality and naturalism against a backdrop of the supernatural and the irrational (LEMUR Paranormal Investigations, n.d.; Medeiros, 2015; Seidman, 2009).

Ghosts as Pseudo-Scientific Discourse

There has always been a tension between purveyors of scientific principles and investigators of ghostly happenings, and today's renaissance of interest in the supernatural takes a turn toward scientific discourse if not epistemology. A scientific investigation of such occurrences would necessarily involve use of accepted positivist research methodologies along with healthy doses of skepticism, critical thinking, and objectivity (Westrum, 1977). An investigation of over 1,000 websites of paranormal investigation teams (Hill, 2012) found a strong use of science-based jargon and equipment but a lack of actual usage of scientific principles. The teams use terms such as "frequency, resonance, energy, quantum, magnetic, environmental, and electricity" (Hill, 2012, ll. 22–23), and expensive technical equipment to legitimate the hobby as research. In fact, their methods are based on accepted forms of data collection: interviews, observations, measurement instruments, and random or systematic sampling. Hill (2012) notes, however, that the investigations lack scientific principles such as documentation of the results, replicability of the methods, triangulation or confirmation of the data, researcher objectivity, and instrument calibration.

The Wine Shop

Deb gives Cris a long look and Cris realizes her mouth must be hanging open at Deb's story.

"Wow!" Cris finally says, "I would have been terrified."

Deb laughs. "Yet, didn't you go ghost hunting last year?"

"That was different," Cris says. "I was in control." She pauses. "Or at least I thought I was."

Deb sits forward. "Tell me about it."

"Well, so," Cris starts. "I participated in two different paranormal investigations last year. One was late into the night at a small town wine shop led by a local paranormal investigation group, and the other was a weekend event at St. Alban's Sanatorium in Radford, Virginia, put on by the stars of the Ghost Hunters International television show."

"A haunted wine shop!" Deb exclaims as she takes a sip from her glass of wine. "Sounds divine!"

Cris laughs. "The Wine Shop is located in a renovated three-story row shop which has at times in its history housed a speakeasy during the Depression and a woman's dress shop during the 1940s–1960s. The woman's dress shop was owned by a woman named Margaret, and the building is reportedly haunted by both Margaret and by the ghosts of gamblers from the building's speakeasy days. Andy and Donna [names have been changed], the husband–wife owners of the Wine Shop, report numerous apparitional sightings throughout the time they've owned the shop and the building. I participated in a paranormal investigation at the Wine Shop from 11 p.m. to 2 a.m. one night last spring."

"Were you there by yourself?" Deb interrupts.

"No," Cris says, "of course Andy and Donna, the owners, were there, and also four men from a local paranormal investigation group who had performed numerous investigations at the Wine Shop previously."

"So, were the owners into the occult or anything like that?" Deb asks.

"No, nothing like that," Cris says. "Donna experienced her first paranormal phenomena shortly after her first husband's sudden death. For the first four or five months after his death, she received phone calls several times a day, every day, from her late husband's cell phone number. When she would pick up the phone, no one was on the other end of the call. 'The experience of a ghost was so comforting to me,' Donna recounted to me, and she said it fit in with her religious beliefs of an afterlife. She was convinced the calls came from her deceased husband who was trying to contact her, and her priest concurred with that interpretation. Donna believed the calls made it easier for her to go through the difficult times after his death and made her less afraid of dying since it served as evidence to her that there is a continuation of ourselves after death. More recently, Donna and Andy have had many paranormal experiences in the Wine Shop. They had not owned it for long when boxes starting mysteriously relocating and unexplained noises sounded when they were working late at night. One afternoon Donna was hanging tissue paper to use for gift wrapping when she saw the paper flutter in the air. Donna explained how this was odd because the door to the building was shut, there were no windows open, and there was no air movement in the building. The fluttering continued for many minutes, long enough that she was able to record it on her phone camera, which she showed to me."

"You saw the video?" Deb asks.

"Yes," Cris nods. "And it looks just like how she described it. Afterwards, Donna and Andy contacted a local paranormal investigation group to investigate. They have since held several paranormal investigations and regularly conduct after-hours ghost tours at the shop. The first time I met Andy and Donna, they showed me the video recording of the fluttering paper and played for me audio recordings of what they said was Margaret, the deceased former owner, talking to them. I heard some unidentified noise on the recording but would not have claimed it was any type of a voice."

"So, then, the investigation," Deb prompts.

> The investigation was several weeks later. The investigators – Mark, Paul, Steve, and Robert [names have been changed] – and I arrived at the Wine Shop around 10 p.m., and Andy and Donna were waiting for us. The investigators took their time meticulously setting up their equipment – electro-magnetic sensors, movement sensors, motion sensors, and audio and videotape recorders. They set up in the two locations that had previously had the most paranormal activity: the basement and the upstairs floor. While they set up, Donna relayed to me a paranormal encounter she'd had just that morning.
>
> "I was unpacking wine bottles," she said, "taking them out of the shipping cartons and putting them on the display racks in the front of the store. I had just taken the last bottle out of the box and was placing it on the shelf when I heard a noise behind me. I turned around just to see out of the corner of my eye. The box flipped itself over."
>
> "Do you think it was Margaret?" I asked her.
>
> "I hope to find out tonight!" Donna answered.
>
> "This should be interesting," I said.
>
> We started our investigation upstairs. In Margaret's 1950s-era dress shop, this floor held the evening gowns, and I could imagine women pirouetting in front of the mirror in their ball attire. It also held Margaret's office and – according to letters found after her death – was reportedly an area with which she had been particularly emotionally attached. We set up a row of folding metal chairs in the middle of the large room. The equipment was scattered around the space – three mag-light flashlights on a counter about 20 feet from our chairs, audio recorders next to them, and motion detectors on the floor a few feet in front of us. The set up was complete around 11 p.m., and Mark, the lead investigator, turned out the lights.
>
> We sat in the dark for a few moments, then Mark called out to Margaret.
>
> "Margaret, can you hear me? Let us know you're here!" he said loudly.
>
> Nothing.
>
> "Margaret, this is Mark. We've talked several times before. I'm here with Andy and Donna. And there's a writer with us tonight named Cris. She wants to write about you. Margaret, if you're here, turn on the flashlight!" he said.

Cris pauses in her story and turns to Deb. "I've since learned that the flash-light activity is quite common in paranormal investigations. The idea is that a spirit can manipulate the energy in a flashlight to turn it on and off at will. Margaret was not cooperating. Mark tried several more times but there was no response."

Cris continues:

> *"Maybe she's not here," he said to me. "I don't know what's wrong. She's always responded when we've been here before."*
>
> *"Maybe she's uncomfortable with my being here," I suggested.*
>
> *"Maybe," he said. He called out to Margaret again.*
>
> *"Margaret, are you quiet because Cris is here? Are you unhappy that Cris is here tonight?"*
>
> *The flashlight beam lit up for a few seconds then turned itself off.*

Cris laughs and explains to Deb, "Great, I thought to myself. The ghost is now talking, and she doesn't like me. I decided to play along and speak to Margaret as if she were a study participant."

> *"Margaret," I said out loud. "I understand your concern. I'm here doing research and I haven't asked your permission to be here. I'm just writing about what Mark and his friends are doing with ghost hunting. I'm not writing anything bad about you, I promise. May I have your permission to be here?"*
>
> *The flashlight lit up again and stayed lit until Mark asked her to turn it off a few minutes later.*
>
> *"Margaret," Mark said. "Cris wants to ask you some questions about what it's like to be a spirit. Margaret, what's it like, being dead. Is it nice over there?"*
>
> *Nothing.*
>
> *"Margaret, you do know you're dead, don't you?"*
>
> *Nothing.*
>
> *Mark started to respond, "Margaret, I hate to break it to you, but ..."*
>
> *I interrupted. "Margaret, I understand you don't feel dead. I mean, you're here talking to us now. Is that right?"*
>
> *The light came on, brighter than before.*
>
> *Mark asked her a few more questions. Margaret confirmed she had turned Donna's box over earlier, just to be playful. After some more "conversation" with Margaret, we moved downstairs to the basement, after thanking Margaret for her time.*
>
> *The basement is now used for storage but during Prohibition it housed a speak-easy and held regular poker games. Mark claimed that during one public ghost tour, they had heard a distinct spirit voice say "I'll raise you," and one of the guests threw down some coins on the ground and within a few minutes the coins had disap-peared. We sat in folding chairs in a circle while Mark tried to call out the spirits,*

hoping for a replay of the previous performance. He was having no luck for the first 30 minutes, but then we heard knocking coming from the front of the basement. I distinctly heard the sounds myself and followed the group to their source in an empty room. The knocking faded after about 10 minutes, and we looked around to try to find their origination. We never saw anything that could be the source of the sound.

"Do you think it was ghosts?" Deb asks Cris.

Cris shrugs. "I left this experience cautious and skeptically wondering if it was possible to remotely control a flashlight and supposing it would be possible to rig an audio recording of knocking in a building in which you regularly conducted tours. I noted Mark's showmanship, calling forth the spirits, putting Margaret's flashlight show on display, performing the gambling routine in the basement. On the other hand, if I was faking it, I would have made Margaret turn on the flashlight much sooner. I'm open to the possibility that there was indeed some sort of paranormal activity going on in the Wine Shop that night."

The Haunted Bridge

"I have another ghost story for you," Deb says as they settle down in their seats on the couch. Evidently the trick-or-treating activity has died down for a while.

It wasn't stormy, or foggy, or particularly dark on the night we decided to try to find the haunted bridge. It was a bright moonlit night, warm enough to leave our coats at home. The only two members of our group who could drive, David Cheshire and Jimmy Belch, best friends their whole lives, were the only ones who knew the location, so David, Jimmy, my best friend Cathy, who dated David, and my boyfriend at the time, Butchie Mangum, piled into David's orange VW bug and off we went.

The Haunted Bridge was located down deep out in Princess Anne County, a rural agricultural area that had once been the largest county in Virginia, but in 1963 was annexed by a small but politically and economically powerful beach resort called Virginia Beach. According to legend, the Haunted Bridge was an old wooden bridge at the edge of the Dismal Swamp. It was not marked or easy to find, but you knew where to turn because of the large white house that stood at the intersection of Princess Anne Road and a narrow, unmarked county road that most locals called Haunted Bridge Road. According to the legend, the large white house had once been a sanatorium, an insane asylum, a hospital for the mentally ill, "the loony bin," as most of the teenagers called it. It had closed, but tales of its harsh medical practices and cruel torture of inmates abounded in local lore. It was said that as former inmates died, their spirits returned – not to the site of their imprisonment and torture, too painful for them to revisit – but instead they traveled to the bridge nearby, a place long denied to them. Supposedly, you could hear their moans, screams and anguished cries when you went to the Haunted Bridge, and if you were particularly lucky, you might see their ghostly lanterns on the road near the bridge, lighting the way for the dead still to come.

On the way to the Haunted Bridge, we regaled each other with ghost stories, haunted tales, and legends. We drank watered-down beer and smoked cigarettes. We laughed, and giggled, and teased each other, trying to outdo each other's stories. On and on we drove, winding through horse pastures and corn fields, wooden post fences and big white wooden farmhouses. We sped around curves while David shifted and downshifted, Black Sabbath in the 8-track, heralding our arrival. The boys talked smack, and Cathy and I rolled our eyes at each other behind their backs. On and on we drove, until finally, in the middle of nowhere, we saw the abandoned, now crumbling white wooden farmhouse on our right, on the corner next to a narrow unmarked road. We didn't need David's "Here we are," to know we were turning onto Haunted Bridge Road.

Stinking collard fields quickly gave way to thick, dark cypress swamp. Twisted black intertwined dense trees lined the road, an impenetrable barrier keeping us from seeing into the swamp. We knew that in the blackwater swamps of the Dismal, the water was dark because of tannins, but we were sure the water became blacker and blacker as we continued to drive. The pungent smell of swamp mud was thick, and as we drove deeper and deeper into the black swamp, the laughter and stories waned and the beer cans fell on the floorboard. David turned off the music. A misty amorphous fog began to gather; it quickened and flitted under and around our car as we drove. We could see it creeping about the trees, hovering above the black water. The car slowed, then stopped, and David pulled the emergency brake, turned around to look at us, and said, "We're here."

We sat there, unmoving. The grasping limbs of low hanging trees seemed to be reaching toward us on either side of the narrow road. The full moon still shone bright. We saw no lights, but ahead of us it was easy to see an old, short wooden bridge spanning a particularly mucky part of the swamp. It was dead quiet. No owls hooting, no leaves rustling, no night cicadas buzzing – just heavy silence. David and Jimmy opened the front doors and began walking toward the bridge, lighting cigarettes as they walked. Cathy, Butchie and I sat in the back wordlessly.

"Y'all goin?" Cathy asked tremulously. Her voice was hushed. Immediately Butchie said, "Hell, yeah!" and leaned forward to get out of the car. I glanced at Cathy and Butchie, and reluctantly said, "Yeah, I'm going." I pushed the front passenger seat forward and climbed out of the front door. Butchie followed. I looked back at Cathy, and she pushed forward the driver's seat and climbed out of the VW. We began slowly walking toward the bridge.

I could feel my heart pounding; I could hear the blood rushing. I tried to control my breathing as I walked. As we got closer to where David and Jimmy were standing on the bridge, leaning over the old, dark wooden rail, we huddled close together and held hands. David and Jimmy straightened from peering over the bridge, saw us coming and David hollered, "Come on!" impatiently, flicking his cigarette over the rails. We continued walking slowly, closer and closer toward the bridge, bunched together, holding each other's hand tightly. Butchie's hand was sweaty in my mine.

At that moment, a horrifying scream pierced the black night. Loud and long, the scream was full of agony, high pitched, desperate. In all my tomboy years spent tromping around the woods and swamps, I'd never heard anything like it. Immediately, Cathy, Butchie, and I dropped hands, turned, and began running. We raced toward the car, and I didn't even realize that David and Jimmy were right behind us until David leapt into the driver's seat, slammed the car in gear, and frantically began trying to execute a three point turn on the narrow bridge, as we all screamed "Hurry! Hurry! Go! Go!" Finally, he got the car turned around, and we began speeding out of the swamp.

"Oh shit, oh shit, oh shit!" repeated Jimmy endlessly, turning his head side to side madly as if searching for whatever was going to come out of the thick black swamp to get us.

"What the fuck was that? What the fuck was that?" yelled Butchie, over and over, rocking back and forth on the console between Cathy and me.

"I don't know, I don't know, I don't know," repeated David as we sped out of the swamp.

I looked behind Butchie at Cathy. She looked back at me. Her eyes were wide; her face was as white as a ghost. I could feel the hot, mottled, red spots of terror on my face. David had stopped repeating "I don't know," and was hurling us down the small narrow road. As we approached the intersection, we looked at the old house on the left. There was one small pinpoint light in one of the windows. We all gasped.

"Did you see that?" asked David, turning quickly away from the road. His face was contorted in fear.

"Yes," I whispered, as David turned back to the road. Wordlessly, we made the long drive home.

St. Albans Sanatorium

"Wow." Cris says. "Sometimes play gets a little too real."

Deb nods. "I've tried to find the place several times since then, but the area is mostly housing developments now." She takes a sip of her wine. "Now tell me about your other paranormal investigation. It was in a former mental hospital?"

Yes, at St. Albans Sanatorium. It's a sprawling four-acre structure in southwestern Virginia. In 1892, the building housed a boy's school and in 1916, the building was converted to a mental hospital. The land itself was once inhabited by several different Native American tribes. It was a location of multiple Civil War battles, and in 1755 was the site of the Draper's Meadow Massacre. In addition, the buildings and grounds have reportedly been the location for other multiple tragedies and deaths from schoolhouse bullying; mental health treatments, including insulin coma therapy, electroconvulsive therapy, hydro shock therapy, and lobotomy; and suicide. The massive St. Albans Sanatorium is now a vacant building and is a popular location for ghost hunting expeditions. I attended a weekend-long paranormal investigation sponsored by the cast of the television show Ghost Hunters International. *Three members from the cast led the investigation and they were assisted by five other investigators from two local paranormal investigation groups. Approximately 80 people attended the weekend. Weekend activities included lectures about paranormal investigations and two overnight explorations of portions of the sanatorium building.*

The Ghost Hunters International *paranormal investigation at St. Albans Sanitorium started with a lecture in the meeting room at the Holiday Inn in which we were all staying. I listened to the piped in Holiday Inn music as I watched people filter in. Approximately 80 people had paid several hundred dollars and traveled from out of town to participate. I was surprised to see that everyone looked pretty normal. There were all ages, ranging from a couple teenagers to an older man with white hair. Most of the people arrived with a partner or friend, but there were a few small groups and a few people alone. There were more women but there was a sizable number of men. All were white. There were jeans and shorts, sneakers, t-shirts and hooded jackets, white hair, brown hair, no hair, and one woman with 1950's bouffant hair. Lots of eyeglasses.*

Britt Griffith, one of the stars of the television show, started the lecture. I noticed I was the only person taking notes. Britt has conducted over 300 paranormal investigations over the past five years. He told his story of how he became interested in paranormal investigations. When he was a teenager, his parents owned a house that was haunted. He used to see a figure walk around the house, his dog would bark wildly at nothing, doors opened and closed on their own. When he told his ghost stories to a friend years later, the friend invited him to join their paranormal investigation group.

Britt gave several pieces of advice to would-be investigators: "Keep a level head. It can suck you in," he said.

"I am not a scientist," he claimed. "We are home inspectors. It's amazing how many people don't know the normal sounds a house can make."

As he fiddled with the audio-visual set up for his lecture and struggled with technical difficulties because his laptop memory was almost full, he described his equipment as he set it up: both analog and digital video recorders and audio recorders, weather and atmospheric sensors, motion detectors, infra-red illuminators, thermal imaging, vibration sensors, carbon monoxide detectors, and facial recognition software. He personally has over $60,000 worth of equipment, he noted. He spent over an hour discussing his equipment and showing us how they set it up and test it ahead of time. He discussed the pros and cons of different types of cameras and how they have to use multiple cameras for differently sized rooms. He described a device called an "Ovulus" with which a ghost can create speech. Britt used it in their investigation at the Stanley Hotel, which was the inspiration for Stephen King's The Shining, and heard it say his full name.

"This is research stuff," he said. "We're looking for fluctuations in the environment that will dial us in on where activity is happening. We're monitoring the environment."

"You don't want too much light for your camera," he noted. "It washes out your evidence."

As he described his expensive equipment, I thought of the equipment I brought, if it could be called "equipment": a flashlight with a D-battery and my cell phone camera. I wondered if they would be adequate for the job, whatever that was.

Britt also suggested listening to your body. "You can feel energy changes," he advised.

"Can we fake it?" he responded to the question I wanted to ask. "Nah. We don't have the time or the budget to fake it. It can be done but that doesn't mean it is being done. Audio and video recorders can be manipulated. Every piece of equipment can be manipulated. But we don't. All we have is our credibility."

I was still skeptical and was glad to know I wasn't not the only one.

"We don't fake it," he continued, "but we have to over-articulate when stuff happens so you will know."

He described their process:

"Get baseline measurements."

They take hours and hours of footage: "This is not about pretty; it's about documentary."

Their tools are "cutting edge."

He told many behind the scenes stories about the show, and during the break, Britt sold and signed t-shirts. "For my kid's college fund," he noted.

He played us some sample EVPs (Electronic Voice Phenomenon) from an investigation. I heard something that might have sounded like a voice but was unable to distinguish words. One woman thought it said, "it's hot in here." I thought she must have an overactive imagination.

"You gotta have fun," Britt advised.

"Show up at 7 p.m. tonight at St. Albans," Britt instructed. I felt a knot in the pit of my stomach. I wasn't sure if it was excitement or fear.

At St. Albans, we were divided into four groups of 20 people. Each group went to a different part of the building for an hour, then we rotated to a new location. I experienced several paranormal phenomena over the course of the night. I saw what I would describe as an eerie iridescent glow on a chair in a hallway. The *air in the chair felt considerably colder than the air next to it and a temperature meter indicated colder air in that spot.*

I had a flashlight conversation in one room. A chair was set up in the middle of the room and on it were placed several flashlights. I put my own flashlight on it to control for any remote-controlled fakery. The flashlights turned on in response to various questions from the group.

"Were you a student here?" No.

"Were you a teacher?" Yes.

"I'm a teacher, too!" I said.

The light became brighter.

"What did you teach? Science?" No.

"Math?" No.

"History?" Yes.

"How do you feel about being part of history?" All the flashlights turned on, bright.

Cris stops. "That's my ghost hunting experience," she says.

"Wow," Deb says.

Thanacommunication

You may wonder why these stories have any pertinence to academic scholarship, epistemology, or cultural understandings. They are, after all, "just" stories: myths and tall tales, often untrue, exaggerated, enhanced, or outright false. Quite the contrary. Our cultural fascination with ghost stories is one reason why thanatourism is so popular. You can look at the stories told about ghosts, ghost hunting, and ghosts sightings, from two different perspectives: from the storylines themselves, and from the way the stories are constructed.

At the first level, these stories construct very specific ideas of behavior, beliefs, and identities. Ghost stories bring history alive, and some serve as cautionary tales that construct appropriate cultural and gender performance, especially for young women. From the ghost story of drowned South Carolina daughter of Vice President Aaron Burr, Theodosia Burr, for instance, whose tragic death forces her to roam the beach searching for her husband to this day; to the myriad of stories of haunted ghosts of the inevitably hanged men and women who'd had the misfortune to fall in love with someone socially considered inferior because of race, class, ethnic, and/or religious differences; to the desperate ghostly mother searching for her babies killed in a carriage accident, shipwreck, or automobile wreck (Pitzer, 2013; Schlosser, 2009), these tales are told with great gusto, often around campfires and kitchen tables. They are often didactic, fables warning us of deviating from the prescribed norms. The tales told describe the penalty for not adhering to culturally approved social constructions – often death, or at the very least, horror and despair. In many ways, then, our ghostly fascinations are identity construction experiences. They let us look at history from a different angle, to understand who we are as humans, as mortals. This then, constructs a different look at history – from the third dimension of time and space.

The same discursive arguments stand out throughout our research on ghostly conversations. Logic, scientific jargon, claims of evidence, and scientific measurements, are all used as rhetorical strategies to prove the existence of life after death. This proof, then, is an emotional and rhetorical comfort to surviving loved ones (as it provides experiences of maintaining relational ties with the deceased), and is a defense against fears of death and dying. Scientific discourse is the primary discourse used by paranormal investigators and it also serves to legitimize the pastime in our post-positivist world.

This ghostly rhetoric constructs a particular kind of questing. This life is too bounded, too narrow, too confining. This rhetoric of otherworldly investigation mirrors the idea of Westward expansion. Paranormal investigators are truly expanding all boundaries. In many ways, it parallels the Star Trek language: "To boldly go where no one has gone before." We are in the midst of a proliferation of experiential tourism: eco-tourism, adventure travel, religious tourism, and thanatourism. Ghost hunting mirrors our cultural fascination in questing and expanding boundaries.

Conclusion

It may not be a coincidence that today's resurgence of interest in the supernatural comes about in a period of time in which death and dying is a frequent discourse in the public sphere. Death permeates human narratives, whether as legends and local lore or as modern popular culture. These experiences are – always have been – storied as pseudo-scientific, pseudo-historical, pseudo-scholarly accounts. What does this construction of the narratives do for us? As these brief narratives reveal, many seek out the ghostly, the paranormal – as children, as adolescents, as young adults, as we age. Death often invites us to visit, reflect, remember, play, learn, grow and exist. We often seek out the macabre, the dark, the supernatural. Anything related to people who are deceased takes on additional significance; as death sanctifies the ordinary. Stories about, visions of, and interactions with, those who have passed to the realm of the dead, remind us of our cultural and interpersonal identities, reify our culturally scripted behaviors, and reinforce our culturally constructed ideas and beliefs about the afterlife.

Note

1 A version of this chapter was presented at the 2017 Southern States Communication Association Annual Conference in Greenville SC and was nominated for best paper in the Language and Social Interaction Division.

References

Bader, C., Mencken, F., & Baker, J. (2010). Paranormal America: Ghost encounters, UFO sightings, Bigfoot hunts, and other curiosities in religion and culture. New York, NY: NYU Press.

Bird, E. S. (2002). It makes sense to us: Cultural identity in local legends of place. Journal of Contemporary Ethnography, 31(5), 519–547.

Fitch, M. E. (2013). Paranormal nation: Why America needs ghosts, UFOs, and Bigfoot. Santa Barbara, CA: Praeger.

Hanks, M. (2015). Haunted heritage: The cultural politics of ghost tourism, populism, and the past. Walnut Creek, CA: Left Coast Press.

Hill, S. (2012). Amateur paranormal research and investigation groups doing "sciency" things. Skeptical Inquirer, 36(2), np. Retrieved from: http://www.csicop.org/si/show/amateur_paranormal_research_and_investigation_groups_doing_sciencey_things

Hill, S. (24 April, 2011). Paranormal TV show listing: Paranormal-themed TV shows. [Web log post]. Retrieved from https://idoubtit.wordpress.com/paranormaltv/

LEMUR Paranormal Investigations (n.d.). Science of ghost hunting. Retrieved from: http://www.lemurteam.com/

Medeiros, M. (2015). Facts and photographs: Visualizing the invisible with spirit and thought photography, communication +1, 4(6), np. Retrieved from: http://scholarworks.umass.edu/cpo/vol4/iss1/6

Pitzer, S. (2013). Haunted Charleston: Scary sites, eerie, encounters, and tall tales. Guilford, CT: Morris.

Schlosser, S. E. (2009). Spooky North Carolina: Tales of hauntings, strange happenings, and other local lore. Guilford, CT: Morris.

Seidman, R. (2009). Ghost Hunters continues ratings success. Retrieved from: http://tvbythenumbers.com/2009/09/04/ghost-hunters-continues-ratings-success/26220

Stone, P. R. (2006). A dark tourism spectrum: Towards a typology of death and macabre related tourist sites, attractions, and exhibitions. Tourism 54(2), 145–160.

Stone, P., & Sharpley, R. (2008). Consuming dark tourism: A thanatological perspective. Journal of Tourism Research 35(2) pp. 574–595. doi: 10.1016/j.annals.2008.02.003

Westrum, R. (1977). Social intelligence about anomalies: The case of UFOs. Social Studies of Science 7(3): 271–302.

Wiseman, R., Watt, C., Stevens, P., Greening, E., & O'Keeffe, C. (2003). An investigation into alleged "hauntings". British Journal of Psychology, 94, 195–211.

4

FIT TO PRINT: COMMUNICATING ABOUT DEATH IN THE NEWS

"Hey, let's check in on the news," Cris suggests during the lull in the trick-or-treaters, turning on the TV and switching the channel to CNN. Cris and Deb are immediately warned by the broadcaster as to the upcoming airing of possible disturbing images. They watch in horror as they hear, "There are multiple fatalities in lower Manhattan after a truck drove the wrong way down a bike path and struck several people, NYPD sources say" (CNN, October 31, 2017). They are engrossed in live video and still photographs of the crime scene. There are children trapped inside a mangled yellow school bus. There are two officers tending to a man whose crumbled body lies motionless. There are pictures of bloodied bodies on the street with their faces blurred by the camera. Deb immediately begins to cry.

"Oh, I can't watch this!" Deb exclaims, averting her eyes as the images flash across the 72-inch screen in jacked up HD color. "Ugh, I just have so many of those images in my head already. I don't want any more mediated horror; they're already seared vividly in my brain." Deb turns off the television and says, "I remember during the Vietnam War, every night my parents would watch the nightly news while my brothers and I cleaned up the kitchen …" Deb's voice trails off. She clears her throat and continues, "I remember that picture of the naked Vietnamese girl running, crying, her clothes burnt off by napalm. The look on her face …" Deb's eyes are far away as she remembers, "… and the Viet Cong soldier with the gun at his head …." She shakes her head and gazes out the dark window.

Cris sighs sympathetically. "I don't remember much about the Vietnam War on television. I was pretty young; maybe we weren't allowed to watch it. I remember the news reporting of President Kennedy's death. The Challenger disaster. The Columbine school shooting. Princess Diana's death and the ongoing coverage of the crash scene. You know what news image haunts me to this day? In January 1982, an Air Florida passenger jet crashed into the icy Potomac River just outside Washington, D.C. It was on the news while I was on a business trip during a time in which I was doing a great deal of flying for work. I couldn't step away from the television, the hours of coverage showing people floating in the river, struggling to stay alive and losing the struggle on camera, rescuers on the banks trying to get to them, finally a helicopter rescue. One heroic bystander jumped into the frigid water to rescue a woman who was too frozen to grab the helicopter rope. In the end, only 5 people out of the 79 passengers on the plane survived. Just watching them struggling to stay alive," Cris shudders. She pauses to think. "Speaking of plane crashes, I was traveling again when the planes crashed on 9/11. As with every American, I think I will never forget the images of the planes crashing into the World Trade Center, first one, then the other, then the building's slow-motion collapse. The worst part, though, was the image of the people – covered in debris, terrified, walking, running, just going anywhere to get away. Their terror was contagious. Later, the people jumping from the burning buildings to their deaths. I think I will remember those images forever."

Deb remembers, "When I first watched that film about the Vietnam War, *The Killing Fields*, based on the experiences of two journalists in Vietnam, there's a scene where the main character looks around a field that's being excavated, and it's full of human skulls, human bones everywhere; it affects you, and after a while it's hard to get those pictures out of your head. They're seared into your brain like a brand."

"Despite those haunting images," Cris interjects, "most studies show that depictions of death in the news are still pretty rare, pretty contested, and their display is fraught with cultural and social conventions that preclude particular types of images being shown in most western societies."

Deb nods. "Perhaps that's why the images that appear in the news have such staying power."

Most war casualties are not shown in news reports of the war; news reports minimize, or omit, war deaths (Silcock et al., 2008). Vietnam was the first war with considerable television coverage. It was called the "living room war;" the first war to bring the reality of war into people's living rooms every night. The three television networks had a Saigon bureau for ongoing covering of the Vietnam War, and had five crews on duty most of the time. Yet, surprisingly, the coverage was fairly tame. Blood and gore were rarely shown. A bit less than a quarter of reports showed the dead or wounded, and these images were not particularly graphic (Patterson III, 1984; Silcock, et al., 2008). Similarly, in the 2003 U.S. invasion of Iraq, only 10% of the images from war scenes actually showed dead or injured people, and after the first three weeks of the war, those images of war dead decreased (Silcock, et al., 2008). Silcock and colleagues concluded that compassion fatigue – a state of burnout from witnessing a large number of deaths and/or tragedies – may play a role in what is covered and what is not.

Academic debate over the depiction of death within western cultures at large, and more specifically within the news, has seesawed between those who assert that "death is dying," as it becomes more removed and sanitized from both cultural discourses and cultural practices, and those who insist that death's imagery is as omnipresent as dying itself, even in the face of modernity and death's subsequent absence from our living rooms and parlors. The factors that influence the depiction of death within the visual news media are complex, diverse, and like death itself, culturally constructed. We suggest that death – and its depictions – are more present in more ways than many of us can see. As we've already observed, death plays alongside us in our children's games and haunts our bedtime stories, inviting moral lessons and nightmares. Like theater's dual-sided masks of tragedy and comedy, life and death always walk hand in hand, and one never appears without the other close nearby.

How common is death's depiction in the news, how does that depiction affect us, and what are the considerations that govern its imagery? As Hanusch (2008) summarizes, "Media place different values on people according to their age, gender, status, nationality, as well as the cause of death" (p. 303). The deaths of public personalities and crime victims are more publicized than the deaths of private individuals (Gray, 2013; Morse, 2014; Walter, et al., 1995) and seem to have more impact on audiences (Ueda, et al., 2017), while there are fewer media representations of those who die from disease (Ueda, et al., 2017; Walter et al., 1995). Those who die alone are portrayed negatively by the media (Seale, 2004). The deaths of mothers, children, and elderly men appear more frequently in the media because their deaths are generally considered more worthy of sympathy (Gerbner, 1980; Hoijer, 2004; Moeller, 1999), and deaths of those who are geographically or culturally distant also appear more frequently, especially in news reporting, and tend to be reported in more graphic terms than the deaths of those consuming that particular media (Campbell, 2004; Petley, 2003.)

Scholars have long agreed that most mainstream media place certain constraints on the display of the dead, gory, or mutilated human body. Morse's (2014) discussion of policies at *Haaretz* mimics many print and broadcast news' policies with regard to the circumstances of publication of particular images: body parts and dead bodies, particularly showing human faces, are not publishable. Hanusch's (2008) study of Australian and German newspapers found that while death was well covered in newspapers, "very few photographs showed death at all" (p. 305). Most of the photographs within his analysis showed the deceased while they were still living, only showed particular circumstances of the death but not the dead body itself, or only included images not associated with the actual demise. Because of these prevailing sentiments regarding the inappropriateness of gory or mutilated images of dead bodies, especially with faces displayed, or the notion that the images were unnecessary to the central news story, Hanusch concludes that "photos of the dead are rare" (p. 307).

Conventions of decency and newsworthy appropriateness aren't the only factors affecting whether and how visual media depicts death, however. The dictates of senior editors, layout and coloring, cropping and distance of shot, circumstances surrounding the death(s), cultural world views, and a host of other factors influence the depiction of dead bodies within news accounts, as well as how they are displayed (Campbell, 2004; Hanusch, 2008; Morse, 2014). While it is the news editors who make the final decisions as to what images will be shown and how those images will be displayed, most news reporters agree that the general rule is to "shoot first and decide later."

Long-time beat and broadcast reporter Kim Schumacher (2017) concurs. As a former journalist for both CBS and ABC affiliates in New York, Georgia, and South Carolina, she's accustomed to having to view, record, and justify her choice to display emotionally disturbing images. Her office is decorated with journalism awards, thank-you notes, and displayed prominently, a picture of her with Dan Rather. Tripods are propped up against her desk. Papers spill over and around each other. Within her lengthy news career, she has covered the Virginia Tech Shootings, the visits of the British Royal family and the Pope, and many other high-profile news events.

Kim explains the editorial demands that often confront a young "beat" reporter who's covering a news occurrence that has resulted in a fatality, whether a crime scene, an accident report, or a suicide:

> *You don't want to come back and have your editor say, "Why didn't you have this?" because you made the decision on your own. You can always make the decision later, and a lot of times there are compromises. You know, we're going to shoot this scene but we're going to blur this part of it. We're not going to shoot the face. There have been times when we've shot video of a body on the ground, and then we were trying to show all the people standing around, and just bring people to what the scene was, but we blurred out the body. You could see it was there, but it was blurred out, you couldn't see the body, but you could see all the people standing around; you could see the people's reaction.*
>
> *Personal Interview*

For many journalists, these decisions represent a continual balancing act. There is a need to balance telling the truth about what's happening in the war, with compassion for people killed in war and for military families (Silcock, et al., 2008). The public's need to know, journalistic responsibility to tell the truth, journalism's constitutional mandates, and standards of human decency are just a few of the factors all journalists and their editors must weigh as they grapple with their duty. As Kim explains:

> *I feel our job is to tell the truth: that's what our job is as journalists, to tell people the truth, and to report it to them in hopefully compelling ways that touches them and helps them understand. That being said, you don't want to go to the point of being sensationalized and abusing that responsibility. So, in my mind you weigh why are we showing this? Is the public going to learn something from this? For example, the Dale Earnhardt autopsy pictures – I don't think anyone should ever see those. There's nothing to be learned. It wasn't a murder, it wasn't spousal abuse …. [On the other hand] another good example is something like 9/11 and the people jumping or falling, not graphic, but emotionally heart wrenching to watch. I mean, my brother was there – he and his girlfriend lived there – and they said they saw it as they were escaping. No one will ever understand unless they were there. But to see those people falling because they can't go any further, or to make the decision to put your head in that space, there is something for the public to understand and there's something for them to learn.*
>
> Personal Interview

These are difficult decisions to make, and news personnel must make them every day. The "Falling Man" image (of a man jumping from the burning World Trade Center) from 9/11 was shown right after the attacks, but today it's difficult to find that picture because the media didn't want to tell this haunting, unresolved story (Drori-Avraham, 2006). From Dale Earnhardt's autopsy pictures to damage from hurricanes to coverage of terrorist actions, journalists weigh purpose, understanding, and the end result in order to choose to display, censor, or prohibit the viewing of particular images. There is also another issue that journalist Kim Schumacher discusses:

> *Just as a person in society, [not as a journalist], I don't want someone else to censor and decide what might be too much to see. Generally speaking, there's the rule that you don't show blood and guts and anything too gory. Once you get past that and start looking at the emotional things that aren't so bloody, you have to be cautious, but you always have to ask "Is there something to be learned from this?" I would rather have them tell me a warning and give me a moment to decide if I want to watch it or not. I don't want them to decide for me when I might have this opportunity to learn. I think people sometimes get upset because they didn't pay attention to the warnings. If the warnings are given and you decide to watch it, or you click, and you see something that upsets you, I feel like you've been warned. I think that people who get upset see a warning, and they disregard it, then they watch or click, and then they get upset. They need to take some personal responsibility. Maybe you didn't want to see it, but I did. The news media has to be cautious and weigh*

whether the benefit of what the public is learning outweighs the sensitivity of the subject.

Personal Interview

There are multiple ways that reporters choose to balance the horror of showing too much with what many of them perceive is a lack of professional responsibility in showing too little. Kim continues:

> *You know if we're showing a car accident and there's been a fatality, there's an arm and half a head hanging out of the car, there's nothing to be learned from that, we don't need to see that, whereas if an escaped prisoner did that and he's still on the loose we might make the choice to show or see that simply because we think that people seeing that might choose to respond, to intervene, to be helpful. There's some stories that I did about child abuse …. I can remember one story I did where the detectives showed me the pictures of the burns all along the arms of the child and along the body, second-degree burns, they trusted me and showed me and let me shoot the video. So I got the pictures and came back and talked to my news director and said that I want to show this on some level. "I know we need to be careful, but I want people to see what this child went through." I think we used like two pictures. There's no face, we didn't show the body, we showed the arm, and blurred the whole arm except for the hand, so you could see how red it was, but you didn't actually see the wound. We showed it once in one segment and didn't show it again. So you have an idea of what this child endured, and what she died from, without having to make it too graphic. I'm just a believer that our job is to tell the truth, and most people think we're just doing it for sensationalism, but I think that the majority of journalists feel like they want the public to understand, and I think the best way to do that is to use good judgment. "Is this going toward further understanding and to help with impact? Or is it just for sensationalism?"*

Personal Interview

The news' depiction of human death impacts us in multiple ways, and none may be more visceral than those delivered via visual media. As long-time newspaper editor Gwen Fowler (2017) asserts, "Words are very powerful, but images can be even more powerful." A former city editor for Greensboro, North Carolina's *Greensboro News and Record* and former Features, News Editorial, and Assistant Managing Editor of Myrtle Beach, South Carolina's *Sun News,* Gwen believes that while some of the journalistic considerations that affect what and how to show graphic and/or disturbing images are similar for all forms of news media, she suggests that some of the constraints that print journalists face may be a bit different from those of broadcast journalists. When Deb visits with her, Gwen is intently editing copy as she sips her coffee in the office she shares with other journalists. Her blonde pixie hair cut and bright blue eyes conceal her ferocious reputation as a news editor. Deb and Gwen chat for a bit and then begin the interview. Gwen's voice becomes more animated as she responds to Deb's questions:

> So I would say particularly with print journalism, where it exists in a permanent format and it's sitting around your house, the general rule that I've always followed is to be cautious. When you're coming in to someone's home, often at breakfast time, you don't want to unnecessarily have gratuitous violence shown or unnecessarily upsetting things …. We often don't truly understand something unless we see it. You know, we can hear about thousands of people dying, but if we see one image that really touches us, it brings it all home for us. And those would be the kinds of cases that I would argue there's a need to show things that might be upsetting to people. And there's also probably a difference – is this something that happened in downtown Greensboro, or did it happen across the country or in another country? If something violent happens, is that person's brother or sister right in town? You know, when things happen locally it takes a little bit more responsibility. I think those same standards apply to news organizations online, except you're not going into someone's home, they have to gain access to the information, and in those cases I don't think you need to be quite so squeamish about some of the images you show. At least then you can say you can give a warning that this might be graphic or disturbing.
>
> Personal Interview

But at what cost are images of death reported, broadcast, and/or displayed? Early studies on the effects of news reports about suicide on subsequent increases in suicide rates, theoretically known as "the Werther effect" (Phillips, 1974; Phillips & Carstensen, 1986; Wasserman, 1984) or "suicide contagion" (Gould & Shaffer, 1986; Gould et al., 1990; Romer, et al., 2006) continue to be replicated and validated within varieties of media – new and old. Generally speaking, televised coverage of suicide deaths results in increased suicide rates among younger populations (Romer et al., 2006; Stack, 1987, 2000; Stack & Gundlach, 1990), while newspaper reports of suicides not only has impact for younger consumers (Mueller, 2017), but also increases suicide rates for those over 44 years of age (Romer et al., 2006). As Romer et al. (2006) conclude, "suicide stories to which a local audience has the greatest exposure are likely to produce contagion" and "local television news is a potent influence on suicidal contagion" (p. 264). Interestingly and most recently, news of suicides reported and transmitted only via social media does not display the same "suicide contagion" effect (Ueda, et al., 2017). Researchers can only speculate right now as to those differences, but we suggest that both the live and pictorial nature of visual broadcast influences these effects.

The display of death for public consumption is a powerful rhetoric. Visual imagery within television and news has not only been linked to increased suicide, but its political power is also well documented (Konstantinidou, 2008; Memou, 2010). George and Shoos (2005) suggest that both photographs and film affect discourse and resulting opinions about varying forms of public execution, influencing death penalty debates. Morse (2014) found that displays of dead bodies within coverage of terrorist attacks were different depending upon the ethnicities of the attackers and the victims, sending powerful visual messages governing notions of human worth and loss. These same visually communicated notions of human worth and loss were important influences in the ways in which the public framed the life and death of Princess Diana (Kitzinger, 1998). Kitzinger argues that Diana herself, like many modern celebrities, essentially became "a creation of the modern mass media" (p. 75) while alive, and her death constituted a sort of public "post mortem" (p. 77).

The display of death affects all of us in multiple ways, but it is our print and broadcast news journalists who face the ramifications of these decisions every day. Not only must they balance the public's need to know, the conventions of human decency, the context and geographic location of the news stories, the political consequences, and the persuasive influences inherent within the coverage, but the potential of the image's inducement toward violence is another factor. *The Charleston Post and Courier* made the decision not to display dead bodies from Dylan Roof's Charleston Massacre for many of these same reasons: the proximity of the site of the murders to that of human survivors in the area, the conventions of human decency, the public's need to know, but in addition to these concerns another consideration emerged, the potential for the incitement of violence (Fowler, 2017).

Coverage of brutal, gruesome, and/or violent news affects journalists. While journalists employ strategies similar to those of many first responders – gallows humor, compartmentalization, and support from one another – the personal, emotional, and mental toll can be taxing. Former broadcast journalist Kim Schumacher (2017) explains:

> *I can turn it off in the moment, and steel myself; I can get the job done. But then when I get home, I sit and think about it. There are some stories though that have really affected me. They haunt me. They stay with me to this day. One of them was a man named Michael Passaro; he was estranged from his second wife, and he had custody of his daughter, her name was Maggie. She was three. He drove her back to his estranged wife's apartment complex and had her in a car seat in the back, and then he poured gasoline all over her and set her on fire, so the ex-wife could look out the window and see. Then when the fire trucks got there, they asked if there was anyone else in the car. He never responded. She died. She was burned alive. Not only did I do that story, but I went through the whole trial from beginning to end. That was just a horrific thing to sit and listen to. He never cried in court; there was no emotion. I remember the prosecuting attorney, Greg Hembree, asked the coroner, "How would you describe that kind of death?"*

and he said, "I can't think of a more painful way to die." Those were his words. I still think of that. I remember that all the time. "I can't think of a more painful way to die." That comes up in my head all the time. Children, elderly people, and animals get me, because they're the most defenseless members of our society.

Personal Interview

Former editor Gwen Fowler (2017) agrees:

Back in the eighties, in Somalia, there were service members dragged through the streets … we did run a photograph of that, and then we had to also run a story explaining why we did that; we had so many former service members in the area …. Beyond the images, it's just being immersed in something so long. I remember after 9/11, I was working I don't know how many hours a day, I was dealing with it on a professional level, but on a personal level, I was traumatized.

Personal Interview

Journalists understand the power of images of death. They also understand their constitutional mandates. Calvert and Torres (2011) suggest that there are at least "four ethical considerations" (p. 3) journalists – both print and broadcast – should reflect upon when grappling with the decision to show images of death:

1   Journalists' ethical obligation as "truth tellers;"
2   Journalists' commitment to "credibility;"
3   Journalists' responsibility to "minimize harm" and remain "sensitive" to others;
4   Journalists' mandate to act "independently" (Calvert & Torres, 2011, pp. 3–6)

They go on to outline First Amendment freedoms that govern the display and graphic images for journalists (pp. 6–10):

1   A commitment to "the marketplace of ideas;"
2   The established "watchdog role of the press in self-governing democracies;"
3   The clash of "familial privacy rights, potential tort liability, and the effects of "shock value" in First Amendment jurisprudence;"
4   Indecency claims

Finally, Calvert and Torres (2011) suggest and provide a rubric for journalists to use that may assist broadcast and print journalists and their editors. It provides five variables that can be ranked numerically:

1   The relationship between the text-based article and the photograph that is under consideration;

2   The newsworthiness of the text-based article if it were not accompanied by the photograph;
3   What is the value of the photograph to the text-based article?
4   What is the "emotional impact" and does it provide "something positive that enhances the overall quality and impact of the story"? and
5   Consider FCC [Federal Communications Commission] factors of "indecency," "graphicness," and "explicitness" (Calvert & Torres, 2011, pp. 11–13).

In his 2006 research study about media reporting of the events of 9/11, Drori-Avraham called media reporting on the event acts of narrating mourning, and suggests that the media did the job of mourning for our country by the way they reported the tragedy (Drori-Avraham, 2006). *The New York Times* told more than 2,000 stories with pictures, of all the people who died in the attack; in essence providing eulogies for the deceased. The photographic images froze time and created their own stories within the big story: first, images of the initial death and destruction, and then the ongoing images of the people who died – the narration of their lives. This juxtaposition of images forever seared the memory of the deceased with the 9/11 attack, turning the families' private grief into public mourning. The media's coverage of the tragedy constructed stories of good victimhood and worthy death (Drori-Avraham, 2006).

The human toll of death in the news has impact on its public and its journalists, on its societies and its cultures. However, "there is a long history of newspapers in the United States publishing compelling images of the dead in connection with newsworthy events" (Calvert & Torres, 2011, p. 13). The images that affect one person may not have the same emotional impact as another; some images have more emotional punch than others. For editor Gwen Fowler (2017), it was a recently published photograph of a young Syrian refugee boy lying dead on the beach in Greece, because "he was about the same age as my grandson." For journalist Kim Schumacher (2017), it was "a kitten that some young boys had set on fire." For residents of Boston, it's the images from the terrorist attack at the Boston Marathon (Williams and Williams, 2015). For Deb, it was the killing fields of Cambodia. For Cris, it was the image of the waiter sobbing in the ballroom where people were gathered waiting for President John F. Kennedy to arrive, with the news trickling in of his assassination, or the image of the taciturn Walter Cronkite wiping a tear from his eye when announcing the death of Kennedy. But perhaps even more evocative were the verbal images evoked by Walter Cronkite's dry narration of the assassination: "[he is] cradled in the arms of his wife," "blood spurting from the President's head," "slumped into the lap of Mrs. Kennedy," "saw blood streaming from his head," and "cut down by the bullet," proving it possible to have a graphic representation of death without showing anyone dead.

The impact of death in the news, just as with our responses to death itself, are socially constructed, highly contested, and intimately individual.

Conclusion

Just because an image could be shown does not mean it should be shown. On the other hand, just because something is upsetting doesn't mean you shouldn't see it. Some might argue the news stories about deaths are overly sensationalistic. Death in the news turns private grief into public mourning and adds to the construction of worthy lives and worthy deaths. The questions of whether and how to report on death are serious questions with serious consequences. Journalists have to balance the very real need for public awareness of horrific events with sensitivity for viewers and readers, and with respect for the dead and their families. Death has always been experienced in the home – in the form of a body laid to rest in the parlor, in emotional deathbed scenes with the family gathered around the dying loved one in his/her own bed. Today, death in the living room is via a large screen television. Some argue that mediated death desensitizes us to it, that death in the media causes compassion fatigue and diverted attention. We suggest that public deaths and narrated tragedies shape our communal and national identity, creating a nationalist context within which we live and die.

References

Calvert, C., & Torres, M. (2011). Staring death in the face during times of war: When ethics, law, and self censorship in the news media hide the morbidity of authenticity. Symposium on Censorship & The Media: Media Self-Censorship. (pp. 1–30). Notre Dame Journal of Law, Ethics & Public Policy.

Campbell, D. (2004). Horrific blindness: Images of death in contemporary media. Journal for Cultural Research, 8, 55–74.

Drori-Avraham, A. (2006). September 11th and the mourning after: Media narrating grief. Continuum: Journal of Media and Cultural Studies, 20(3), 289–297.

Fowler, G. (2017, August 31). Personal Interview. Conway, South Carolina.

George, D., & Shoos, D. (2005). Deflecting the political in the visual images of execution and the death penalty debate. College English, 67(6), 587–609.

Gerbner, D. (1980). Death in prime time: Notes on the symbolic functions of dying in the mass media. Annals of the American Academy of Political and Social Science, 447, 64–70.

Gould, M. S., & Shaffer, D. (1986). The impact of suicide in television movies: Evidence of imitation. New England Journal of Medicine, 315, 690–694.

Gould, M. S., Wallenstein, S., & Kleinman, M. (1990). Time-space clustering of teenage suicide. American Journal of Epidemiology, 131, 71–78.

Gray, O. (March 26, 2013). The death of television news. Moderate Voice. Available at Point of View Reference Center. Accession Number: 86696703. http://themoderatevoice.com/179663/the-death-of-television-news/anchorman/

Hanusch, F. (2008). Graphic deaths in the news media: Present or absent? Mortality, 13(4), 301–317. doi: 10/1080/13576270802383840.

Hoijer, B. (2004). The discourse of global compassion: The audience and media reporting of human suffering. Media, Culture and Society, 26, 513–531.

Kitzinger, J. (1998). Image: Diana Princess of Wales. Screen, 39(1), 73–79.

Konstantinidou, C. (2008). Spectacle of suffering and death: The photographic representation of war in Greek newspapers. Visual Communication, 7(2), 143–169.

Memou, A. (2010). "When It Bleeds, It Leads": Death and press photography in the anti-capitalist protests in Genoa 2001. Third Text, 24(3), 341–351.

Moeller, S. D. (1999). Compassion fatigue: How the media sell disease, famine, war, and death. London: Routledge.

Morse, T. (2014). Covering the dead: Death images in Israeli newspapers. Journalism Studies, 15(1), 98–113.

Mueller, A. S. (2017). Does the media matter to suicide?: Examining the social dynamics surrounding media reporting on suicide in a suicide-prone community. Social Science & Medicine, 180, 152–159.

Patterson III, O. (1984). Television's living room war in print: Vietnam in the news magazines. Journalism Quarterly, 61(1), 35–39, 136.

Petley, J. (2003). War without death: Responses to distant suffering. Journal for Crime, Conflict and the Media, 1, 172–185.

Phillips, D. (1974). The influence of suggestion on suicide: Substantive and theoretical implications of the Werther effect. American Sociological Review, 39, 340–354.

Phillips, D., & Carstensen, L. L. (1986). Clustering of teenage suicides after television news stories about suicide. New England Journal of Medicine, 315, 685–689.

Romer, D., Jamieson, P. E., & Jamieson, K. H. (2006). Are news reports of suicide contagious? A stringent test in six U. S. cities. Journal of Communication, 56, 258–270. doi: 10.1111/j.1460–2466.2006.00018.x.

Schumacher, K. (2017, August 31). Personal Interview. Conway, South Carolina.

Seale, C. F. (2004). Media constructions of dying alone: A form of "bad death." Social Science & Medicine, 58, 967–974.

Silcock, B. W., Schwalbe, C. B., & Keith, S. (2008). "Secret" casualties: Images of injury and death in the Iraq War across media platforms. Journal of Mass Media Ethics, 23, 36–50. doi: 10.1080/08900520701753205.

Stack, S. (1987). Celebrities and suicide: A taxonomy and analysis, 1948–1983. American Sociological Review, 52, 401–412.

Stack, S. (2000). Media impacts on suicide: A quantitative review of 293 findings. Social Science Quarterly, 81, 957–971.

Stack, S., & Gundlach, J. (1990). The effect of hyper media coverage of suicide, the case of New York City. Social Science Quarterly, 71, 619–627.

Ueda, M.; Mori, K.; Matsubayashi, T.; & Sawada, Y. (2017 in press). Tweeting celebrity suicides: Users' reaction to prominent suicide deaths on Twitter and subsequent increases in actual suicides. Social Science & Medicine, 1–9. Available at http://dx.doi.org/10.1016/j.socscimed.201.06.032.0277-9536/C2017 Elsevior Press.

Walter, T., Littlewood, J., & Pickering, M. (1995). Death in the news: The public invigilation of private emotion. Sociology, 29, 579–596.

Wasserman, I. (1984). Imitation and suicide: A reexamination of the Werther effect. American Sociological Review, 49, 427–436.

Williams, B., & Williams, P. (5 January, 2015). NBC Nightly News. Available from Points of View Reference Center. Accession Number 32U13115165606NNN.

5

ANGELS OF DEATH: COMMUNICATING ABOUT DEATH IN MEDICAL SETTINGS

Deb clicks off the television and puts the remote down on the coffee table. "You know," she says, "if the doctor would have just told my family earlier that my mom didn't have much longer to live, that would have made the last year so much easier."

"Yeah," Cris says. "I know you had a lot of angst as a family around when and how to continue or discontinue treatment. Was it difficult until the very end?"

Deb nods. "My mom couldn't eat on her own and some of my family members wanted to force-feed her. I wanted to just let her die in peace. We had terrible fights about it for months and it was agonizing to see her just get worse and worse. Some of my family thought she would still be alive for many more years and were unprepared when she did die." Deb takes a sip of her wine. "I know Alzheimer's is a terminal disease. I also know that it's hard for doctors to know when an Alzheimer's patient is nearing the end, especially when she's non-communicative, non-functional, and people are force feeding her." She gazes off into the distance. It's clear this is still hard for her to talk about. "You know, Cris, my mom was diagnosed in 2005, but she had begun exhibiting symptoms several years before."

"I know you said when you went to Italy you noticed a lot of warning signs. I remember you telling me all those stories about her getting lost in the hotels!" Cris and Deb reminisce together, and Deb says, "Yeah, it got to the point where I wasn't comfortable with her being alone. I'd hold her hand when we'd cross the streets. She couldn't remember to look both ways." Deb drains her wine glass. "When we went to New York, she couldn't find her way back to the hotel room from the hair stylist, just downstairs. She stopped driving, voluntarily, in 2004; we all knew then something was wrong, and we knew that she knew."

"Telling patients and families that their condition is terminal might be the most difficult conversation medical providers and their patients and families have," Cris says. "And from my personal experience with my parents, even when a doctor gives you the bad news directly, it's really difficult to absorb the meaning. That's the way it was with my dad when he was diagnosed with cancer."

Cris's voice fades off as she remembers:

> As I type these words, my thoughts float back to a hospital room in 1989. Dad has cancer. Cancer. The word hangs in the air, on the page, as I type it. I'm with Dad when Dr. Walker gives us the news. Dad and I have never really been close, but I'm glad I'm there when the doctor comes in. It's strange; I feel a sense of protectiveness toward him while we listen to the doctor. Dad had cancer ten years earlier – throat cancer – and was cured. We're prepared for another diagnosis of cancer; we know it's a possibility. But I'm not prepared for the language Dr. Walker is using. I wait to hear the prescribed treatment. But it's strange; he says some strange things.
>
> "It's prostate cancer, but it's spread to the bladder and the kidneys."
> "We can do surgery to slow the growth of the cancer."
> "We'll try to slow it down."
> "We can't tell how slow or quickly the cancer will continue to grow."
>
> I struggle to hear words about curing the cancer, about getting rid of it, but he doesn't say them. He talks about slowing it down. He talks about maintaining quality of life as long as possible. But he doesn't say "cure." My mind tries to understand, but I struggle with the concept. Through the whole visit, Dad acts very odd – strangely quiet and calm. I ask a lot of questions, but he doesn't seem to have any. After the doctor leaves, I feel confused. My brain feels as if it's full of cotton candy, making my thoughts sticky and slow. The news isn't computing; it doesn't fit into my version of reality. Dad seems resigned to the news. Just like that. He doesn't seem to be upset or concerned. He acts as if he already knew. Dad doesn't have much to say to me after the doctor leaves but asks me to go by their house and tell Mom after I leave the hospital. I tell her; she doesn't say much either. I call my friend Jane. She's a nurse, and she always answers my medical questions.
>
> "Don't worry," she says. "Prostate cancer is a slow growing cancer. Most people with prostate cancer end up dying of something else first." Somehow, this seems reassuring.
>
> Davis, 2010, pp. 4–5.

"Of course," Cris continues, "that's if you can get a doctor to give you the news directly. In my research, I've found that healthcare providers are reluctant to give bad news and don't know how. Families frequently feel let down by doctors' failure to take charge of the situation and be clear about prognosis and making recommendations for palliative care. Most physicians wait for the family to bring up the topic, but families rarely do. Providing information on terminal prognoses is difficult for medical providers because families' wants and needs are contradictory. Families want information related to patients' personhood rather than pathology (Russ & Kaufman, 2005), and healthcare providers are more comfortable with pathological language rather than seeing the patient holistically."

"Families want to be given information about their loved one's medical condition," Cris continues, "but the information must include guidance in interpreting what the doctor is telling them, and if they get too much information, they can feel overwhelmed. And, regardless of what information they get, they feel ill-prepared to make the decisions they need to make about their loved one's care (Russ & Kaufman, 2005). Of course, that assumes the family is present when the bad news is even given. In the hospital or at medical appointments, the terminal conversations may take place with only the patient; the family may be left out if they are not present when the physician is available to have the conversation (Russ & Kaufman, 2005)."

Cris pauses to find a file on her laptop. "I wrote about this in my story about my dad. Here," she reads:

> *Marian shifts her position in her hospital bed. She's still groggy from her surgery, but right now, this is a blessing. Sleep takes her mind off of her pain. She dozes off. Lying there in the liminal space between consciousness and unconsciousness, in the deep recesses of her brain, she hears a voice in the room. She's too tired to open her eyes, and the voice floats over her like a cloud. She hears a curt male voice. "This is Dr. Curtis." the voice says. "I have a patient I want to admit to hospice. Marian Powell. She is appropriate for hospice care at this time." Hospice. The words hang in the air, and her mind slowly takes them in. Appropriate for hospice. She doesn't have to think about what that meant. She knows. It's a death sentence.*
>
> Davis, 2010, p. 6

"That came from a research project I did with a hospice and it reflects an actual experience a patient had. It's important to tell people and their families they are dying," Cris says. "It allows them to say and do what they need to so that they can die peacefully."

People are afraid of death – they're afraid of dying, they're afraid they will be trapped without good choices at the end of life, they're afraid they will lose control or be shamed or lose their dignity. They're afraid they will be alone when they die, and they're afraid that, when they get to the end of their life, they will find that their life was wasted. Basically, people are afraid of the unknown and death is very unknown to us (Neimeyer, 1995). Therefore, patients and families are ambivalent in their orientation toward end of life conversations with healthcare providers (Russ & Kaufman, 2005). Families want to know the doctor's prognosis, but they also want to be given hope. A good death is a death filled with hope. Families want realistic hope, though, not false hope, which is especially difficult when the news is not particularly hopeful. Nuland (1993) asserts that it is the doctor's job to never allow "his patients to lose hope, even when they are obviously dying" (p. 222). The physician giving the terminal prognosis has the power to offer hope, withhold it, or even to take it away, but seeing hope as simply offering a cure is unnecessarily restricting. Hope is not just a reassurance of life, and hope doesn't necessarily mean "cure," but hope is also believing that you have the ability to influence outcomes in your life and that you have choices in life (Averill et al., 1990; Nuland, 1993). Thus, a good death also involves hope, even in the face of a seemingly hopeless situation, in the midst of adversity, because hope is related to the significance we give to our situation, to holding an inner strength and having the determination to endure whatever happens (Averill et al., 1990; Davis, 2014; Groopman, 2004). Hope can be thought of as a protective factor that helps people deal with chronically stressful situations (Groopman, 2004; King et al., 2003; Richardson, 2002). Hope results in positive outcomes not just for the hopeful person, but also for those around him or her through indirect communal benefits (Snyder, 2000). We should point out that hope does hold a key to physical benefits as well as these mental and emotional ones – for seriously ill patients, hope has been found to block pain receptors in the brain and change neurochemistry in the body (Groopman, 2004; Richardson, 2002; Snyder, 2000). A good death occurs when the patient and family are fully informed (Webb, 1997), and this is why communicating with patients and families is so important – for patients with a terminal prognosis, hope might be related to accomplishing certain things before the end of their lives, or might be in the form of a promise by the physician that no futile attempts will be made to save their life, or that "no man or woman will be left to die alone" (Nuland, 1993, p. 243). A good death also occurs when a person is allowed to die with as much dignity and comfort as possible, as quickly as possible, with no pain and no prolonged suffering (Webb, 1997).

Cultural attitudes towards death concern our beliefs, fears, behaviors, about what a good death is. Cultural attitudes toward death affect our dying experiences. In our culture, in which the dying are traditionally separated from the rest of "healthy" society, caring for a terminally ill loved one is a severe disruption of the family's lifestyle. Just as serious illness is a dramatic loss of the hopes and dreams that had guided a person's life (Frank, 1995), death and terminal illness of a loved one is a serious disruption in the trajectory of a family's life, and it's not unusual for people in our society to find themselves completely unprepared for the death of a loved one. Everything turns upside down when a loved one is terminally ill. Life turns into death. Health turns into illness. Living rooms turn into bedrooms. Spouses turn into caregivers. Love turns into loss. Treatment turns into acceptance. Movement forward becomes frozen in time. Cultural attitudes toward pain and suffering also affect our end of life experiences. People in our society are not used to being in pain; we have medications and treatments that get rid of pain at the first sign. Perhaps the most difficult thing for families to deal with, when caring for a terminally ill loved one, is pain or suffering on the part of the patient. Death is hard and it is especially hard when the loved one suffers either emotionally, physically, or socially toward the end of their life. In addition, cultural attitudes toward caregiving for loved ones also play into how we experience the death of loved ones. Caring for a loved one with a terminal illness is both emotionally and physically very difficult, but it's considered a filial duty to provide care for parents, for instance, at their end of life (Davis, 2010).

"I experienced the agony of my mother's pain at the end of her life," Cris says to Deb. She tells the story:

> I can hear her yelling as soon as I walk in the front door at Hospice. "Oh, oh, oh, oh, oh, oh, oh!" I hear echo down the hallway. I am amazed that other patients have not begun complaining.
>
> "Hi, Mom," I try to say cheerfully as I walk into her room. "How are you feeling?" She looks at me with tears in her eyes and moans.
>
> "Oh!" she responds. "Pain! Pain!" I can see it on her face. I don't care what the doctor said. She is in pain.
>
> "Mom, I'm so sorry!" I pat her left hand. I notice that her right arm is drawn up against her chest and her hand is curled under toward her chin. I resist the urge to run out of the room. I don't know how long I can stand watching her like this. She grabs my hand.
>
> "Help me!" she implores.
>
> "Mom, we're doing the best we can!" I try to explain, but the explanation is not enough.
>
> "Pain!" she repeats. "Help me!"
>
> I am rooted in this spot next to her bed, unable to help her, forced to watch her, suffocated by feelings of helplessness, impotence, powerlessness. I don't know what to do. The doctor won't give her pain medication. He says it is the morphine that caused this condition. He says we have to get it out of her system. He says she is not in pain. But she is in pain. I can see it. I can feel it. I can feel it through my body, in my nerve endings, in my muscles, joints, bones. Sharp and throbbing, aching and stabbing. I am the pain. At this instant, I am utterly convinced that there is a hell, and I am in it.
>
> I escape into her bathroom. I close the door firmly behind me and turn on the fan and the faucet to drown out noise. I fall to my knees and cry, trying to hold back the sobs so I can't be heard, struggling to breathe between the sobs rising from my gut, from deep inside me, from my soul. Over the fan and the water, I can hear her moan. "Oh, God," I pray. "Help me! Make it stop! Oh, please, make it stop!" I rock back and forth and pray, "Make it stop. Make it stop!"

Suddenly, I hear a voice say, "Hi, Mom!"

"Jerry!" I hear Mom yell, loudly and clearly. "Help me, Jerry!"

"Where's Cris?" I hear Jerry ask.

I wipe my eyes and turn off the water. I come out of the bathroom just as Mom yells loudly, "Help me!"

"Mom!" I say, exasperation and frustration boiling over. "We're doing the best we can!"

This catches her attention and she looks directly at me, as if seeing me for the first time. "I love you!" she shouts loudly.

I take a deep breath. "I love you too, Mom," I answer.

Davis, 2005, pp. 403–403

Families and patients also need to know prognostic information in order to make crucial decisions about end of life care or withdrawal of treatments, and physician's refusal or inability to prognosticate a timeframe to death is a source of frustration to families (Russ & Kaufman, 2005).

"It's too bad you weren't able to convince your family to bring in hospice services earlier," Cris says.

"Well, to be fair, we didn't know hospice was an option unless 'death was imminent.' Finally, my dad found out that we could use them because of their focus on palliative care, and it really was a godsend. They'd come every other day, help get mom dressed, and feed her breakfast. Hospice paid for a lot of things that Mom's insurance wouldn't cover. I can't remember how many years it was, but then hospice discontinued services, because she didn't die fast enough. Then, we were able to use them again. It was really hard, and became complicated."

"What do you mean?" asks Cris.

"Well, on the days hospice came, the caregivers wouldn't get mom out of bed, because they knew that the hospice worker would do it. But sometimes the hospice worker would be late, or be sick, or there'd be some complication, and there my mom would lie. My dad came one day for lunch, and she was still in bed in her soiled nightgown, because the caregivers just assumed hospice was coming. It got frustrating, and then when they sort of fired her because she didn't die fast enough, I got pretty angry." Deb shakes her head. "It was just a horrible time."

Cris nods sympathetically. "It's hard, because people think of hospice as giving up, but that's not really true. And research reports that the earlier hospice is called in, the better the end of life experience for the patient and the family."

"Yeah, and I don't think that people even know what services hospice offers," Deb says.

"I agree. Besides the obvious one that most people know about, palliative care – pain and symptom management – hospice also provides nursing and physician care, social work services, bereavement services, spiritual care, home health aides, and housekeeping services. They provide families with needed information and explanations about their loved one's diagnosis and prognosis; they help the families understand what the medical providers are telling them. And, they provide these services at home, in nursing homes or hospitals, or – at the very end of a person's life – in an end-stage hospice facility (Davis, 2010)."

Most people have limited knowledge of hospice care until they or their loved ones have a need for their services. Most people are correctly aware that hospice care is for people with a terminal illness who have a prognosis of six months or less to live. Many hospices also provide palliative care – pain and symptom management – for chronic conditions or terminal conditions that have a prognosis longer than six months. Hospice's array of services includes providing equipment; running errands; managing pain; providing emotional care; and providing medical and paramedical care from social workers, doctors, and nurses. They provide care 24–7, and their assistance is especially appreciated at times of crisis. Hospice staff provide both physical and emotional support that is all-encompassing and ever-present, for both patients and families (Davis, 2010).

Our society values experts and professionals, and hospice staff are the "death experts." One of the most important things they do is to provide information to families and patients about the dying experience. This information seems to help patients and families cope with and accept the unfamiliar changes they are undergoing. Family members typically have concerns about "doing it right" for their loved one, and hospice provides information to help them. Hospice has an uncanny knowledge about death and dying. Providing information is one way that hospice facilitates a "good death" by helping patients and families find a sense of coherence and control in the midst of chaos (Davis, 2010).

Cris wipes a tear from her eye. "I experienced hospice's expertise with death when my mother died in a hospice home," she says. "The day she died:"

> Later that evening the nurse gave us the news. Mom's oxygen saturation level had dropped to 47%. The end was surely near. Probably tonight. We called family and friends, and we all rallied around. And watched. And waited. By 2:00 a.m., the night nurse sent us home. Mom had stabilized. She's not going to die tonight, at least not while we're there. Another day passed, Thursday night. Mom was in a coma, but there was no telling how long she would stay that way. Exhaustion set in, from days of watching her sleep, waiting for her to die. We went home around 11:00 p.m.
>
> They called just after midnight. We dragged back to Hospice, to say goodbye to her body, to comfort each other, to find feeling in the numbness of death.

The nurse on duty gave me paperwork to sign. I glanced at the date of death: 12/3. December 3. My birthday.

"Thanks a lot, Mom," I thought. "You died on my birthday. What a thing to remember every year!"

I looked again at the form. Next to the date was the time of death. 12:03. What?

"She died at 12:03 on 12/3," I said, not believing what I was reading. "12/3 at 12:03."

"Yes, isn't that strange?" The Hospice nurse paused from her paperwork. "I'm sure of the time, too." She leaned in and spoke with that mystical voice that Hospice nurses get when they talk about death. "I was in another room and I had a feeling that I just HAD to go to her room. I looked at my watch. She had JUST died. I'm sure of the time of death."

12/3 at 12:03. My birthday. You might find that to be a coincidence. I prefer to think of it as Mom's ultimate dialogue, her way of telling me every birthday, forever, "Happy Birthday," and "I love you."

Davis, 2003, pp. 212

Hospice care goes beyond merely providing medical care to providing care that would be termed as "love." Hospice's treatment of patients goes well beyond seeing them in their "sick role," as, for example, "my cancer patient." Hospice's treatment of patients could be characterized as an interpersonal relationship, in which the patient is seen and treated as a unique human being with individual wants, needs, and tastes, and a dialogic relationship in which the patient is lifted up and made to feel better about themselves by virtue of the way they are treated by hospice staff. Even in the midst of what could be embarrassing and degrading care, hospice helps the patients and family maintain their dignity, and, therefore, their humanity. They treat them as fully human, as more than simply their illness or their symptoms (Davis, 2010).

Hospice treats families as fully human by respecting their voice, their thoughts and opinions, and their rights to make their own choice for themselves and their loved ones. Our society tends to sanctify dying people, treating them as saints after they are dead and speaking of the deceased in reverent terms. In the same way, we seem to sanctify hospice. Perhaps this is because hospice staff provides care that, in our society, only a family member or friend would do; perhaps it's because since insurance or Medicare usually pays for the services, they appear to be doing it for free; perhaps it's because hospice staff deal with what our society deems to be untouchable and unclean; or perhaps it's because our society sanctifies the dead and hospice staff are given what might be called a courtesy sanctification. Hospice staff are thought of as saints because they provide care in taboo matters and don't judge or blame the family for not providing that care themselves (Davis, 2010).

If you think about the concept of social constructionism – that our communication constructs certain experiences, you could say that hospice constructs
humanness for patients. Much of medical care can be really dehumanizing. For
instance, in the hospital, people are frequently treated as if they are the sum of
their symptoms or bodily parts instead of a holistic human being with thoughts
and fears, feelings and experiences, histories and stories. Hospice staff, in contrast, are intentional about treating their patients more holistically. For example,
when they talk about patients in team meetings, they tell their life stories,
moving beyond listing their medical symptoms to talk about their interests,
their families, their stories, and their personalities. Perhaps most importantly,
they talk about the patients' lives before they became ill (Davis, 2010). They
move beyond patienthood to see patients as holistic beings, de-medicalizing
the patients to see them for who they really are beyond their medical problems
and infirm bodies (Hyde, 2005).

Here's an example of this from Davis, 2010, telling the story of a hospice
team meeting:

> Barbara begins in a monotone voice. "Clyde Jones, lung C.A., mets to the bone.
> 75-year old white male, wife at home, married daughter who is caregiver. Nurse,
> once a week, counselor, one time. No volunteer, home health aide three times, no
> chaplain, no homemaker."
>
> While she talks in her language of clinical reasoning and case presentation
> bullets (Good & Good, 2000), everyone is shuffling paperwork, filling out forms,
> and piling them around the table. Susan interrupts her paperwork to tell his story.
> "He was playing golf three times a week until he got sick. His wife is disabled.
> They've been married for 49 years. They have one daughter. They have an ador-
> able golden retriever they're going to need to give away."
>
> Barbara adds to the story. "As I said, he's got lung cancer. He has the most
> beautiful orange grove. The problem is, his daughter works full-time, and she's
> trying to care for both him and his wife. The wife is unable to get around. She is
> in a wheelchair most of the time herself. I think she's coping though."
>
> Home Health Aide Karen objects. "She's not coping. The two times I've been
> there she's fallen to pieces."
>
> I notice how this discussion now almost sounds like gossiping. Their voice
> tones are lively and animated. As they talk, these faceless names come to life.
> They become people with stories, personalities, and relationships.
>
> The admissions discussion is interrupted when Dr. Cameron arrives. The dis-
> cussion changes to very clinical language. Sentences become clipped, with shorter
> exchanges. This is the "edited version" of the patient's story (Good & Good,
> 2000).
>
> "Mrs. Smith?"
> "65-year old female. Multiple myeloma. Brain mets."
> "Symptoms?"

"She's having problems with her bowels. She's taking Senna."

This exchange has a list-like quality, with a staccato-tone and curt sentences between her and the nurses. I am surprised at the abrupt change in their "formal reporting" (Ellingson, 2003), but within a few minutes, Dr. Cameron is joining in the chatting and friendly conversation about the patients. "She seems to be getting confused. She was embarrassed about forgetting my name."

Susan adds. "Going to the bathroom seems to be becoming a problem for her. It's making her reluctant to leave home."

The nurses make several recommendations to the doctor, which she considers and seems to accept.

"Will her daughter handle her death okay?"

"No, there's a suicide risk on her."

"We'd better keep an eye on her then."

Davis, 2010, pp. 21–22.

Hospice also constructs humanness by treating patients and families with dignity. Even in the midst of providing very undignified care for patients, team members find ways to maintain their patients' dignity. Hospice team members help patients maintain their personal agency, respecting their lives and their decisions, even if they don't agree with them, and by encouraging them to take responsibility for themselves, as much as they are able (Davis, 2010). The following excerpt is taken from an observation of a hospice patient–provider interaction:

Marian usually has read the morning paper when Karen, her home health aide arrives. This morning, Karen already has her coffee ready before the aroma wakes Marian up. "Good morning!" Karen greets her as she stands at the foot of her bed. "How are you feeling this morning?"

"Not so good, honey. A lot of aches and pains this morning. I'm not sure I'm up for a bath this morning."

"Don't you worry, Mrs. Powell. We'll fix you up. I'll get you some breakfast, you'll feel better after you eat."

"I'm not really hungry."

"Just a little. I brought you some grapes. I know they're your favorite."

Marian hesitates. She really feels weak this morning and she can't decide if eating will make her feel better or worse.

"I'll peel them for you. I know you like them that way." Karen offers as she goes into the kitchen without waiting for a response.

"What are we going to do today?" Karen asks as she watches Marian eat. "Whatever you want, you're the boss today."

"My nephew is coming to visit this afternoon," Marian says. "I want to be up and dressed when he comes."

"We'll get you a bath and fix up your hair. You'll feel better after that."

"Karen, honey, I can't believe you're having to do this for me. I never thought I'd be having someone bathe me and clean me up."

"Mrs. Powell, you're like my grandmother. It's okay," Karen reassures her.

"Karen, honey, you take such good care of me! I don't know what I'd do without you!"

"Oh, Mrs. Powell," Karen responds, "you're my favorite patient!" She carefully helps Marian into, then out of, the bathtub, making sure to keep her from falling while at the same time expertly using two separate towels to keep her covered. "Tell me about your nephew."

"He's such a fine boy. He's going to bring me dinner today," Marian says as Karen helps her [lie] on the bed. "When are your nieces coming to town?"

Karen rubs lotion into her back. "Now for the massage. They're coming in tomorrow. I can't wait. It's been months since I've seen them."

"Oh, that feels so good!" Marian savors the feeling of the massage. "Fix my hair up pretty today; I want to look good for Jimmy."

"It's good for your circulation," Karen says as she finished rubbing in the lotion. "Mrs. Powell, I'll fix you up special. We'll put on your favorite lipstick."

"Help me in the sunroom, honey. I don't want Jimmy seeing me in bed," Marian instructs as Karen helped her get dressed.

"You look really nice, Mrs. Powell. Real dressed up today."

Marian glances in the mirror. "You've fixed me up so nice, I don't look like I'm sick! That makes me feel really good!"

Davis, 2010, pp. 51–52

Team members are also very open about acknowledging flaws in patients and families. They see them as they are, with both good qualities and bad qualities, and they accept them that way. They don't sugarcoat them and make them better than they are, but they don't make them out to be worse than they are, either. Even with people who are difficult to care for, team members manage to provide care and compassion. If they like a patient, they say so. If they don't, they say that too. There's none of the "sanctifying the dead" you often see after people die. They story them in all their humanity, good and bad. This serves as confirmation (Buber, 1965) to the patients, acknowledging their personhood, affirming them as they are, affirming that they are okay – appropriate, even, for hospice – just the way they are. From another hospice team meeting:

Karen's report is eventful. "Mrs. Long pulled out a steak knife on me." I listen, shocked, as she tells the story matter-of-factly. "I don't take it personally. I'm concerned about her safety. She said she'd kill me if I didn't leave, and I said, 'I'll leave when you put the knife down!' I couldn't leave her alone. She might hurt herself!"

Davis, 2010, p. 76

Reciprocity of Relationships

Hospice relationships are reciprocal. Team members open themselves up to patients and families. They practice reciprocal communication, and share parts of their lives while patients share parts of theirs. They build a reciprocal relationship with patients and families, sharing their own lives and their own selves. This act of sharing communicates to patients that they have something to offer, something still to give to others. We all have a need to be needed, and team members provide patients and families with the gift of receiving what they have to offer (Davis, 2010).

Hospice interactions with patients and families are relaxed. In the best, most "human" interactions, team members take their time. Doctors and nurses don't wear white. They talk to patients as a friend might (Davis, 2010). The next two excerpts are from observations of hospice patient–provider interactions, first with a volunteer, then with the physician.

> *"Here you are, Mrs. Powell." Lisa hands Marian her cup of hot tea. Marian is always cold, and Lisa hopes that sipping this will make her feel a little better. Now that Marian has let Lisa make herself at home in her kitchen, Lisa's beginning to feel like she can be of some help to her. She sits down next to Marian on the couch.*
>
> *"Susan was just leaving as I was coming in," she observes. "What are your visits with her like?"*
>
> *"I just see her as a normal person. She's just another normal person that comes to visit. We just sit and talk. As if there's nothing wrong, she's just visiting. That's the way I feel she is. Sometimes I'm upset and we talk about that. I think that mainly gets me through the day because, except for you, I have nobody else to talk to, about my situation. She's somebody I can talk to. Like I've known her all my life. To talk to somebody about my feelings."*
>
> *Lisa nods. "Like a friend," she reflects.*
>
> *"You, Susan, Karen, Barbara," Marian continues. "It always feels good. Seeing somebody come in. Because I feel there's somebody that cares for me. Sometimes I don't really think about y'all being hospice. I feel that you're just a friend, coming for a visit. Someone to confide in. I try not to think of y'all being hospice."*
>
> *Marian hands Lisa her empty tea cup as she continues talking. "Y'all don't treat me like I'm on death row. You don't treat me like I'm dying."*
>
> *Lisa smiles. "What do we treat you like?" she asks.*
>
> *"You treat me like everyday people treat everybody."*
>
> *Davis, 2010, p. 63*

Hospice team members take bedside manners to a new level, by taking time to talk to them, to listen to them.

> *Dr. Cameron walks over to Marian's bed and begins taking her vital signs as Marian sits up on her pillow. Dr. Cameron's voice is focused. "We're concerned*

about the pain you've been having. We want to do some tests right away." Marian nods but doesn't say anything. The doctor continues. "We think the cancer has spread to your spine. We want to do a CT scan and MRI. Right away."

Marian dabs at her cheeks as her tears wet them. Dr. Cameron kneels by her bed. She stays there for quite some time, silently, holding Marian's hand, patting her, rubbing her back, letting her cry. When Marian's tears begin to stop, Dr. Cameron speaks again. Softly, still kneeling, but looking directly into her eyes. "Describe your pain," she asks.

Davis, 2010, p. 66

Team members talk to patients about everything and everybody in their lives, and in so doing, they connect with them at a deep level of understanding. They "read" them, understanding their emotional and spiritual needs, sometimes even before the patient herself knows she has the need. They are not afraid to get close to their patients, and, despite the emotional toll that such closeness plays on team members, they build a mutual trust between them and the patients (Davis, 2010).

Patients as Worthwhile Human Beings

Hospice team members communicate to patients and families that they care, through both words and nonverbal communication such as touch. Hospice patients feel loved and appreciated, and feel accepted where they are, for who they are. Through hospice's caring communication, patients are constructed as worthwhile human beings, worthy of being loved and cared for, and grieved for (Davis, 2010). From a hospice team meeting, a nurse's report on a patient who just died:

"The patient died peacefully. She woke up, the continuous care nurse gave her permission to go, and she died. I don't know if I ever told her it was okay to go." Barbara reaches for the Kleenex and wipes her eyes before she continues. "We told each other how much we loved each other. Kisses and hugs."

Davis, 2010, pp. 67–68

Patients are treated as fully human when hospice team members acknowledge them as people who are worth grieving over, worth feeling sad for (Davis, 2010). From an interview with a home health aide:

I sit next to Karen at Vallartas. We're continuing our interview between bites. "Do you cry when they die?" I ask her.

"Oh, my gosh," is her response.

"Yet you keep going back and doing it again." This is more of a statement than a question.

"Oh yeah."
"Why?"
"Because they need love and I have love for all of them."

Davis, 2010 p. 89

Compassionate Honesty

Patients' suffering is recognized and affirmed. Yet, they are not coddled. Hospice team members are honest with them, giving them information when they need it, as they are ready to hear it, teaching them what they need to know when they need to know it. Patients cope with illness through information management. Collaborative sharing of information between doctors and patients creates an equal relationship between them, and gives patients coping opportunities. Being honest with patients and families acknowledges their death and in so doing, acknowledges their life (Davis, 2010). It provides them "with an environment where their voice can be heard and responded to in a genuine way" (Hyde, 2005, p. 46). Following is a conversation between a daughter of a hospice patient and the hospice social worker:

> *"You know, Susan, here's my concern. Mom's so far outlived the doctor's prognosis in the hospital. She doesn't seem to be getting any worse. She seems to be rallying. They never did a biopsy in the hospital. Maybe she doesn't even have cancer. Is it possible they made a mistake? Is it possible she's not ready for hospice? She seems to be feeling better this week. We have plans to go out this afternoon!"*
>
> *Susan hesitates before answering. This is always a difficult conversation to have. She's not sure what Katherine is ready to hear, so she decides to answer the question indirectly. "Regardless of Marian's prognosis, she's still a good candidate for hospice. Because of her age, because of her oxygen problems, she's still very appropriate for hospice." Susan can tell that this isn't the answer Katherine is looking for. They sip their coffee in silence.*
>
> *Davis, 2010, p. 59*

Conclusion

Aging, illness, and dying are rites of passage within which we need to create new meanings for our lives. In the midst of this liminal state, we can move outside of ourselves to find meaning in our shared humanity. Hospice provides life to patients who are involved in the process of death. In the face of possible social death, hospice sometimes provides the only source of life to dying patients. Being under the care of hospice means that life is valued and acknowledged – for the patients, a new phase of living has just begun (Davis, 2010).

References

Averill, J. R., Catlin, G., & Chon, K. K. (1990). Rules of hope. New York: Springer-Verlag.

Buber, M. (1965). The knowledge of man: Selected essays. Trans. by Friedman, M., & Smith, R. G. London, U.K.: Allen & Unwin.

Davis, C. S. (2003). A dialogic farewell: Enhancing the "I-Thou" quality of a parent-child relationship. Journal of Loss and Trauma, 8(3), 201–215.

Davis, C. S. (2005). Home. Qualitative Inquiry, 11(2), 392–409.

Davis, C. S. (2010). Death: The beginning of a relationship. Cresskill, NJ: Hampton Press.

Davis, C. S. (2014). Communicating hope: An ethnography of a children's mental health care team. New York, NY: Routledge.

Ellingson, L. L. (2003). Interdisciplinary health care teamwork in the clinic backstage. Journal of Applied Communication Research, 31(2), 93–117.

Frank, A. W. (1995). The wounded storyteller. Chicago, IL: University of Chicago Press.

Good, B. J., & Good, M. D. (2000). "Fiction" and "historicity" in doctor's stories: Social and narrative dimensions of learning medicine. In Mattingly, C., & Garro, L. C. (Eds.), Narrative and the cultural construction of illness and healing. pp. 50–69. Los Angeles, CA: University of California Press.

Groopman, J. (2004). The anatomy of hope: How people prevail in the face of illness. New York: Random House.

Hyde, M. J. (2005). The life-giving gift of acknowledgement: A philosophical and rhetorical inquiry. West Lafayette, IN: Perdue University Press.

King, G., Cathers, T., Brown, E., Specht, J. A., Willoughby, C., Polgar, J. M., MacKinnon, E., Smith, L. K., & Havens, L. (2003). Turning points and protective processes in the lives of people with chronic disabilities. Qualitative Health Research, 13, 184–206.

Neimeyer, R. A. (1995). Death anxiety. In Wass, H., Bernardo, F., & Neimeyer, R. (Eds.), Dying: Facing the facts. pp. 49–88. Washington, D.C.: Taylor & Francis.

Nuland, S. B. (1993). How we die: Reflections on life's final chapter. New York, NY: Vintage.

Richardson, G. E. (2002). The metatheory of resilience and resiliency. Journal of Clinical Psychology, 58, 307–321.

Russ, A. J., & Kaufman, S. R., (2005). Family perceptions of prognosis, silence, and the "suddenness" of death. Culture, Medicine, and Psychiatry, 29(1), 103–123. doi: 10.1007/s11013-11005-4625-4626

Snyder, C. R. (2000). The past and possible futures of hope. Journal of Social and Clinical Psychology, 19, 11–28.

Webb, M. (1997). The good death: The new American search to reshape the end of life. New York, NY: Bantam.

6

TALK TO ME: COMMUNICATING ABOUT DEATH IN FAMILY SETTINGS

"Have you and Jerry planned for your deaths?" Deb asks Cris, curled up sipping on a warm beverage, switched from the earlier wine.

"What do you mean? Like a will or living will? We have a will and a living will explaining that we don't want to be kept alive by artificial means. As Jerry likes to say, 'just pull the plug.'"

"Lenny and I have too. Neither of us wants our deaths delayed by medical interventions such as respirators or forced feeding; we've even discussed the circumstances of chest compressions in CPR. We'd like to be kept comfortable and allowed to die. But I'm more interested right now in your plans for your funeral. Have you written your own obituary or talked to each other about your funeral plans?"

"Oh! Well, yes and no. We have not written our obituaries, although we've talked about it. We've discussed my funeral wishes frequently but I've never written it down and I'm not sure Jerry would remember when the time came. We even have a form to fill out that we got from our church that would let us fill in our funeral wishes, but neither of us have filled it in." Cris sits thoughtfully for a minute. "I definitely want a church funeral then a reception afterwards. There are some favorite hymns I want sung at my funeral; they evoke comforting imagery to me. On the other hand, I would want my iPhone playlist played at the reception afterwards – lots of Bruce Springsteen, Bonnie Raitt, and Rolling Stones sending me off. I have an idea of Bible verses I want read at my funeral and I know the liturgy I want used. But I'm not sure if I've told Jerry. All he's told me is that he wants to be cremated and his ashes scattered someplace he enjoyed being. That's kind of open ended. How 'bout you?" Cris asks, standing up to clear cups from the coffee table.

"Oh, yeah!" Deb grins, leans forward, and begins to talk excitedly. "Lenny's under strict instructions. I'll have a wake, with a lot of alcohol, and cheese …"

"Cheese?" Cris interrupts, beginning to giggle.

"Girl, you know I love me some cheese!" Cris giggles and nods. "The food will be fabulous, and there must be lots of cheesy yummies. *Saturday Night Live* reruns will continually play on a televised loop inside the venue, and I want everyone to tell funny stories and have a great time. There will be very fine bourbon, and I want lots of toasts. Hell, maybe I'll even suggest throwing toast, like in *The Rocky Horror Picture Show*!" Deb's laughing now, and throws a piece of Halloween candy at Cris. She laughs too and tosses the candy back to Deb, who pops it in her mouth.

"Are you going to be cremated or buried?"

Deb leans back and sighs. "You know, I always wanted to be buried. It really bothered me when I was younger that my mother's parents both opted to be cremated. As you know, I have wonderful memories of visiting my father's family graves – first with my brothers then with my cousin – and there was nowhere to visit my maternal grandparents. Then, their names were carved in the Knights of Columbus memorial at St. Mary's Catholic Cemetery in Norfolk, Virginia, so I was finally able to visit. There was a stone bench in front of the marble, engraved monument that held the names of all of the "sultans" and "sultanas."' I used to love to go there with my brothers, and we would tell stories about Nanny and Granddaddy Ferlauto and reminisce." She pauses and looks puzzled.

"What?" queries Cris.

"Well, it's just that, now, I'm not sure. I don't have children, and most of the people who love me, I expect, may already be dead by then. All my grandparents, aunts, and my mom, are already dead; by then I expect my father, all my brothers maybe, and I don't think my nephews or goddaughters are the type to visit graves. Hell, it's everything I can do to get 'em to spend time with me now – they're young people! They have their own lives!" Deb laughs, and Cris joins in. "In-ground burials are so expensive; if there are people still alive who care when I'm dead, I don't want them to worry about expense. I'm leaning now toward cremation, even though my mom and I always swore we'd never be cremated!"

Cris is quiet for a minute. Then, she says, "Yeah, I definitely want to be cremated. All our parents are cremated, and their ashes are in their church columbarium. So we can visit them just like we used to visit our grandparents' graves. I think the odds are that I, too, will have few people to visit my grave. I expect I will outlive many of my family and friends. This has really got me thinking – when I get home, Jerry and I will have to talk about this and write down our wishes."

End of Life Conversations

These "final conversations" are not as common as one might think. While 2,626,418 peopled died last year in the United States alone (Centers for

Disease Control, 2017), most literature – whether scholarly or journalistic – agrees that a majority of people do not talk overtly about their own or their loved ones' deaths. These end of life conversations are also rather clearly classified and specified within such literature. "Final conversations" are defined as "all interactions, verbal and nonverbal, that an individual has with another who is terminally ill from the moment of a terminal diagnosis to the point of death" (Keeley & Generous, 2015, p. 378; 2017, p. 2). Final conversations can take the form of farewell behavior – saying goodbye to terminally ill loved ones through gifts, talking, and formal goodbyes (Kellehear & Lewin, 1989), or lasting words – intergenerational communication that passes on advice, moral guidance, and memories (Kastenbaum, 1997). Keeley and Generous (2017) have identified five overarching themes within their research summary on final conversations: "love, identity, religious/spiritual messages, everyday talk, and difficult relationship talk" (p. 2) as well as "instrumental" topics such as funeral planning. For them as well as other researchers, nonverbal communication within such final conversations is especially important, as verbal communication may grow increasingly difficult for those at the end of life. Webb (1997) asserts that open conversations can "bring closure to life when a cure is no longer likely" (p. xxix). Most of us do not talk about our own impending deaths until we're diagnosed with a terminal illness, yet, suggests Webb, "families that can talk these normal feelings through can come out of the long illness and death of one of their members still healthy and intact" (p. 213).

Lifelong Conversations About Death

Discussions between and among the healthy about death, however, are not so easily categorized. These conversations, as we have observed, begin among children fascinated by "what happens to us when we die" and are fostered, relationally and interpersonally, through storytelling, ghostly play, and socially constructed experiences within their lives, such as funerals of loved ones. They are also centered within our mediated, cultural, and social discourses and ways of being such as social media, computer gaming, news, entertainment, sport, religion, tradition(s), holidays, conversations, rituals, and a host of sites of symbolic interaction within our human milieu. From our childhood games, to our stories and legends, to our arts and entertainment, and influencing even our social and cultural norms, extending to our most integral institutions, death winds its way throughout all of our lives while we live, not just as we age, become ill, or confront our deaths in more visceral ways such as in war, within violence, or in near-death experiences. Death is always a part of life, even if we don't notice it all of the time.

For Cris and Deb, their personal and professional lives have been intertwined with Death for a very long time. Death is omnipresent in their lives.

Both raised in faiths that promulgate notions of an afterlife, subsuming death with the promise of a life after death, death has accompanied their religious and familial upbringings. Cris lost her mother and father by her 42nd birthday, and has already lost her first grandchild, all of her grandparents, and parent-in-laws; and in the course of writing this book, Deb has lost her mother, her mother's sister, her godmother, a brother, and several uncles. They have both lost many friends, family members, and professional colleagues. But their losses are generally relatively typical of women their age. As Deb likes to remind people, the natural progress of a life course dictates that we survive our grandparents, our parents, our older aunts, uncles, siblings. The alternative – parents who survive their children, especially young children whom they have lost, whether due to biological causes such as illness or due to human intervention such as accident or violence – is an abomination. Cris' loss of her grandchild is one such aberration.

For communication researchers as well as for families, communication is important in all facets of our lives, but especially as we prepare for death. We, along with other researchers (Kwak et al., 2014), recommend that end of life conversations are ongoing and begin early in one's life, proceed at developmentally appropriate paces, and become more instrumentally directed throughout the life course. Deb has talked with her three nephews about death throughout their lives. From asking them questions like "What kind of party would you like everyone to have after you die?" to openly answering questions about family deaths, rituals, funerals, and burials, she tries to make death a part of their lives, albeit in specific and age appropriate ways. Deb describes this:

> *I stand over my grandmother's casket. She looks beautiful. Her skin is like wrinkled parchment. I think to myself how much she would love the way her silver hair is curled and how good she looks with that pink shade of lipstick. I reach out to touch her hand, folded over a small Bible. It is ice cold to the touch. I withdraw my hand and shiver. I hear my brother, Ed's, voice in the background, and turn away from Nanny to greet my brother and my oldest nephew, Eddie. Eddie is only four or five at the time, and he is hanging back, tugging at Ed's hand, trying to move away from the viewing room. I can tell he's scared. I kneel down and engulf him in my arms, showering enthusiastic kisses all over his face, just like my mom always did to me. He giggles, squinches his face, pulls away from me a bit, and asks loudly, "Why's Nanny asleep in that box?"*
>
> *I burst out laughing. Ed begins to shush him, but I quickly shake my head. I smile broadly at Eddie and say, "Nanny's really tired. She had to go to sleep."*
>
> *Eddie furrows his brow. He cocks his head. He gazes at the casket and asks, "When will she wake up?"*
>
> *I hold his shoulders, and look into his eyes. "I don't know, Eddie. I don't know how long she's going to sleep, and I don't know where she'll be when she wakes up. She might not be here anymore when she wakes up."*

"Well, where would she be? Where would she go? She's right here with us. She needs to be right here with us." He looks at me, pleadingly, and starts to cry. I pull him in to me and hug him, rubbing his shoulders. I move his body away from mine, but I keep my hands on his shoulders, and look into his eyes. "She might wake up in heaven. She might wake up in another place. She might come back here to visit us. She might sleep for a very long time. We just don't know, baby. No one knows." I feel hot tears in my own eyes. My lips begin to tremble. Eddie is looking down at his shoes, my hands still on his shoulders. He looks up at me, hopefully, wistfully. I compose myself and say, "She's been very busy for a long time, Eddie. She's very tired."

He nods. "Poor Nanny." Eddie says. "She needs to sleep." I nod. He pulls away from me, walks over to the casket, and pats it. He says, "Sleep tight, Nanny. Don't let the bed bugs bite." I smile. It's the same refrain we've said to him at bedtime for most of his life. He turns away and sits in a corner. He begins to play with his toys. I walk outside and begin to cry.

As the years passed, the number of Deb's nephews increased, as did her interventions to help them understand and cope with death. They visited haunted houses and made scary videos; when her nephews became teenagers, they talked about different cultures' death and funeral rituals and went to Day of the Dead celebrations; and now that two of them are young adults, they watch horror movies together and talk endlessly about end of life, and their own end of life plans. Deb's parents' instructions and directives about their deaths, and other family members' open and specific conversations about these topics, have made these discussions seem commonplace.

Reluctance to Acknowledge Death

Death is surely one continuous and final social construction, even if we don't want to acknowledge it. And many people don't want to acknowledge it. Researchers (Ferrell et al., 2004; Kale et al., 2016; Mori et al., 2017; Vander Geest et. al., 2015) have found that as many as 66% of family members of those who are dying don't want to talk about the impending death of their child or terminally ill family member with that ill family member. Reasons are varied: protection of the ill, especially with regard to the very young and the very old; apprehension, unease, worry, incomprehension, disorientation, denial, disconcertment, extreme sense of caution, lack of modeling, general fear of the unknown, terror (Becker 1973; Keeley & Generous, 2015, 2017; Keeley et al., 2014; Wiener et. al., 2008). However, those decisions have long-term consequences. Some of these same studies reveal that as many as 33% of participants regretted their decision to refuse to talk about impending deaths with family members who were dying (Mori et al., 2017; Ferrell et al., 2004), while only up to 6% of participants regretted engaging in "final conversations" with loved ones (Mori et al., 2017). Sadly, studies also show that 68% of patients in palliative care wished that they would have engaged family members in final conversations much earlier in the course of their illness (Rabow et al., 2003; Steinhauser et. al., 2001). "Death talk" topics they wished had been discussed included the assignment of a health care surrogate who knew what to expect and could make decisions regarding treatment options; a financial affairs surrogate and/or power of attorney who could help them get their financial affairs in order; and someone to help them plan their funerals (Steinhauser et. al., 2001). Even more disturbing, perhaps, is research that suggests that as many as 80% of clinicians miss opportunities to discuss advance planning and/or end of life care with their patients (Ahluwalia et al., 2012).

Final Conversation Behaviors

In a survey of 74 relatively healthy older adults conducted by Cris and colleague Randy Boyles (Davis & Boyles, 1999), 80% had engaged in some sort of farewell behavior, defined as behavior that had been performed "as a way of saying goodbye to your children, family, friends, or other loved ones, in preparation for your death sometime in the future." The most common form of written farewell behavior reported was written memoirs, cited by 41% of the participants. Almost half (43%) of the participants had given a gift as a remembrance, while approximately one-third had given a gift of money (26%) or exchanged affection (37%) as a form of farewell behavior. The gifts reportedly given fall into the following categories: jewelry (19% of those giving gifts), household items (19%), and keepsakes/personal items/heirlooms/trinkets (9%). Approximately four out of ten participants verbally told their loved ones their life story (43%), and gave verbal advice (39%). One-third (35%) gave a verbal goodbye to loved ones. Other farewell behaviors included personal business and legally related discussions: discussion of end of life issues (power of attorney, living will, caregiving issues) (6%), discussion of and preparation of their will and life insurance (4%), donation of their body (4%), and making their funeral and final arrangements (4%). Eight percent of participants considered the passing on of values and advice to be their farewell behavior to their families and loved ones. Six percent of participants commented that they thought open communication about death is important. Conversely, 6% stated that they were not yet ready to discuss their death with their loved ones and would do so when the time became more imminent. One participant stated she looks forward to a formal goodbye with her family gathered around her deathbed. Some participants wrote in comments indicating that they were not ready to face the reality of saying goodbye:

> *If I anticipate death, I would do all of the above but if death isn't expected, I hope I have told them during my lifetime. To do it too early would be upsetting to my children.*

I think about dying sometimes, but I don't dwell on it nor do I discuss it with family. Jokingly I tell them what I want to be buried in, whether they do or not is up to them.

One participant recognized that the time to say goodbye is now:

I try to communicate with my children all along, not holding back something for close to death time. I would like to become very comfortable discussing death as time goes on. I guess that should be now, however, since we never know.

Sometimes, reluctance to say goodbye comes from the loved ones and not the older adult:

I am open with my children and friends on death and other subjects. We have certainly had conversations concerning death, but my children refuse to let me discuss this subject at length. Since their father's [sudden] death six years ago, they are more reluctant to have these discussions. Hopefully, the situation will become easier to talk about.

A few participants wrote in comments illustrating the value of giving advice and moral principles as farewell behavior, suggestive of Kastenbaum's lasting words (1997): "Write and speak of my values in life and speculation of life in the new dimension of being after death."

Affective Conversations at End of Life

Most people with a terminal diagnosis plan to say goodbye to loved ones before they die (Kellehear & Lewin, 1989), but a sizable number intend to wait for deathbed farewells. In addition to the very instrumental topics within final conversations, researchers have also identified more affective and emotional themes. As we've stated, these familial death farewells provide opportunities for families to say goodbye, say what needs to be said, achieve closure and make amends, and provide family members and loved ones with expressions of affection, reassurance, acceptance, reaffirmation, support, and, simply more time with their loved one (Keeley and Generous, 2017; Kellehear & Lewin, 1989). According to Schenker et al. (2012), health care surrogates routinely discuss three emotional needs that often conflict with decision making and made certain conversations more difficult than others. Those include not wanting to feel responsible for a loved one's death; the need to allow the loved one to pursue recovery, and a desire to maintain family well-being and unity.

Cris wrote about and identified several types of farewell behavior in her communication with her parents as they moved closer to their ultimate deaths. In this paper, she suggested this communication approached dialogic communication, a deep level of interpersonal communication and shared connection. Here is an example of a song serving as dialogic farewell communication:

> *It was the week before Thanksgiving, 1999. It was two weeks before my mom's death, but, of course, we didn't know that yet. What we did know was that Mom had idiopathic pulmonary fibrosis, which meant that her lungs couldn't pull oxygen out of the air. She was on a double-oxygen cannula full-time, and had begun using a more powerful oxygen mask at night. She was a difficult and demanding patient. My sister Kelli, who was caring full-time for Mom, called to give me an update. "Mom is getting harder and harder to deal with," she complained. "She's not sleeping through the night, and she won't let me sleep, either. She calls me every hour and wakes me up! When I come into her room, there's nothing I can do for her. I think she's just afraid to go to sleep!"*
>
> *I worried about Kelli's state of mind. Several months of sleep deprivation from my mom's constant demands was taking its toll. Mom's blood oxygen level was getting dangerously low, resulting in confusion and irritability. She had always been a critical mother, but now her oxygen deprivation made her even more so.*
>
> *"Then, you won't believe what she did last night! She was up singing at 3 a.m.! Singing! In the middle of the night! I don't know what she thought she was doing!"*
>
> *"I'll come over tomorrow and spend some time with her," I offered, hoping this time spent with Mom would ease Kelli's burden and my guilt. I showed up the next afternoon. Mom was in bed when I arrived, but insisted on coming into the living room to sit with me. I waited patiently while we slowly got her into her motorized wheelchair, wheeled her down the hall, and transferred her to the couch. We sat there in silence for a minute as she caught her breath, sucking in air from her oxygen cannula, recovering from the exertion. I tried to think of conversation, to take her mind off of her health. "So, Mom," I said casually. "I understand you were up last night, singing." I expected to observe a flash of dementia, another step in the decline of her oxygen-deprived brain.*
>
> *"Well, yes, I was," she replied, quite coherently.*
>
> *"Uh, why?" I didn't know what else to say.*
>
> *"Because I couldn't sleep and I was bored!" she said matter-of-factly. This made sense to me. Mom had always been a night person, and while we were growing up, she had often stayed up late at night to do housework.*
>
> *This clear logic took me aback. "What were you singing?" I asked, still waiting to hear symptoms of confusion.*
>
> *"I'll show you," she began, and she sang. She sang songs from my childhood, songs she had sung to me, to sing me to sleep, when I was a small child. She sang songs she and my grandmother used to sing together. This woman, who minutes earlier couldn't catch her breath, sang! Fully, beautifully! "Red, Red Robin." "Sidewalks of New York." "Ragtime Cowboy Joe." "How Much Is That Doggy*

*in the Window?" "You Are My Sunshine." "It's a Long Way to Tipperary."
"My Funny Valentine." She sang my favorite, "Bye, Bye, Blackbird." She sang,
and I went back in time. Back before she got sick. Back before our years and
years of arguments and hard feelings. Back before my rebellious teenage years.
Back before the many years of her disparaging words cut me so cruelly. I went
back to being the small child who lay tucked in bed, listening intently to Mommy
singing, and begging, "Just one more song, Mommy, one more, before I have to
go to sleep!"*

*"Oh, Mom!" I said. "That really takes me back to when I was three years
old!"*

*"Me too," she replied, patting my arm. "Only I'm sorry that now I'm not
able to hold you in my arms and rock you while I'm singing."*

*Tears stung my eyes. "That's okay, Mom," I said, as I took her hand. We sat
there, holding hands, singing together, mother and child.*

Pack up all my cares and woes,
Here I go, singing low,
Bye bye blackbird
Where somebody waits for me,
Sugar's sweet,
So is he/she,
Bye bye blackbird
No one here to love and understand me,
Oh what hard luck stories they all hand me,
Make my bed and light the light,
I'll arrive late tonight,
Blackbird, bye bye.
                    Henderson & Dixon, 1926.

In this paper, Davis (2003) identified song, verbal farewells, gestures, gifts, and
death itself as types of dialogic farewell communication. Here is an example of
gestures as dialogic communication between Cris and her father on his deathbed:

*"He's in a coma. He can't hear you." My sister sat on the far side of my dad's
hospital bed. I looked at my dad. His eyes were glassy; the pupils covered over
with a frosty glaze, staring, unfocused on the ceiling. His skin was as white as
his sheet, and his whole being seemed focused on his breath coming in and out
of his pursed lips. This was my daily visit to see him. He was at home, dying
of cancer. He had been dying for months, and I had been making a daily trek
to sit with him. The end seemed near, but we had been saying that for a long
time and it hadn't come yet. I ignored my sister's advice and took his hand a
little too eagerly, and he winced in pain.*

"Oh my God," I panicked. "Now I've hurt him." I looked at his face. He was back to his unfocused look. I calmed down. "Hi, Dad! It's Cris. I've come to visit."

His head moved ever so slightly. I sat there holding his hand. My sister left the room, and I was alone with Dad. I looked at him. He looked like a concentration camp refugee. The disease had left him with little but thin, fragile skin covering his bones. He was still alive, but his body didn't seem to know that. He reeked of decomposing skin from the bed sores that even the most loving care couldn't prevent, and his neck was no longer capable of holding his head upright, so his head leaned heavily against his right shoulder.

"How much longer, God?" I asked, no longer expecting an answer or even a hearing. "How much longer are you going to put my dad through this?" I sat thoughtfully. I had to say it. I'd been trying to say this for weeks, but couldn't bring myself to say it. Now it was time.

"Dad," I began. "You know, if you have to go, if you have to go, it's okay." I took a breath and began again. "Dad, if it's your time to go, it's okay to go." He didn't respond. I couldn't tell if he heard me or not. At least I said it.

I sat there for awhile in silence until my husband poked his head in the door. "Cris, it's time to go. Let's go." We had nothing to do, nowhere to be, but the hours loomed long sitting in this place of death.

"Okay." Every day when I left, I had told my dad, "I'll see you tomorrow." He had always responded with "Yes, I'll see you tomorrow." Today I couldn't bring myself to say it. Instead, I paused at the door and looked back at him. "Goodbye, Dad. I love you."

He lifted his index finger in response.

We got the call at 11:00 that night. For some reason, I was surprised.

Davis, 2003, p. 208

Communication and a Good Death

Among people who have a terminal prognosis, impending death forces them to downsize their lives – to let go of everything but the most important things in life (Keeley, 2007). People with a terminal prognosis frequently focus much of their attention on their close relationships. When people know they are dying, they and their loved ones have an opportunity to strengthen their relationship (Keeley, 2007). A "good death" involves saying what you need to say – I love you, I'm sorry – before you die. Communication at end of life can give people an opportunity to deal with the past and talk about things they couldn't talk about previously, share important moments, say a meaningful and heartfelt goodbye, acknowledge fears and concerns about death and about a life without one another, forgive past hurts, deepen their love, resolve conflicts, and achieve closure in relationships (Keeley, 2007).

One of the most important needs of the dying person is to feel heard and to maintain human connection, yet, as loved ones, our ability to listen to loved ones who are dying is often clouded by fear, confusion, helplessness, and guilt (Vora & Vora, 2008). In addition, foreknowledge of a loved one's death helps the family deal with anticipatory grief – the grieving period prior to a loved one's death. Anticipatory grief begins at the diagnosis of a loved one's terminal illness, and it's characterized by disorientation and suffering by the relational partner but is also often accompanied by an increased feeling of attachment, closeness, tenderness, and a desire to be with the dying loved one during the time that is left.

Relational Communication at End of Life

Ellis (1995) suggests that final conversations allow for a re-imagining and re-articulation of individual identities and interpersonal relationships. Most research-ers agree that the ability to have end of life conversations allows those who are confronting their own deaths to regain some level of control by being able to decide and articulate their preferences ahead of time (Wiener et al., 2008; Zeyti-noglu, 2011), and are necessary to both those facing impending death and their loved ones (Gardner, 2012; Scott & Caughlin, 2015). We suggest these communi-cative interventions in the course of a loved one's death assist with both the death of the terminally ill patient as well as the grieving process for survivors.

Reasons for failure to engage in final conversations differ a bit based on the perspectives of the dying and the surviving. Survivors often worry about inadvertently betraying negative aspects of prognosis to the dying family member, upsetting the patient and/or other family members, and often express uncertainty about the impetus, timing, topic, and appropri-ateness of final conversations (Keely & Generous, 2017; Mori et al., 2017; Vander Geest et al., 2015). Patients worry about when and how to initiate such conversations (Rabow et al., 2003) and wish to shield their loved ones from pain. Many researchers identify cultural and ethnic gaps in the litera-ture as well. Some cultures and ethnicities find talking about death a taboo subject (Kwak et al., 2014) and express reluctance to broach the subject with family members. Understandings of these issues are complicated by a lack of empirical research among those who are of non-Caucasian descent; for example, scholars have documented absences in the literature among populations who identify as Latina/o, African or Caribbean American, and/ or Asian (Berkman & Ko, 2009; Carr, 2011; Johnstone & Kanitsaki, 2009; Keeley & Generous, 2015, 2017; Kwak, 2014; Moller, 1996; Pitts qtd. in Grant, 2017; Yonashiro-Cho et al., 2016).

However, Faulkner (1997) points to a wide body of research that suggests that "children involved in open communication about their own or a family member's impending death are less likely to experience anxiety, withdrawal, and isolation than those who are "protected" from such knowledge" (p. 64). Imber-Black (2014) argues that any family secrets are harmful, fostering a lack of family communication and problem solving that leads to distrust, but that secrecy in the context of illness is especially damaging within interpersonal and familial relationships. She suggests that "maintaining a secret that lives and breathes every day in a family – cancer, diabetes, alcoholism, drug abuse, impending death – requires the skills of a high wire acrobat," necessitating family members to "organize their lives to preserve secrecy while pretending not to notice" (p. 157). The ramifications to family cohesion, maintenance, meaning making, and communication are devastating. In her work with families shaken by terminal illness, she uses a model developed by Wright and Bell (2009) that assists family members in confronting "illness secrets," allowing for meaning making through shared narratives, myths, rituals, and open discussion about "taboo issues" (pp. 160–161). We suggest these conversations are necessary to our individual, familial, and collective mental, physical, emotional, and social health.

Advance Planning

Early preparation of advance care planning documents (Schenker et. al., 2012; Wiener et. al., 2008) and family members' communal planning of end of life celebrations (Kwak et al., 2014; Schenker, 2012) are also helpful for families reluctant to incorporate the surety and finality of death into their lives.

Many researchers and practitioners also recommend that care managers, family members, and other professionals – especially clinicians – advocate for formal advance planning (Kwak et al., 2014; Schenker et al., 2012). Maltby and Finns (2004) argue that our present day contractual models of advance health care planning and decision making ignore the long-term realities of relational proxy care. They advocate a "covenantal model" that incorporates their "educational kit, *Fidelity, Wisdom and Love: Patients and Proxies in Partnership*, which can be used by individuals or in a group setting to help people execute effective advance care planning" (p. 353). Briggs (2004) and her colleagues at The Respecting Choices® Advance Care Planning (ACP) team at Gundersen Lutheran Medical Center apply a "representational approach" (pp. 342–343) using interactional interviews to foster culturally sensitive and experientially useful advance planning techniques among diverse populations. Modan and Brill (2014) use constructed dialogues, narratives, and other storytelling mechanisms to facilitate advance planning as well as final conversations. Governmental, medical, and not for profit initiatives can also be helpful to promote ongoing discussions about end of life, advance care planning, and final conversations, such as the National Healthcare Decisions Day Initiative (Black, 2010).

Conclusion

On July 1, 2017, the Institute on Culture, Religion and World Affairs at Boston University announced the death of sociologist Peter Berger (Berger, 2017). Co-author of *The Social Construction of Reality: A Treatise in the Sociology of Knowledge* (1966), Berger argued that common social and cultural experiences affirm, enrich, and shape our everyday experiences. Berger understood the magnitude of the all-encompassing symbolic meanings to our everyday lives, as do we, and we advocate grabbing Death by the horns and wrestling it to the ground. Our co-existence with Death does not negate it; that is not possible; however, confronting death does seem to tame the enormity of its effects – just a bit.

References

Ahluwalia, S. C.; Levin, J. R.; Lorenz, K. A.; & Gordon, G. S. (2012). Missed opportunities for Advance Care Planning communication during outpatient clinic visits. Journal of General Internal Medicine, 27(4), 445–451.

Becker, E. (1973). The denial of death. New York: Free Press.

Berger, J. (2017, July 1). Theologian fought "God is Dead" movement. [Obituary originally published in the New York Times]. The Sun News, p. 9A.

Berger, P., & Luckmann, T. (1966) The Social Construction of Reality: A Treatise in the Sociology of Knowledge. New York, NY: Penguin.

Berkman C. S., & Ko, E. (2009). Preferences for disclosure of information about serious illness among older Korean American immigrants in New York City. Journal of Palliative Medicine, 12(4), 351–357.

Black, K. (2010). Promoting advance care planning through the National Healthcare Decisions Day Initiative. Journal of Social Work in End-of-Life & Palliative Care, 6, 11–26. doi: 10.1080/15524256.2010.489220.

Briggs, L. (2004). Shifting the focus of Advance Care Planning: Using an in-depth interview to build and strengthen relationships. Journal of Palliative Medicine, 7(2), 341–349.

Carr, D. (2011). Racial differences in end of life planning: Why don't Blacks and Latinos prepare for the inevitable? Omega, 63(1), 1–20.

Centers for Disease Control. (2017). Deaths and mortality. Available at https://www.cdc.gov/nchs/fastats/deaths.htm

Davis, C. S., & Boyles, R. (1999). Farewell behavior and communication apprehension. Unpublished manuscript.

Davis, C. S. (2003). A dialogic farewell: Enhancing the "I-Thou" quality of a parent-child relationship. Journal of Loss and Trauma, 8(3), 201–215.

Ellis, C. (1995). Final negotiations: A story of love, loss, and chronic illness. Philadelphia, PA: Temple University Press.

Faulkner, K. W. (1997). Dealing with death: Talking about death with a dying child. The American Journal of Nursing, 97(6), 64–69.

Ferrell, B., Kreicbergs, U., & Squire, C. (2004) Talking with dying children about death: Patients who talked to their children had no regrets. Patient Education Management, 11(12), 139–141.

Gardner, D. B. (2012). Quality in life and death: Can we have the conversations? Nursing Economics, 30(4), 224–232.

Grant, M. (2017). Understanding cultural gaps and disparities in advanced illness care. Generations – Journal of the American Society on Aging, 41(1), 10–15.

Imber-Black, E. (2014). Will talking about it make it worse? Facilitating family conversations in the context of chronic and life-shortening illness. Journal of Family Nursing, 20(2), 151–163. doi: 10.1177/1074840714530087.

Johnstone, M. J., & Kanitsaki, O. (2009). Ethics and Advance Care Planning in a culturally diverse society. Journal of Transcultural Nursing, 20(4), 405–416.

Kale, M. S., Ornstein, K. A., Smith, C. B., & Kelley, A. S. (2016). End of life discussions with older adults. Journal of the American Geriatrics Society, 64(10), 1962–1967.

Kastenbaum, R. (1997). Lasting words as a channel for intergenerational communication. Ageing and Society, 17, 21–39.

Keeley, M. P. (2007). "Turning toward death together": The functions of messages during final conversations in close relationships. Journal of Social & Personal Relationships, 24(2), 225–253. doi:10.1177/0265407507075412

Keeley, M. P., Generous, M. A., and Baldwin, P. K.(2014). Exploring children's final conversations with dying family members. Journal of Family Communication, 14, 208–229. doi: 10.1080/15267432014.908198.

Keeley, M. P., & Generous, M. A. (2015). The challenges of final conversations: Dialectical tensions during end-of-life family communication. Southern Communication Journal, 80(5), 377–387. doi: 10.1080/1041794X.2015.1081975.

Keeley, M. P., & Generous, M.A. (2017). Final conversations: Overview and practical implications for patients, families, and healthcare workers. Behavioral Sciences, 7(17), 1–9, doi: 10.3390/bs7020017.

Kellehear, A., & Lewin, T. (1989). Farewells by the dying: A sociological study. Omega – Journal of Death and Dying, 19(4), 274–292.

Kwak, J., Ko, E., & Kramer, B. J. (2014). Facilitating advance care planning with ethnically diverse groups of frail, low-income elders in the USA: Perspectives of care managers on challenges and recommendations, Health & Social Care In The Community, 22(2), 69–77. doi: 10.1111/hsc.12073.

Maltby, B. S., & Fins, J. J. (2004). Informing the patient-proxy covenant: An educational approach for Advance Care Planning. Journal of Palliative Medicine, 7(2), 351–355.

Modan, G., & Brill, S. B. (2014). Engaging death: Narrative and constructed dialogue in Advance Care Planning discussions. Communication & Medicine, 11(2), 153–165.

Moller, D. W. (1996). Confronting death: Values, institutions, & human morality. New York, NY: Oxford University Press.

Mori, M.; Yoshida, S.; Shiozaki, M.; Baba, M.; Monta, T.; Aoyama, M.; Kizawa, Y.; Tsuneto, S.; Shima, Y.; & Miyashita, M. (2017 in press). Talking about death with terminally ill cancer patients: What contributes to the regret of a bereaved family member? Journal of Pain and Symptom Management.

Rabow, M. W.; Schanche, K.; Peterson, J.; Dibble, S. L.; & McPhee, S. J. (2003). Patient perceptions of an outpatient palliative care intervention: "It had been on my mind before, but I did not know how to start talking about death." Journal of Pain and Symptom Management, 26(5), 1010–1015.

Schenker, Y., Crowley-Matoka, M.; Dohan, D.; Tiver, G. A.; Arnold, R. M.; & White D. B. (2012). "I don't want to be the one saying 'we should just let him die'": Intrapersonal tensions experienced by surrogate decision makers in the ICU. Journal of General Internal Medicine, 27(12), 1657–1665.

Scott, A. M., & Caughlin, J. P. (2015). Communication non-accommodation in family conversations about end of life decisions. Health Communication, 30, 144–153. doi: 10.1080/10410236.2014.974128.

Steinhauser, K. E.; Christakis, N. A.; Clipp, E. C.; McNeally, M.; Granbow, S.; Parker, J.; & Tulisky, J. A. (2001). Preparing for the end of life: Preferences of patients, families, physicians, and other care providers. Journal of Pain and Symptom Management, 22(3), 727–737.

Vander Geest, I. M. M.; van den Hewel-Eibrick, M.M., van vliet, L. M.; Pluim, S. M. F.; Streng, I. C.; Michiels, E. M. C.; Pieters, R.; & Darlington, A. S. E. (2015). Talking about death with children with incurable cancer: Perspectives from parents. Journal of Pediatrics, 167(6), 1320–1326.

Vora, E., & Vora, A. (2008). A contingency framework for listening to the dying. The International Journal of Listening, 22, 59–72. doi: 10.1080/10904010701808458.

Webb, M. (1997). The good death: The new American search to reshape the end of life. New York: Bantam Books.

Wiener, L.; Ballard, E.; Brennan, T.; Battles, H.; Martinez, P.; & Pao, M. (2008). How I wish to be remembered: The use of an Advance Care Planning document in adolescent and young adult populations. Journal of Palliative Medicine, 11(10), 1309–1313. doi: 10.1089/jpm.2008.0126.

Wright, L. M., & Bell, J. M. (2009). Beliefs and illness: A model for healing. Calgary: 4th Floor Press.

Yonashiro-Cho, J., Cote, S., & Enguidanos, S. (2016). Knowledge about and perceptions of advance care planning and communication of Chinese-American older adults. Journal of the American Geriatrics Society, 64(9), 1884–1889.

Zeytinoglu, M. (2011). Talking it out: Helping our patients live better while dying. Annals of Internal Medicine, 154(12), 830–832.

7

BETWEEN THE LINES: COMMUNICATING ABOUT DEATH IN OBITUARIES[1]

The doorbell rings. Deb opens the door, and a tall trick-or-treater dressed as a skeleton stands on the doorstep grinning. "Trick or Treat!" he singsongs.

"You might be the last trick-or-treater of the night!" Deb says as she dumps a handful of candy in his bag and closes the door. Sitting back down, Deb grabs the big backpack propped up next to the couch, rummages through it, and pulls out a folder.

"Did you wanna' see my mom's obituary?" Deb asks, passing Cris the stark black and white single-spaced sheet of paper.

"Absolutely!" Cris responds, folding her legs underneath her, settling in, and beginning to read:

> *Wife, mother, grandmother, daughter, sister, godmother, aunt, Devout Roman Catholic, proud Sicilian, faithful and loyal friend – Our "little Italian girl," Our "yankee southern girl." Always laughing with a joy de vivre. Eclectic, fashionable, and a lover of life. Our beloved Marguerite Maria Carmelita Ferlauto Cunningham has left us. Born in New York City, New York on February 21, ___, transplanted to Tidewater, Virginia, and died in Virginia Beach, Virginia on August 21, 2016. She is survived by her devoted husband and childhood sweetheart, Edward Earl Cunningham; her children, Dr. Deborah Cunningham Breede and her husband, Lenny; Edward Earl Cunningham, Jr. and his wife, Tammy; and her "baby," John Thomas Cunningham and his wife, Kathy. Cherished by her grandchildren, Edward Earl Cunningham, III, and his fiancé, Jessica Sevin; Brandon ___ Cunningham; Tyler ___ Cunningham; and Kristen Creekmore; she is also mourned by her sister, Joan Ferlauto Pape and her husband, Brian; her nephew Patrick Beemer and his daughters Gillian and Stella; her goddaughter Lisa Marie Pierozzi and her mother, Marcia Pierozzi; and Godson(s) Peter*

_____ and _____; and a host of dear friends, neighbors, colleagues, acquaintances, and strangers whose lives she touched over _____ years. Marguerite, or "Megs" as most everyone knew her, was predeceased by her parents, Thomas Anthony Ferlauto and Melina Daraio Ferlauto; her parents in law, John Drummond Cunningham and Nell Cotton Cunningham, and a large_ extended family ... that included dozens of uncles, aunts, cousins, and other hangers on and no accounts ☺... ok ... _extended family. Megs had too many gifts, talents, and extraordinary qualities to mention here, but many of them revolved around her commitment to friends and family; her delightful sense of adventure; her ability to make every person who came into her life feel as though they were her best friend; and her pride in all things she loved – her friends and family, her faithless Redskins, but most especially the life and home that she created with her adored Ed. She was a lauded hostess; a voracious reader and explorer; a singer, dancer, and fashionista; and a film buff and fierce trivia opponent. Her time on this earth was marked by service to others, excitement at every new turn, and an unwavering sense of faith. She was our hero, our compass, and our life. Her last years were difficult, and were made more loving and comforting by the presence of people Megs could never thank in words but did so every day in spirit: the incredible staff at The Memory Center in Virginia Beach, Virginia – especially Jackie, Nia, Kathy, weird singing guy, and friends she made there and lost – Ms. Shirley, Ms. _____, and her roommate Darlene; Jim Federer and the staff at Holy Family Catholic Church; and her best friends for sixty years, Pat Harp and Violet Forrest and their husbands, Reno and Bob. A viewing and memorial will be held at Hollomon Brown Funeral Home,_ insert address, insert date. _A Catholic Sacramental Mass will be held at Holy Family Catholic Church,_ insert address, insert date. _There will be a reception at the Broad Bay Country Club,_ insert address, _immediately following Mass. Arrangements for the family are being handled by Hollomon Brown Funeral Home,_ insert other details. _Megs loved flowers, but she would also love memorial donations in her name to The Alzheimer's Foundation; St. Mary's Home for Women and Children in Norfolk,_ The Memory Center? Holy Family? Anyone/anything else? _Online condolences can be left at Hollomon Brown Funeral Home_ insert address. End with quote – maybe "phenomenal woman?" Bible? Thoughts?

"Of course, that's not the final version, the one that was published," Deb says, handing Cris a second single-spaced sheet of paper.

"Really?" She looks up over her reading glasses, takes the second sheet of paper and begins to read.

Wife, mother, grandmother, daughter, sister, godmother, aunt, devout Roman Catholic of proud Sicilian heritage, and friend. Our "little Italian yankee southern belle," who was always laughing, always eclectic, fashionable, and a lover of life. Our beloved has been taken from us. Born in New York City, on February

21, 1934, transplanted to Tidewater, and died in Virginia Beach, on August 21, 2016. She is survived by her devoted husband and childhood sweetheart for over 65 years, Edward Earl Cunningham; their children, Dr. Deborah Cunningham Breede and her husband, Lenny; Edward Earl Cunningham, Jr. and his wife, Tammy; John Thomas Cunningham and his wife, Kathy. Cherished by her grandchildren, Edward Earl Cunningham, III, and his fiancée, Jessica Sevin; Brandon John Cunningham; Tyler Thomas Cunningham; and Kristen Yocum; she is also mourned by her sister, Joan Ferlauto Pape and her husband, Brian. Marguerite, or "Megs" as most everyone knew her, was predeceased by her parents, Thomas Anthony Ferlauto and Melina Daraio Ferlauto; her parents in law, John Drummond Cunningham and Nell Cotton Cunningham, and a large extended family. Megs had too many gifts, talents, and extraordinary qualities to mention here, but many of them revolved around her commitment to friends and family; her delightful sense of adventure; her ability to make every person who came into her life feel as though they were her best friend; and her pride in all things she loved, most especially the life and home that she created with and for her adored Ed. She was a lauded hostess; a voracious reader; a singer, dancer, and fashionista; and a film buff and fierce trivia opponent. Her time on this earth was marked by a committed service to others, excitement at every turn, and an unwavering sense of faith. She was our hero, our compass, and our life. Her last years were difficult, and made more bearable and comforting by the presence of people Megs could never thank in words but did so every day in spirit: the incredible, loving staff at The Memory Center, Jim Fedor of Holy Family Catholic Church; and her best friends for over 60 years, Pat Harp and Violet Forrest and their husbands, Reno and Bob. The family will receive visitors at Hollomon Brown Funeral Home, 1264 N. Great Neck Rd., Virginia Beach, on Monday, August 29, 2016, from 6:30 to 8:30 p.m. A Catholic Sacramental Mass will be held at Church of the Holy Family Catholic Church, 1279 N. Great Neck Rd., Virginia Beach on Tuesday, August 30, 2016, at 10:30 a.m. followed by interment at Princess Anne Memorial Park, 1110 N. Great Neck Rd. There will be a reception at the Broad Bay Country Club, 2120 Lords Landing, Virginia Beach, immediately following interment. In lieu of flowers please make memorial donations in her name to The Norfolk Sports Club Scholarship Foundation. Online condolences can be left at www.hollomonbrown.com. Goodbye Mama, Nanny, Friend! Goodbye Megs!

Framing of Death

The differences between these two obituaries illustrate just a few of the social constructions implicit and explicit within the framing of death. It is a team jousting match, with all of the complexities of life and love; marriage and divorce; oppression and freedom; family and gender; relationships strong as iron, and those lost like our spectacles; class and religion; and hope and despair – all wielded as are the weapons of a tournament, like a ringside seat at Medieval Times – complete with a fairy tale love story, joy and heartbreak, cruel destruction, unrelenting remorse, and – like all happy endings – a partial and incomplete resolution – because that's what you get in real life, not the bows that precede the encore.

Obituaries, especially those appearing in print newspapers, seem to be a dying art. They are both victims of the same murderers. They are castoffs, anachronisms, vestiges from a pre-digital place. The same criticism of newspapers is discussed over morning coffee, laptop and device screens, the new fences and gates between us, instead of the old print newspapers held aloft, splashing as the pages turn: "Why should I pay for this when I can read it now for free?" In the case of obituaries, the intent is the same, the wording is the only thing newly wired: "Why should I pay for an obituary in a newspaper, which nobody reads any more, when the funeral home will post it on their website for free?"

There are many answers to that question, but for some families, it's because the deceased wanted it, the family could afford it, and the 80- and 90-year-old circle of friends that constituted a primary culture for this decedent and family still read the paper newspaper faithfully every morning over coffee. Privilege saturates these choices like a wet sponge. But it's more than privilege. It's more than class. It's age and technology and choice and whim and more. Many elites choose to only have an online obituary, or none at all, and for those in the public eye, their obituaries become news. For many who are "wired," internet and digitally engaged, who access books on Kindle rather than between paper pages, they correctly assume that many will not see the obituary in the printed paper, but will notice it when they skim the online obituaries of home town newspapers, new town newspapers, in-between newspapers, all online.

One could suggest that these varying opinions and choices don't end up mattering much anyway. While the epitaphs on tombstones may be the Twitter version of a life story, obituaries – whether printed or online – are often the survivors' version of a life story, unless of course, the deceased has written their own obituary. One might assume that they then become the author of their own final life stories, but that's just funny. While we may be the authors of our own obituaries, that does not ever mean that we are freed from the constraints of all of those jousts over the details, all of those social constructions, and more: intent and reality, nostalgia and desire, power and narcissism, joy and regret – they weave their way through the obituaries as well, but they are sometimes written with secret ink that begins to appear between the lines.

It is a bewildering place to be in. An empty house, a bereft family, a dead human being, a hole in space. A beloved wife, mother, grandmother, aunt, sister, friend. A happy matriarch, our "little Italian girl," "our yankee southern belle." In the family discussions over Deb's mom's obituary, some insisted these were all one long descriptor, one compound adjective. Some constructed them as two separate narratives, partitioned by time, relationship, and context.

The "little Italian girl" was a term of endearment used by her spouse for more than half a century. "Our yankee southern belle" was a goal, described to Deb's mom, Megs, in great detail by a new friend from South Carolina, who took it upon herself to school Megs in becoming a "True Southern Belle," which apparently, after decades living in southern Virginia, Megs had still not achieved. Megs became a string of adjectives. All references to cousins were deleted. Contributions were sent to the Norfolk Sports Club instead of St. Mary's Home for Women and Children. Each of these choices necessitated lengthy discussions, a few arguments, and finally, what to some felt like agreement and to others capitulation. Much like death, the construction of an obituary is a compromise, a giving in, a surrender, an acknowledgement of the futility of more effort. We always give in, one way or another.

Obituaries as Socially Constructed Life Stories

Like many of you, Cris and Deb have lost many beloveds to death, some of them among the people loved most in this world: adored grandmothers and grandfathers, mothers, Cris' father, mothers and fathers-in laws, best friends, godmothers, aunts, cousins, colleagues, neighbors, casual acquaintances, friends of friends. Death surrounds humans like the pages of the newspapers that surround the obituaries. They are scribbled shrouds. Some of these loved ones did not have published obituaries, either online or in print newspapers. But the ones who did all produced and presented life stories for those obituaries that were socially constructed in contested and conflicted ways.

For example, Deb's Aunt Joan's obituary, written by her second husband, her only son, and the son's girlfriend, sounds like a religious pilgrimage culminating with an immaculate conception:

> *Joan Emma Pape was born in the Bronx borough of New York to Carmelina Maria Daraio and Gaetano Ambrosia Ferlauto on February 8, 1939. Her father, a marble and stone artisan, later moved the family to Norfolk, Virginia, where she graduated from Norfolk Catholic High in 1956. Joan's first job was with the Norfolk newspaper, which she left, to work at Oceana Naval Air Station. Always up for an adventure, she then moved across the country to Bremerton, Washington for another position with the Navy. In 1964, she returned to Norfolk to give birth to her only child, Patrick. In 1973, Joan married naval officer Brian Pape in Norfolk, Virginia. She was very proud of Brian and loved meeting people from around the world via his long tenure in the Naval Reserve. Joan and her family moved to Chicago and then California before settling in the Pacific Northwest. There, she pursued her dream of helping others by studying social work and going on to work in community services with King County and Providence Hospital. After moving to Bellingham, Joan co-founded Hope House, a non-denominational charity serving the poor and homeless. Nominated for the*

annual Hunhausen Humanitarian Award in 2001, Joan served on the boards
of many non-profits. A devout Catholic all her life, Joan was always very active
in her church community. Joan generously supported the Whatcom Symphony
Orchestra, Mt. Baker Theater, Bel Porto Lodge Sons of Italy, and the Bell-
ingham Golf & Country Club, and her vivacious personality made her many
friends. A proud Sicilian, she'll always be remembered for her love of cooking,
parties, jazz, opera, classical music, ballet, and Broadway shows. Joan is survived
by her husband, Brian, son Patrick, stepson Scott, stepdaughter Debra, and her
beloved grandchildren, Gillian, Stella, Matthew, Mark, Brittany, Breana, Jenna,
and Scott Jr. Mass of Christian Burial will be held at ....

While Aunt Joan did travel across the country working, she primarily did so
as a "trailing spouse," following the career of Tom, her first husband, and the
father of her child, who is never mentioned in her obituary. She left Virginia
and returned with a child, with no explanation of how she got the child or
what happened to the child's father. Tom's absence from the obituary is almost
Orwellian. It is a social construction not of her life, but of an idealized, socially
acceptable, and desired life. Desire overcame reality. It is a more culturally
acceptable life than the messy divorce, violent fights, infidelity, excommuni-
cation, and subsequent socially acceptable redemption that Deb's Aunt Joan
actually lived. We suggest such absences, half-truths, exaggerations, semantic
compromises, graceful choices, and downright lies are commonplace in the
construction of an obituary, whether self-authored or not.

None of these are unusual or necessarily uncontested notions. The obituary moves beyond a simple accounting of one's life, a tally of deeds and
accomplishments. Hume (2000) suggests that not only do obituaries "reflect
the worth of a life" (p. 150) but "are powerful commemorations that focus
on social values" (p. 151). A distinct genre of its own (Afful, 2010; Ondimu,
2014), the obituary, is of course, a social construction, but it is also many
other things: a family tree, a family Bible, a betrothal, a divorce, *The Grand
Tour*, a boast, a fact, a fiction, an academic yearbook, a professional resume,
a "*corpa vitae*," a contest of memory, a public record, a genealogical chroni-
cle, an "instant and authoritative biography, ... an erratic record of [sexual]
proclivity" (Starck, 2009, p. 338), a wish, a dream, a desire, a lament – a swan
song delivered with agony and beauty – and more. Obituaries not only
recall and evoke individual memories of one who has died, but they also
serve as sites of public and collective memory (Fowler, 2004, 2007; Fowler &
Bielsa, 2007; Gavriely-Nuri & Lachover, 2012; Lachover & Gavriely-Nuri,
2011; McElroy, 2013; Wasserman, 1998), and sites of collective and individual healing (Wallace, 2003; Wasserman, 1998). They report, analyze, and
interpret history (Fennell, 2014; Wasserman, 1998) and valorize the victims
of terrorist atrocities and military attacks (Hume, 2003; Lee et al., 2014;
Wasserman, 1998).

Obituaries as Cultural Reifications of Values and Social Norms

Researchers (Albert et al., 2016; Crespo, 2007; Fernandez, 2007) have identified two types of obituaries – informative, which share important details
about the decedent's life, death, and/or funeral arrangements, and opinative,
which are more personal, intimate, and are designed to create a specific effect
for the audience. These categorizations, while useful, seem a bit reductionist.
With "a resounding cultural voice" (Hume, 2003, p. 167), obituaries often
communicate, idealize, and reify cultural values, social norms, and the notions
inherent within civic life (Barth et al., 2013; Wasserman, 1998). They transmit and reflect the ideology espoused by the media which publicizes them
(Dilevko & Gottlieb, 2004; Epstein & Epstein, 2013; Fowler & Bielsa, 2007;
Gavriely-Nuri & Lachover, 2012; Johnson, 2006; Moore, 2002; Phillips, 2007),
but they also transmit and reflect the ideology/ies of cultures writ large and
small, particular places in time and space, and ways of being both common
and contested (Albert et al., 2016; Barth et al., 2013; Chaudhry et al., 2014;
Fowler, 2004; Hume, 2000; Ondimu, 2014; Phillips, 2007; Starck, 2009). They
present depictions of professional life (Dilevko & Gottlieb, 2004; Fowler &
Bielsa, 2007), and because of the ways in which obituaries create, reflect, and
reify social structures and cultural norms, we agree with Phillips' (2007) con-
tention that "obituaries are rituals" (p. 330), cultural texts that are transformed
through time, reflecting not only temporal social conventions but also those
affected by geographies, politics, standpoints, and ways of being (Wasserman,
1998). As Fowler (2004) suggests, "We might think of obituaries as commemorative pacts that help explain the inertia – the continuous reproductive re-
enactment – of social structures" (p. 148). Fowler goes on to assert, following
Connerton (1989), that whenever and whatever we are remembering, we are
always also forgetting. This dialectic between remembering and forgetting is
always present in memorializing (Hume, 2000).

Obituaries are the beginning of this journey forward, but they are also an
accounting backward. They are an itinerary in reverse, a travelogue written
in hindsight. They cost by the word, and so their recollections are brief and
abbreviated, often lacking the details that turn black and white into Techni-
color. Increasingly, however, obituaries in the South reveal modernities, cultural norms, and details that not only allow for a changing social landscape,
but also reify some of the traditional ways of being still common for many
living "south of the border." An analysis of obituaries in a small southern
newspaper elucidates many of these tensions and shifts.

Myrtle Beach, South Carolina, has been a tourist destination since its
inception as a day trip for families living in the swamps and pine forests of
South Carolina. First only accessible by the "side-wheeler" river boats that
plied the narrow and shallow Carolina rivers, then by train, it is now several

roads' end point, bringing carloads of summer tourists from the north, west, and south. Home to dozens of golf clubs and courses and, at one time, the site of a large Air Force base, Myrtle Beach and its adjacent "Grand Strand" area has now become a retirement haven, snow bird destination, and fast-growing municipality, surrounded by an increasingly populated but formerly primarily rural county. It is one of the fastest growing cities, and one of the most popular summer tourism destinations, in the country.

As is always the case, an analysis of obituaries in *The Sun News*, the only daily newspaper serving the entire Grand Strand region, identifies social constructions historically common in the Carolinas, and yet such an analysis also reveals increasingly modern influences and constructions that sometimes smack against the norm. There are also glaring absences and omissions in *The Sun News* obituaries that are rather typical of traditional southern living. It is these presences and absences within the obituaries that allow us to examine culture writ large and small in this area.

Previous researchers have noted absences in obituaries that often reflect absences in representations of cultural life generally. Obituaries for women, non-professionals, non-elites, the uneducated, and people of color are largely lacking in newspapers prior to the late 20th century (Dilevko & Gottlieb, 2004; Epstein & Epstein, 2013; Fowler, 2004; Fowler & Bielsa, 2007; Hume, 2000, 2003), and in some countries, are still the exception to the norm (Albert et al., 2016). In our analysis of daily obituaries published in the Myrtle Beach *Sun News* between May 18, 2016 and August 18, 2016, we found a much more inclusive and representative population included in the obituaries. Although this was primarily a convenience sample, we also assumed that such a small town southern newspaper would reflect multiple ways of being in the South, both historic and evolving. While we did not quantify our qualitative, thematic analysis, we did note that women and people of color were included and widely represented, and even though professional and educational achievements were lauded, many of those mourned in the pages of our daily newspaper were secretaries and salespeople, pharmacists and fishermen, farmers and factory workers, veterans and vendors, managers and musicians, beauticians and bartenders, firefighters and freemasons, teachers and truckers, engineers and emergency dispatchers, debutantes and delivery drivers, homemakers and health care workers. With only a few exceptions (beautician, debutante, homemaker, and mason), these occupations crossed gender and racial lines. Traditional gender and racial norms as reflected in occupational status in the south are certainly evolving.

But not all social and cultural mores are changing. During the summer of 2016, notable absences in the obituaries carried in *The Sun News* included any identification of same sex couples or those who label themselves GLBTQ, and while some national and ethnic differences were noted, for the most part, the obituaries in Myrtle Beach, South Carolina are predominantly of white and European American or black and African American people. It would be foolish to claim that only straight people die in Myrtle Beach, so the lack of obituaries referencing sexual orientations other than heteronormative seems a nod not only to individual preference but also to social acceptability.

With only a few exceptions, representations of ethnic diversity were limited. With small but thriving Korean, Vietnamese, Cambodian, Nigerian, Russian, Jewish, Lebanese, Turkish, Syrian, Egyptian, Polish, Romanian, and other, communities, and much larger Hispanic, Caribbean, and Greek co-cultures present in Myrtle Beach, the lack of representation in the newspaper obituaries – and culture at large – is surprising. However, depictions of religious differences were limited as well. Almost every obituary highlights membership in a Christian church, and the "in lieu of flowers" donation suggestions are overwhelmingly Christian places of worship. Good Shepherd Anglican Church; South Strand Assembly of God; Calvary, First, Lakeside, Langston, Little Bethel, North Conway, Pleasant Union, Salem, and Wando Baptist Churches; St. John's and St. Michael's Catholic Churches; Grand Strand and Pawleys Island Community Churches; Our Lady Star of the Sea and The Shepherd of the Sea Lutheran Churches; Belin, Faith Wesleyan, Good Hope United, Union, St. Paul's Waccamaw United, and Surfside Methodist Churches; and many more are mentioned as possible donation recipients. South Carolinians may be dying, but God is alive and well in their obituaries. While the reader is occasionally invited to donate to a "charity of one's choice," these options are limited, and certainly less frequent and common than Christian churches or veterans, animal, or literacy organizations. One notable exception, and one that certainly reflects current death and dying trends, is the frequent suggestion for memorials to go to the Hospice, Alzheimer's or American Cancer Associations, a random clue of cause of death within a genre always full of euphemistic ambiguity.

These invitations to donate funds are often some of the only ways we may assume cause of death. Prior to the mid-20th century, discussions of cause of death in obituaries were common and often included extensive descriptions of the deceased's last days (Crespo, 2007; Phillips, 2007; Starck, 2009). As more current research has indicated (Albert et al., 2016; Barth et al., 2013; Johnson, 2006; Phillips, 2007; Starck, 2009), currently, statements of cause of death are often ambiguous, stating that death has occurred "suddenly" or "after a long illness." The exception is the death – or battle against death – characterized as heroic: "passed away peacefully after a brave and courageous 10-year battle with cancer," or "died following a long courageous fight against ALS."

Obituaries as Reflection of Relational Constructions

Furthermore, death often occurs "surrounded by [loving] family." Family, an oft noted trope in obituaries (Barth et al., 2013; Hume, 2000;

Ondimu, 2014), is alluded to frequently in the obituaries we analyzed, and was clearly important to both men and women, another differing gender norm, especially in the South. While it is still common for women to "have no greater joy in life than her family," men were also frequently depicted as grounded in the home:

> *"he loved spending time with his family,"*
> *he spent time enjoying "his grandchildren,"*
> *he died "following a long life filled with love and service."*

These familial descriptions often extended to others outside of the immediate family:

> *"Marvin was a special adopted father to many."*
> *"Big Rob belonged to many families as well as his immediate family."*
> *"His proudest accomplishment, however, was his daughter."*

Historically these values, expected and lauded in women, were lacking in obituaries for men (Hume, 2000), yet today seem much more widespread and commonplace.

The history of family, and the subsequent naming of family and individual, is important to all families, and by extension to the state (Bourdieu, 1998). Families work "to perpetuate their social being" through "reproduction strategies" that include "fertility, matrimony, succession, economy, and education" (p. 19). Obituaries serve to record, transmit, reify, and authorize these modes of reproduction. These matters are especially important in the American South. Characterized by long histories – often fraught with division – and even longer familial ties, family name is an important element of the southern obituary. For men, constructions such as "He was the son of John Cribb, who served on the South Carolina Commission of Forestry for 44 years" are common. For women, who almost always take their husband's last name in this area, "Nee" (formerly), with the woman's maiden name following, is a common construction; i.e., Nee Hinchcliffe, Nee Edge, Nee Sutton, Nee Trapper. Nicknames are frequent and clearly gendered: Taffy, Radar, Lil Will, Tootie, Queenie, Dee, Peg, Dooley, Hutch, Bob and Bobby, Bill and Billy, Rick and Ricky, Sam and Sammy, R. W. and B. W. Memberships in long standing familial organizations such as the Daughters of the American Revolution or the Daughters of the Confederacy are frequently noted. Whether you were born and raised in the South, or moved here from "up north," the social constructions typical of the South are the social constructions typical of the southern obituary.

These familial constructions are especially true within depictions of married life. In obituaries, marriages are often long, happy, and blissful. They last many years: from 15 to 77 years, and spouses are often preceded by descriptive positive adjectives: "cherished wife," "loving husband," "devoted wife." Possible and/or suspected lovers are "long time companions" and "close friends." In the southern obituary world, marriages are always happy. Infidelity and violence rarely occurs. Wives are adored and husbands are revered. Faith, family, and football.

Football, the South's metaphor for sport, is a frequent theme appearing in obituaries for women and men. These notations were often related to themes of origin. For example, "never forgetting his roots, he was an avid fan of both Penn State Football and the Pittsburgh Steelers" or "Prior to her retirement, she coached field hockey and softball." While men still love to hunt and fish, and women's interest in sport still seems grounded in traditional "women's" sport, these recreations are increasingly common for both women and men:

> "Ms. Usher enjoyed bowling, swimming and golfing"
> "Margaret was very fond of Boston sport teams and grey horses"
> "She ... graduated from University of Tennessee (GO VOLS!)"

We wonder about these depictions, though. Throughout their lives, Cris' and Deb's mothers and mothers-in-law engaged in multiple activities they didn't love, or really like all that much, because they were expected – and wanted – to be good wives. Deb's mother sat with her father and watched Washington Redskins football, Old Dominion University basketball, and PGA golf every weekend. She labeled herself a fan and bought and wore team gear on game days. But she sat in a lawn chair and read a book when they went to the Master's tournament in Augusta, Georgia, and spent more time outside the basketball arena gossiping and eating hot dogs than she did watching the game. She was constantly shushed during family fishing trips where she never picked up a fishing pole, and she never watched any of these sporting events when home alone. She was a fan because she loved her husband, not because she loved sport. The exception was boxing, which she adored, mainly because her beloved father took her to the matches in Madison Square Garden in New York City as a child. But even a boxing match went unviewed if Megs' father or grandfather weren't around. Cris' mother-in-law wore a dress, hose, and heels every day of her life: during the endless camping trips with her husband and three sons, during the occasional visits to the beach, during the fiftieth anniversary wedding cruise that her husband planned for her. Like many women, these mothers participated, observed, or engaged in sport to build relationships; they didn't use relationships to further a love of sport. There is a difference depicted in these obituaries if you read between the lines.

"Faith, family and football," the cultural trilogy of the South, certainly still represents important ways of being in the South, but the ways in which the trilogy layers across gender lines in obituaries is especially interesting. Football isn't just for men, family isn't just for women, and faith spans sex, gender, and other standpoints. Both women and men often have long military service, and many are characterized as "proud veterans." Often, these chronicles of military service read like a catalog or travelogue:

> *"Harold enlisted in the US Air Force, and after 2 years attended the US Military Academy at West Point; he was later assigned to FT Bragg, NC; FT Sill, OK; FT Bliss, TX, Redstone Arsenal, AL …. After serving in Vietnam as a subsector advisor, in 1966 he returned to Redstone Arsenal until 1970, then attended General Staff School in FT Leavenworth, KS. His last assignment until his military retirement in 1973 was with the Concepts Analysis Agency in Bethesda, MD."*
>
> *"Connie retired as resource manager for the US Army Security Assistance Command in 1991 after over 28 years of dedicated service. Connie was a former officer of the VFW Auxiliary."*
>
> *"William served in the US Army, first The Norfolk Military University, then at FT Lawson, WA and was stationed at the Shemya Air Force Base in the Alaskan Aleutian Islands."*

Conclusion

Obituaries in the Myrtle Beach *Sun News* reflect many of the changes in the "new south:" an increasingly transient population characterized by exponential migration from the north, growing diversity in employment options for women and men, new visibility for people of color, and personal traits and characterizations that cross gender and class lines. However, they also represent social constructions of both past and present norms. Traditional values with regard to marriage, family, religion, and country still predominate. Marriage is still between a man and woman, nuclear and extended families are still bound by long standing kinship ties, God and football equally share Sundays, and boys go to war, some returning as heroes, some not returning at all. Fluid, dynamic, and intersectional, the obituary – for the most part – remains a specific genre that constructs our lives and deaths in socially acceptable ways.

Note

1 A version of this chapter was presented at the 2018 Southern States Communication Association Annual Conference in Nashville TN and was awarded the 2018 "Top Paper" Award by SSCA's Ethnography Interest Group.

References

Afful, J. (2010). A genre analysis of death announcements in Ghanaian newspapers. Available at: http://www.language-and-society.org/journal/1–2/7_afful.pdf (accessed 20 August 2016).

Albert, A. O.; Anthony, A.; & Lateif, A. (2016). Understanding the life course through newspaper obituaries. Indian Journal of Gerontology, 30(4), 452–460.

Barth, S.;Van Hoof,J.J.; & Beldad,A. (2013). Reading between the lines:A comparison of 480 German and Dutch obituaries. Omega – Journal of Death and Dying, 68(2), 161–181.

Bourdieu, P. (1998). Practical reason. Stanford, CA: Stanford University Press.

Chaudhry, S. M.; Christopher, A. A.; & Krishnasamy, H. (2014). Gender discrimination in death reportage: Reconnoitering disparities through a comparative analysis of male and female paid obituaries of Pakistani English newspapers. Advances in Language and Literary Studies, 5(2), 29–34.

Connerton, P. (1989). How societies remember. Cambridge: Cambridge University Press.

Crespo, F. E.(2007). Linguistic devices coping with death in Victorian obituaries. Revista Alicantina de Estudios Ingleses, 20, 7–21.

Dilevko, J., & Gottlieb, L. (2004). The portrayal of librarians in obituaries at the end of the Twentieth century. Library Quarterly, 74(2), 152–180.

Epstein, C. R., & Epstein, R. J. (2013). Death in *The New York Times*: The price of fame is a faster flame. QJM: The Monthly Journal of the Association of Physicians, 106(6), 517–521.

Fennell, V. L. (2014). A tale of two obits: Reading the Cold War through the obituaries of W.E. B.DuBois and Chairman Mao Tse-tung. International Journal of Communication, 8, 301–318.

Fernandez, E. C. (2007). Linguistics devices coping with death in Victorian obituaries. Revista Alicantina de Estudios Ingleses, 20, 7–21.

Fowler, B. (2004). Mapping the obituary: Notes towards a Bourdieusian interpretation. The Sociological Review, 52, 148–171.

Fowler, B. (2007). The obituary as collective memory. New York: Routledge.

Fowler, B., & Bielsa, E. (2007). The lives we choose to remember: A quantitative analysis of newspaper obituaries. Sociological Review, 55(2) 203–226.

Gavriely-Nuri, D., & Lachover, E. (2012). Reframing the past as a cosmopolitan memory: Obituaries in the Israeli daily Haaretz. Communication Theory, 22, 48–65.

Hume, J. (2000). Obituaries in American culture. Jackson, MS: University Press of Mississippi.

Hume, J. (2003). "Portraits of Grief," reflections of values: *The New York Times* remembers victims of September 11. Journalism & Mass Communication Quarterly, 80(1), 166–182.

Johnson, M. (2006). The dead beat and the perverse pleasures of obituaries. New York: Harper Collins Publishers.

Lachover, E., & Gavriely-Nuri, D. (2011). Requiem to nationalism? Shaping a collective Israeli identity through obituaries. Global Media Journal, Mediterranean Edition, 6(1), 24–39.

Lee, W. S.; Shim, J. C.; & Yoo, J. W.(2014). Reflecting absence: Representing the extraordinary deaths of ordinary sailors in the media. Journal of Loss and Trauma, 19(5) 416–425.

McElroy, K. (2013). "You must remember this:" Obituaries and the Civil Rights Movement. Journal of Black Studies, 44, (4), 335–355.

Moore, S. H. (2002). Disinterring ideology from a corpus of obituaries: A critical post mortem. Discourse & Society, 13(4), 495–537.

Ondimu, J. (2014). A socio-cultural understanding of death: A genre analysis of obituaries in a Kenyan newspaper. Language Matters, 45(1), 3–22.

Phillips, J. B. (2007). The changing presentation of death in the obituary, 1899–1999. Omega – Journal of Death and Dying, 55(4), 325–346.

Starck, N. (2009). Sex after death: The obituary as an erratic record of proclivity. Mortality, 19(4), 338–354.

Wallace, J. (2003). "We can't make more dirt …": Tragedy and the excavated body. The Cambridge Quarterly, 32(2), 103–111.

Wasserman, J. (1998). To trace the shifting sands: Community, ritual, and the memorial landscape. Landscape Journal, 17(1), 42–61.

8

PERFORMING LIVES: COMMUNICATING ABOUT DEATH IN FUNERALS AND EULOGIES

"What was your mom's funeral like?" asks Cris.

"It was beautiful," Deb says, tearing up.

"My parents' funerals were really meaningful also," says Cris. "My mom picked out her favorite hymns ahead of time, and the pastor gave a beautiful eulogy based on talking to my mom before she died, and my sisters and me after she died."

Deb smiles. "That's so nice! As you know, my mom was a devout Roman Catholic, so we only had a few choices within her ceremony. Of course, she wanted the Roman Catholic sacramental Mass, which we all knew, and while it's a lovely ceremony, it's quite scripted since it represents the last of the seven sacraments that Catholics try to achieve."

"It is a beautiful ceremony," Cris agrees.

Deb continues. "My dad, of course, chose the readings and the music, and I thought they were really representative of what my mom would have wanted. The music was all Pavarotti, whom she adored, and the readings were all appropriate Bible verses. I spoke, my brother John spoke, and close family friends did the readings." Deb starts laughing. "I was so nervous walking up to the lectern to deliver my mom's eulogy! I just knew I was going to trip – you know me, Cris … "

"Grace personified," Cris agrees and laughs along with Deb.

"Miraculously, I did not trip, or slur my words, or misstep in any way. I feel like my mom was with me." Deb smiles, then begins to laugh again. "On the other hand, my friend Darlene wanted to do a reading, and while she was walking up, she tripped, stumbled, and started to say 'Oh, shit,' 'cause you know, Darlene cusses like a sailor!"

Cris smiles knowingly. "Truly, a delicate flower …"

Deb starts laughing. "I'm told it happens often."

"Yes, it does!" Cris agrees. "I've seen a lot of funerals," Cris adds. "I used to be executive director of a non-profit organization that served older adults. In that capacity, I attended funerals of volunteers and participants fairly frequently.

"Didn't you also write a paper about funerals?"

"Yes, and for that project, I attended several funerals and also interviewed people about their experiences with funerals. I have some sad funeral stories and also some funny ones."

"Funny?" Deb asks.

"Yeah, I guess funny in a 'black humor' sort of way. One time, I was planning on attending a funeral of a volunteer named Jean. The morning of the funeral, another volunteer, Carolyn, came by and asked me if I knew that Jean had died. I replied that I did, and was planning to attend her funeral that afternoon. Carolyn said, 'Her funeral was yesterday.' I paused, confused, because I was sure that I had read it in the morning's paper that it was that afternoon. Carolyn insisted that it was yesterday, and said that she had in fact attended the funeral yesterday! I pulled out the newspaper, and read that it was that afternoon, so I called the funeral home and verified that, in fact, it was that afternoon. Carolyn's response was, 'I wonder what I attended yesterday.' The thought of somebody attending the wrong funeral was quite amusing to me, and Carolyn and I reflected on how she could have attended the wrong funeral without realizing it. She said that she had arrived late, and there wasn't a casket, and, in fact, since the service was all in Latin – it, too, was a Catholic service – she wasn't even sure that it was a funeral she had attended! Since the focus of our behavior is our meaning of what happened, and not the 'objective reality,' Carolyn would have been quite happy not knowing that she attended the wrong funeral. The service had all of the ritualistic elements necessary to convince her that she had in fact said goodbye to Jean, and she was quite content until I told her otherwise (see Davis, 2008). That still makes me laugh when I think about it, not to be mean, but – honestly – it could have happened to any of us!"

Deb chuckles. "What's your other funny funeral story?"

"I was conducting interviews for my research, and one of the pastors I interviewed told me this story:

> They had the casket open, and were getting ready to start the funeral, and the funeral director comes down and tries to shut the lid and they kept pushing on it. They finally remembered there was a little thing you had to lower on it, to lower the deceased's head inside the casket, and when they pick the lid back up to close it again, there's like this shroud, where you can like see [an image of] the person's face on the lid. Can you imagine sitting there watching this? Clear as can be was his impression."

Personal Interview

"The backstage side of funerals is not something you want to be visible," Deb says, laughing.

Funeral Practices

Public Performances of End of Life

Death rituals differ greatly across time and cultures, even within the U.S., and it is therefore very difficult to make generalizations about them, but regardless of origin, funerals and related burial rituals reflect, reconstruct, and reinforce a culture's meaning of death and life. More traditional western Christian-influenced death rituals typically involve funerals, memorial ceremonies, and burial rites, all "liturgical, formal, poetic, communal, and biblical expression[s] of personal and community loss and grief as well as comfort and hope" (Langford, 2010, p. 2). Definitionally, funerals are ceremonies at which the remains of the deceased are present; many conclude with a burial or commitment of the bodily remains, while memorial services do not have the remains at the ceremony (Langford, 2010). Funerals are highly ritualized forms of communication and cultural performance; the rituals themselves providing a sense of permanence, familiarity, and security in the midst of the social and personal upheaval of a loved one's death. As with other rituals, funeral rituals have a performative nature, in which the act of performing is socially negotiated and provides specific symbolic meaning (Davis, 2008; Rappaport, 1980).

Framed through a culture-specific lens, modern funeral practices include a variety of opportunities to celebrate the life of the deceased individual while also confronting the associated emotions of the living. Funerals are public expressions of faith and grief and offer a very tangible confirmation of a loved one's death, along with an affirmation of support from the community. Times of death are liminal times, spaces in which both the deceased and their surviving loved ones are perceived to be between life and death, between relationship and loss.

Death represents a shift in one's relational identity, and funeral and other end of life rituals provide a tangible way to deal with the liminality of this shifting identity (Davis et al., 2016; Seale, 1998). Funerals and related end of life rituals are rites of passage, marking this stage of life much as baptisms or christenings, bar/bat mitzvahs or confirmations, and weddings, mark time through other liminal stages of life. End of life rites and rituals, from the Middle Ages to modern times, repeat familiar rituals, laments, gestures, and symbols, offering a comforting familiarity to expressions of grief and mourning (Ariès, 1981). Funerals as rites of passage formalize this stage by providing a structured way in which the survivors can talk about their deceased loved one and focus on the faith, community, and family they can still hold on to for comfort (Davis, 2008; Davis et al., 2016; Rappaport, 1980).

Throughout time, funeral practices have helped bridge the liminal gap between the survivor and his/her deceased loved ones through reminders of the deceased's life, elements of relational closure, and a reorientation toward a new life without the ongoing relationship with the deceased (Danforth & Tsiaras, 1982; Davis, 2008; Davis et al., 2016; Seale, 1998). During the funeral itself, loved ones have a moment to pause and reflect upon the ways in which their lives have been changed by this death. Thus, funerals give surviving loved ones an opportunity to begin to create a new relational story with a new coherence that incorporates their changed relational status (Davis, 2008; Davis et al., 2016). Funerals are for the living, as the saying goes. Whether Christian or non-Christian, traditional or alternative, all end of life rituals provide a space for the grieving loved ones to process their loss (Green, 2014).

Funeral rituals from various religious traditions function to honor the deceased, comfort the surviving loved ones, and publicly grieve, but also to reify beliefs surrounding death and the afterlife (Langford, 2010). The religious statements of belief serve as proxy affirmations of faith for the deceased (Davis, 2008; Davis et al., 2016).

Funeral services venerate the deceased, communicating that the person was worthy of respect and mourning. They provide a public recognition of and tribute to the life of the deceased. Funerals also bring closure to a person's life – they are, literally, the final public statement made about a person.

Public Performances of Grief and Social Support

Funerals confirm the death, forcing reluctant mourners to face the cold reality of death. In so doing, funerals open space for the community to comfort the mourners and the mourners to comfort each other. They also provide social support for the survivors and give the community a venue through which to say goodbye to their loved one. They facilitate expressions of grief for the mourners and are an opportunity to provide succor to the bereaved. As with other faith traditions, the Christian faith leader's role in such a religious ritual is to comfort the family and to "convey the love of God" (Langford, 2010, p. 4) to those present. In many ways, funerals and related end of life ceremonies construct a comforting and supportive sense of community for the grieving loved ones (Davis, 2008). Through stories or photographs, formal eulogies or informal sharing, talking about memories of our deceased loved ones with others in the community helps people reorient themselves to their new identity without their deceased loved one (Davis, 2008; Davis et al., 2016; Seale, 1998). Shared stories also connect both the deceased and the survivors to the ancestors who had previously died – connecting them to a familial lineage that is comforting and represents the circle of life (Davis, 2008; Davis et al., 2016). This continuity reinforces the sense of community for the grieving survivors and paints a vivid comforting picture of "a connection … to the ancestors who had gone on before" (Davis, 2008, p. 419).

Funerals and related end of life ceremonies pull the community together, connect private and public grief, and bridge the theological gap between the human and the divine – offering a way in which to embody the spirit of the deceased at the same time they sanctify the body. Funerals join the past, present, and future together as they invoke all of our deceased loved ones. They remind all participants of our own mortality but offer hope through reification of our shared belief systems. They incorporate the voices of the entire community through ritualistic and participatory elements, and they bring meaning and order to the perceived chaos of death and dying by incorporating familiar elements with the strangeness of death. Funerals help us create meaning out of the chaos of the illness or accident, the unfamiliarity of the death itself, and the stress of planning the services. The funeral service is an opportunity to remain connected with the deceased while the grieving loved ones get used to the loss and their change in relational status. In all these ways, funerals are rites of passage to move the survivors through the massive relational transformation of death (Davis, 2008).

Other purposes of end of life rituals include helping survivors cope with their own fear of death, offering rituals and procedures with which to dispose of the body, assisting the deceased in the afterlife; and reestablishing, reaffirming, and reconnecting with social networks.

Familiar Traditions

In our western culture, most end of life rituals include common characteristics which are heavily proscribed by religious or cultural traditions: a room crowded with people, some sort of confession or repentance, an anointing, perhaps a death watch, a wake of some sort, a wreath hanging on the door of the home, a body on display and frequently beautification of the corpse, a funeral procession, wearing black or specific – usually somber – colors, mourners who cry and wail, flowers, specific music, and sprinkling of water, oil, or incense. Various religious traditions also have elements that are symbolic of specific beliefs. For instance, some Christian funerals incorporate the use of a cloth called a "pall," which symbolizes the baptism of the person who died, making reference to – according to a minister quoted in Davis (2008) – "you are covered in life and death by your baptism, … raised into a new reality" (p. 412).

Familiar rituals, recitations of memorable religious readings or passages from holy texts, and singing recognizable religious songs are comforting for their familiarity and also from the reminder that people of this specific religious or cultural tradition have been saying or singing these same things for generations back. The perceived presence of a long line of cultural and spiritual ancestors is a comforting image for mourners (Davis, 2008). The familiarity of this rite of passage reminds us of our own loved ones' funerals, connecting us through our collective mourning into a larger communal body (Davis, 2008).

Deb shares her earliest funeral memories:

> *As a young child growing up in the 1950s and 60s in southern Virginia, I vividly remember the discussions among my grandmother, her sisters, and her aunts as they planned their obituaries and funerals. By the time I was old enough to peer over the windowsill, I knew that yellow roses were the preferred color and genus for funeral flowers, that black was the expected shade and style of dress at the service, and there was a corresponding relationship among the yellow roses, black clad people, and perceived popularity of the decedent. Food and punch choices were debated among my aunts as hotly as the cakes and casseroles emerging from the ovens on the day of the funeral, and in those times of limited air-conditioning, talc and handkerchiefs were a part of funeral attire, stuffed in between the ample bosoms of the women in my family. Cremations were rare, and usually, the viewing and church service were part of a larger ritual that included a graveside service consisting of the lowering of the casket and a reception at a family member's house afterward. It was always a long day, interrupted by intermittent excitement and long stretches of boredom. I liked the food. Afterward, families visited the cemetery on particular days, bringing flowers and memories with them, and lying them gently on the gravesite, dusting off the dead leaves and cloth remnants of offerings left previously. My father still visits my mother's crypt every Thursday. He replaces dead flowers with live ones, and sits on the bench in front of the mausoleum and talks to her, telling her how much he misses her. My brothers go on Mother's Day. I only go when someone wants me to.*

In addition to formal church services commemorating the life and commending the body of a loved one, there are a myriad of ancient and innovative ways people express closure at a loved one's death. More traditional ceremonies may be held at a funeral home, place of worship, or at the graveside or columbarium (resting place for cremated ashes), but more contemporary ceremonies may be held at home or outdoors, at a park or museum (Green, 2014; Marsh, 2017).

Traditionally, funeral rituals include symbolic elements such as specific colors (perhaps white for purity, black for mourning, green for life after death); white candles (to symbolize light in the darkness); objects meaningful to the deceased or the family such as a picture of the deceased or possessions of value; music that is significant to the deceased or family or to the religious tradition; creeds or ritualistic readings; readings from religious texts; and flowers as a sign of respect (Langford, 2010). Funerals or memorial services in many religious and ethnic traditions include eulogies – extended statements about the deceased spoken extemporaneously or read either by the presiding clergy or by friends or family members. Many traditions include a wake, visitation, or family vigil prior to the more formal funeral service. Sometimes these are held at the family home, others are held at the funeral home or at the church. Frequently these include a viewing of the deceased's body in an open casket; they may include food or refreshments; they typically involve informal condolence conversations with the surviving family members (Langford, 2010).

Funerals are a performance of one's life, and as with all performances, audiences are required to complete the performer–audience link. A funeral without mourners would be an empty ceremony indeed. In Davis (2008, p. 410), a pastor is quoted sharing what may be the saddest funeral story ever:

> *The loneliest funeral I ever did was one of the first ones I ever did. The only people at this funeral, was the funeral director, the person who died, and me. And why they even had a funeral service, I'll never know. But he had outlived all his family members, all his friends, nobody knew him.*
>
> *Personal Interview*

Protestant Funeral Customs

A typical Protestant (Christian) funeral service might have the following order of service (Langford, 2010; Moravian Book of Worship, 1995):

Prelude
Welcome
Hymn
Liturgy
Hymn
Scripture and Prayer
Special Music
Memoir or Eulogy
Hymn
Postlude

In the Moravian church – a small Christian Protestant denomination – a funeral service includes the following responsive reading in their "Liturgy of the Moravian Church for the Burial of the Dead." Typically, a minister or workshop leader reads the lines in normal type and the congregation, or participants, respond with the lines in bold type:

> Lord, our God, in whom we live, and move, and have our being.
> **Have mercy upon us.**
> Lord, our God, you do not willingly bring affliction or grief to your children.
> **Leave your peace with us.**

Lord, our God, you have raised Christ from death as the assurance that those who sleep in death will also be raised.

Bless and comfort us, we humbly pray.

Eternal God, accept us as your children in your beloved Son, Jesus Christ, who came into the world from you, was born a human being, and lived among us. He took the role of a servant, and has redeemed us from all sin and from death, with his holy and precious blood, and with his innocent suffering and dying. Christ has done this so that we may be his own, live in his kingdom, and serve him in eternal righteousness, innocence, and happiness, since he, being risen from the dead, lives and reigns, forever and ever.

Amen

Our Savior has said: Whoever hears my words and believes the one who sent me has eternal life and will not be judged, but has already passed from death into life.

Savior of the world, lead us in paths of righteousness for your name's sake.

We do not live to ourselves and we do not die to ourselves. If we live, it is for the Lord that we live; and if we die, it is for the Lord that we die. So whether we live or die, we belong to the Lord, for Christ died, rose from death, and lives again in order to be Lord of the living and of the dead.

Living Redeemer, we find our hope in you.

As a father has compassion on his children, so God has compassion on those who honor him; for he knows how we were formed, he remembers that we are dust. As a mother comforts her children, so will I comfort you, says the Lord. The Lord lifts up those who are bowed down, and sustains those who are bereaved. And God will wipe away all tears from their eyes.

The steadfast love of the Lord lasts forever, and his goodness endures for all generations.

Glory be to the Father, and to the Son, and to the Holy Spirit.

As it was in the beginning, is now, and ever shall be, world without end.

Amen

Continuing with the "Conclusion of a Memorial Service," the liturgy reads:

I am the Resurrection and the Life, says the Lord. Those who believe in me will live, even though they die, and those who live and believe in me will never die. Therefore, blessed are the dead who die in the Lord. Yes, says the Spirit, they will rest from their labor. Where, death, is your victory? Where, grave, is your sting? It is sin which gives death its power, and it is the Law which gives sin its strength. All thanks to God, who delivered us from the fear of death, the power of sin, and the condemnation of the Law. Thanks be to God, who gives us the victory through our Lord

Jesus Christ. Keep us in everlasting fellowship with the heavenly Church Triumphant, and let us rest together in your presence from our labors.
Hear us, gracious Lord and God.
Glory be to him who is the Resurrection and the Life. Even though we die, he gives us life now and forever. Glory be to Christ, in the church which waits for him on earth, and in the church which is around him in heaven, forever and ever.
Amen

Moravian Book of Worship, 1995, pp. 177–178.

The service concludes with a "commitment," or burial service, at the graveyard, which ends with the following liturgical statements:

I am the Resurrection and the life, says the Lord. Those who believe in me will live, even though they die; and those who live and believe in me will never die. Therefore, blessed are the dead who die in the Lord. Yes, says the Sprit, they will rest from their labor. Where, death, is your victory? Where, grave, is your sting? It is sin which gives death its power, and it is the Law which gives sin its strength. All thanks to God, who delivered us from the fear of death, the power of sin, and the condemnation of the Law. Thanks be to God, who gives us the victory through our Lord Jesus Christ …
We now commit this body to the ground, in sure and certain hope of the resurrection of all believers to eternal life through our Lord Jesus Christ. He shall change our weak, mortal bodies and make them like his own glorious body, using that power by which he is able to bring all things under his rule. Keep us in everlasting fellowship with the heavenly Church Triumphant, and let us rest together in your presence from our labors.
Hear us, gracious Lord and God.
Glory be to him who is the Resurrection and the Life. Even though we die, he gives us life now and forever.
Glory be to Christ, in the church which waits for him on earth, and in the church which is around him in heaven, forever and ever

Moravian Book of Worship, 1995, p. 180.

Jewish Funeral Customs

Jewish funeral practices include a purification ritual called a Tharah in which the body is ritually cleaned and purified in water, then dressed in a white shroud called a tachrichim – white as a sign of purity and holiness. Jewish families, rather than participate in a wake or visitation prior to the funeral, gather in a ritual that involves tearing their clothes or wearing a black ribbon over their heart. The funeral service, called a Levayah, typically includes prayers, eulogies, and scripture readings – frequently a recitation of Psalms from the Torah. In Jewish funerals, loved ones might pray the Dayan HaEmet, translated as: "Blessed are You, Lord our G-d, King of the universe, the True Judge" (http://www.chabad.org/library/article_cdo/aid/386958/jewish/Dayan-HaEmet-The-True-Judge-Blessing.htm), or the Mourner's Blessing ("Mourner's Kaddish"), translated into English as:

> Glorified and sanctified be God's great name throughout the world
> which He has created according to His will.
> May He establish His kingdom in your lifetime and during your days,
> and within the life of the entire House of Israel, speedily and soon;
> and say, Amen.
> May His great name be blessed forever and to all eternity.
> Blessed and praised, glorified and exalted, extolled and honored,
> adored and lauded be the name of the Holy One, blessed be He,
> beyond all the blessings and hymns, praises and consolations that
> are ever spoken in the world; and say, Amen.
> May there be abundant peace from heaven, and life, for us
> and for all Israel; and say, Amen.
> He who creates peace in His celestial heights,
> may He create peace for us and for all Israel;
> and say, Amen
>
> *Mourner's Kaddish*

A Jewish funeral may close with the Prayer for the Soul of the Departed (Kel Maleh Rachamim):

> O G-d, full of compassion, Who dwells on high, grant true rest
> upon the wings of the Shechinah (Divine Presence), in the exalted
> spheres of the holy and pure, who shine as the resplendence of the
> firmament, to the soul of [*mention her Hebrew name and that of her father*]
> who has gone to her [supernal] world, for charity has been donated
> in remembrance of her soul; may her place of rest be in Gan Eden.
> Therefore, may the All-Merciful One shelter her with the cover of
> His wings forever, and bind her soul in the bond of life. The Lord is
> her heritage; may she rest in her resting-place in peace; and let us say:
> Amen
>
> *Kel Maleh Rachamim*

Following the funeral service, the family and loved ones will participate in a procession to the burial, signifying respect and support for both the deceased and the surviving loved one.

After the services, families gather to eat a special condolence meal and then participate in a seven-day period of mourning, called Shivah, in which they remain home and refrain from work ("sit Shivah") while they receive visitors from the community who light candles and offer prayers and consolation (http://www.chabad.org/library/article_cdo/aid/282506/jewish/Soul-Talk.htm). Practicing Jews are not usually embalmed and are sometimes cremated but usually buried in a plain pine box (http://www.chabad.org/library/article_cdo/aid/386958/jewish/Dayan-HaEmet-The-True-Judge-Blessing.htm; https://www.everplans.com/articles/jewish-funeral-traditions).

Islamic Funeral Customs

Islamic funeral customs include a service at the mosque; readings from their holy book, the Koran; recitation of prayers for the soul of the deceased (called "Salat al-Janazah") in the courtyard of the mosque; a closed casket; and a funeral procession to the graveyard. Muslims are not cremated and are usually not embalmed. In Islamic tradition, the body is bathed by family members in a ritual called "Ghusl," and covered in a white cotton shroud called "Kafan." Ghusl involves at least three washings in a specified order, and bodies are shrouded with their arms in a praying position. Muslims are buried in an easterly direction facing Mecca. Mourners go from the burial to the family home for a meal and informal consolation. During the 40-day period of mourning after the death, family members wear black (https://www.funeralwise.com/customs/islam/; https://www.everplans.com/articles/muslim-funeral-traditions).

Funeral Traditions

Note how all of these funeral traditions reify the belief system of those reciting them, affirm their beliefs in their specific version of an afterlife, and offer comfort to the mourning loved ones. Specific behaviors such as cleansing or preparation of the body, songs or hymns at the funeral, funeral processions, and mourning behaviors all honor the deceased. Elements such as prayers for the deceased or deathbed confessions offer social and spiritual support for the dying person, while wakes and visitations after the death offer social support for the surviving loved ones, as does music or hymns sung at funerals. Funeral processions also offer social support for the mourners, and they also serve to remind the survivors that they are part of a continual march of the past, present, and future, part of the lineage of ancestors and descendants (Davis, 2008) – that death is a natural part of life. Funeral processions (and recessions – the family leaving the funeral processionally ahead of the other mourners) are performative and public expressions of grief (Davis, 2008). All of these familiar rituals are markers of constancy in the midst of the shifting reality when a loved one dies (Davis, 2008).

Open caskets at a visitation or funeral confirm the death and help to bridge the liminal space between life and death (Davis, 2008). As we've stated previously in this book, all forms of communication have heightened symbolism when they concern a death, and that holds true for funerals and related end of life rituals. Who attends and who does not, who is invited to provide a eulogy, who sits with the family and who doesn't are all decisions fraught with personal and relational politics (Davis, 2008).

Today, seeming traditionally oriented funeral or memorial services include more modern elements, such as video tributes to the deceased loved one and online guest books on the funeral home website. You can replay a video of the funeral service or, if you can't attend, you can watch a live streaming of the service. In addition to or in lieu of more traditional funeral or memorial services, surviving family members are opting for making videotaped eulogies or publishing eulogies online rather than delivering them at a funeral service, memorializing a loved one in a blog or Facebook post, or lighting virtual candles on websites (https://www.huffingtonpost.com/2012/06/04/technology-funeral-rituals_n_1567545.html?ncid=edlinkusaolp00000003). Jewish mourners can sign up for email reminders of the anniversary of the loved one's death (called a "yahrtzeit") from ShivaConnect.com.

In fact, many families forego a formally ritualized ceremony, as fewer and fewer people hold regular churchgoing practices, and as families and loved ones live geographically scattered lives. As people embrace a more individualistic lifestyle, the services reflect this – you can have a funeral personalized with a movie-theme, for instance (Green, 2014).

Eulogies: Retrospective Sensemaking

Most funeral or memorial services include some sort of eulogies, some delivered by clergy and others delivered by friends or family; some extemporaneously informal and others written and read. Eulogies are a form of ceremonial rhetoric, and are characterized by being planned in advance, for the purpose of a performance of praise for its subject, consolation for the audience and speaker, identification with the audience (which is characterized by having a relationship with the deceased), and a statement on the character of the deceased (Davis et al., 2016). Eulogies are important ceremonial aspects of a funeral service in which, suggest Davis et al. (2016), the speaker performs both him/herself and his/her deceased loved one, in an attempt to frame his/her loved one's life retrospectively within the social frame allowed by funeral and eulogy codes. Eulogies specifically and funerals generally provide the penultimate performance of one's life, constructing retrospective meaning for loved ones' lives and reconstructing meaning for survivors in light of their loss, reconstructing our social identities in the face of the loss of a loved one (Davis et al., 2016). Davis et al. (2016) found that eulogies affirm and reconstruct our relational identity through specific ritualized forms of communication in which the bereaved loved ones focus on self-identity as they articulate their experience of grief. When relationships are lost, people who are bereaved have to reframe their relationships with the deceased and their surviving loved ones. Eulogies are one way we do this, suggest Davis et al. (2016), through various types of discourse. Loss discourse, the expression of the sense of relational loss by survivors, is exemplified in the following eulogy:

> *Dear [SON], I am a Tom Waits fan. For whatever reason, his music fits well with me and moves me. There is no doubt we would have spent lots of time listening to his songs together .... Given your passing, [SON], I'd like to focus on one short verse that has a new meaning for me. It goes like this ... "The things you can't remember tell the things you can't forget that history puts a saint in every dream." [Father about Infant Son].*
>
> *Davis et al., 2016, p. 321*

Relational discourse, explicitly referring to the relationship between the deceased and their loved ones, or recalling events that contribute to family or community identity, is exemplified in this eulogy:

> *We are all here today to honor the memory of [DECEASED] who has touched all our lives as a mother, grandmother, neighbor, friend, and dear wife. My name is [EULOGIST], a lifelong student of [DECEASED]. [Student of Deceased].*
>
> *Davis et al., 2016, p. 321*

Virtues discourse is discourse that refers to positive characteristics – primarily relational virtues – held by the deceased. Here is a eulogy that falls under this category:

> *When you think about [DECEASED], what do you remember? I remember her contagious smile, her laughter, and her beautiful face. Everyone remembers her for her beautiful, sunny smile. I remember that strong will that made her into the beautiful, graceful dancer and the great softball player that she was ... I also remember that [DECEASED] was a selfless, kind-hearted soul and was always willing to lend a hand even during her toughest of times. [Female friend of Deceased].*
>
> *Davis et al., 2016, p. 322*

Legacy discourse, discourse that refers to the ways the life of the person giving the eulogy was changed by the deceased, or to values or lessons learned from the deceased, is exemplified by:

> *As I am about to begin my marriage, I will use my parents' love and devotion to one another as a model for my future marriage and family life. [Daughter about Mother].*
>
> *Davis et al., 2016, p. 323*

Transcendence discourse refers to the discursive construction of a "good death" by sanctifying the deceased, referring to how the deceased is better off, accepted death, or will be seen again, or addressing a mystery or dilemma surrounding the death. Following is an example of transcendence discourse:

> *The morning he died, I know he said, "God please take me home." And knowing he is there happy with God makes it a little easier. [Grandson about grandfather].*
>
> *Davis et al., 2016, p. 323*

The final type of eulogy discourse identified by Davis et al., 2016 is social discourse, expressions of acknowledgement and gratitude or requesting social support. This is an example of social discourse in a eulogy:

> *Our family has been overwhelmed at the outpouring of prayers, love, and support throughout this difficult journey. It has helped tremendously to be surrounded by so many who, like us, absolutely adored our beautiful [MOTHER]. [Daughter about Mother].*
>
> *Davis et al., 2016, p. 324*

Say Davis et al. (2016):

> *We all die in the middle of a story, and eulogies attempt to encapsulate these unfinished narratives. Eulogies go further, however, than simply summarizing lives into end stories. Eulogies are written retrospectively but set the stage for a re-imagined future. Eulogies serve a sensemaking function, but relationally – they help us make sense of a loved one's death, and of us and our relationship, in the face of a loved one's death – through many different types of discourse …. Death creates a relational liminality in which the surviving loved one is in a state of social liminality – between social roles, relationships, and contexts. Eulogies help survivors to move through this liminal state into a newly constructed identity. Eulogies … represent our public attempts to both memorialize the deceased and construct meaning out of their life and out of their death, both for them and for us. Eulogies give word to that which may be thought of as wordless – the ultimate ending, loss of self, loss of voice, loss of identity.*
>
> *pp. 324–326*

Back to the Basics: The Green Movement

"I just remembered," Cris says suddenly. "I met a guy recently who told me about another type of funeral – a home funeral! It's a movement!"

"A home funeral!" says Deb. "I've heard of that. Kind of like natural childbirth – taking back the power of life transitions from the licensed gatekeepers."

"Exactly," Cris says. "The home funeral movement is a social movement that bypasses the traditional funeral homes, mortuaries, embalming, or churches. If a person dies at home from natural causes, the family can clean and dress her body and put her in bed or place her in the living room. If the body is packed with ice and the air-conditioning is turned up, the body can stay there for a couple days while loved ones come in and say their goodbyes. They might even have the funeral at home with the body there. When it is time to dispose of the body, she can be wrapped in a shroud or placed in a wooden casket and, depending on state laws, may be able to be buried in the family's back yard, or can be buried in a green cemetery or picked up by an agreeable funeral home. There are even crematoriums where you yourself can take your loved one's body to be cremated. Some will even let you push the button to start the cremation process (Personal Interview; https://www.huffingtonpost.com/2013/01/25/home-funerals-death-mortician_n_2534934.html)."

"You can do that, legally?"

"In most states home funerals and home burials are legal," Cris says.

"What a way to be close to a loved one's death," Deb says.

"Yes, it's a very hands-on way to participate in a loved one's end. Proponents say it's a good way to begin the grieving process. And it's counter-cultural."

"It seems like it's a response to the high costs of funerals," says Deb.

"Yes," says Cris, "and, ironically, it's modern, but of course it's a return to the more traditional methods of death and dying."

"Seems like it would be a way for people to retain control over their own deaths and the deaths of loved ones. It lets them spend more time with the loved one's body than they would if a mortuary was involved," Deb says thoughtfully.

"I would think that would be difficult for a family member to do," says Cris. "Cleaning the body, keeping the body in the home for several days, having the service in the home. But the guy I was talking to said it actually helps the family come to terms with their grief. He does say it's very emotional, but it's a very tangible way to acknowledge a loved one's death which helps with the grieving process. It's a very tender way to say goodbye."

"A tender goodbye," Deb repeats. "That sounds like a very loving way to go."

Conclusion

Funerals are the penultimate final performance of our lives, but one in which we are not actually ourselves present. A key part of funerals, eulogies are a specific type of discourse in which we make sense of our deceased loved ones' lives and the newly changed relational lives of surviving loved ones. Funerals – and eulogies – represent the life of the deceased in a myriad of personal, cultural, relational, and religious ways, as they carry the deceased from life to afterlife by wrapping up their life story in a tidy narrative of retrospective public sensemaking and memorialization. Funerals and eulogies also carry the surviving loved ones from that chapter of their relational story into the next. Davis et al. (2016) say:

> *The bereaved is, among other things, a performer in a cultural drama that asserts basic ides about the nature of life and death. These eulogies are identity performances that tell us who we are and how we are supposed to live our lives. They are guidebooks for our lives constructed from the lives of our deceased loved ones. Thus, eulogies do not just make sense of the lives of the deceased; they make sense of our lives as well, in the face of – in relation to – the lives of the deceased.*
>
> *p. 326*

References

Ariès, P. (1981). The hour of our death: The classic history of Western attitudes toward death over the last one thousand years. New York, NY: Vintage.

Danforth, L. M., & Tsiaras, A. (1982). The death rituals of rural Greece. Princeton, NJ: Princeton University Press.

Davis, C. S. (2008). A funeral liturgy: Death rituals as symbolic communication. Journal of Loss and Trauma, 13(5), 406–452.

Davis, C. S., Quinlan, M., & Baker, D. K. (2016). Constructing the dead: Retrospective framing and sensemaking in eulogies. Death Studies, 40(5), 316–328. doi: 10.1080/07481187.20106.1141261

Green, E. (2014, August 19). Burying your dead without religion. The Atlantic. Retrieved from https://theatlantic.com

Kel Maleh Rachamim (n.d.) http://www.chabad.org/library/article_cdo/aid/367837/jewish/Kel-Maleh-Rachamim.htm.

Langford, A. (2010). Christian funerals. Nashville, TN: Abington Press.

Marsh, T. D. (2017, October 27). Life after death: Americans are embracing new ways to leave their remains. The Conversation. Retrieved from https://theconversation.com

Moravian Book of Worship. (1995). Bethlehem, PA: Interprovincial Board of Publication and Communications.

Mourner's Kaddish (n.d.) Available at https://www.myjewishlearning.com/article/text-of-the-mourners-kaddish/

Rappaport, R. A. (1980). Concluding comments on ritual and reflexivity. Semiotica, 30, 181–193.

Seale, C. (1998). Constructing death: The sociology of dying and bereavement. Cambridge, UK: Cambridge University Press.

9

RHETORIC OF DECAY: COMMUNICATING ABOUT DEATH IN CEMETERIES AND BURIALS

Deb stares outside at a family strolling home on the darkened street, costumed in their Halloween attire. They remind her of tourists strolling down the Washington Mall or a resort town's boardwalk.

Deb turns to Cris and says, "You know, Cris, as we travel to tourism and heritage sites for our research, explore and investigate, eat out in nice restaurants and see the landmarks, we really become more tourists than researchers."

Cris nods as she reaches into the candy bucket and pulls out a piece of candy. She nibbles on it as Deb continues, "We cruise graves. We wander cemeteries leisurely, strolling, as if they are parks or boardwalks. We're sightseers in foreign realms. We consult guidebooks, take pictures, and compare attractions. We do it now for both work and leisure, for social and religious rituals, and for family and community gatherings …"

Cris interrupts thoughtfully. "We've always done it. Funerals and burials, and then the obligatory holiday visits, were important familial, social, and cultural norms when we were children. Our memories of life are interwoven with memories of death. The celebrations that hover around both life and death are important to us all, although some suggest there is a waning, a paling, in some culture's immersion in death – no longer so interwoven, no longer so revered. I think now more than ever many are consumed with death."

Deb reaches for a piece of candy, and murmurs, "Thus the focus of this book. It seems odd, perhaps, in some ways, our fascination with death and the celebrations that surround it, but it's not. Death and the cultural rituals associated with it, after all, are celebrations of life."

"My memories of cemetery visits have often been ritualistic, familial, and celebratory," agrees Cris. "Growing up, we went to visit Nana and Granddad's grave in Forest Lawn Cemetery in Los Angeles regularly. The last time I went

I was 16, when my dad and I were visiting L.A., six years after we moved away. I sat on the closely mown ground and remembered when I was a child sitting on that grass picking dandelions. In the winter the flowers were dried and white, and we would blow them away like soap bubbles. In the summer they were yellow, and we would tie a slip knot around the end and launch them at each other. This time it was summer, and the grass was green and lush. We parked at a curb near the graves, and the walk from the car was short. All the grave markers were metal, about three by five inches, flat on the ground. It was my job to pick the grass from around the edges of the marker because even though the cemetery kept the grass mowed they didn't trim around the edges and the grass threatened to overtake the graves, hiding the names and dates that reminded us that this was a person, this was a life once lived. Next to each marker was a hole in the ground which held a cylindrical container in which you put flowers. As Dad and I put our flowers in the container and picked away the errant grass, we reminisced about how we always visited on every occasion – birthdays, Memorial Day, Mother's Day, Father's Day – when we lived here."

Cris sighs at the memory and Deb sits quietly as she gathers her thoughts.

"'Don't come to my grave,' my dad told me. 'When I die,' he said, 'don't come to my grave. Don't put flowers on my grave. It's just a waste of time and money.'"

"What did you say to that?" Deb asks.

"I said nothing, except I mentally noted the paradox of being so faithful to put flowers on these graves while strongly believing the practice was a waste of time."

"Yeah," Deb says.

Cris continues her story. "We left the grave section of Forest Lawn and went to another part of the huge cemetery, seemingly far from Nana and Granddad's graves. Aunt Cassie was buried in the mausoleum, a stone structure that looked like a condo for coffins, with large stone walls in which rows and columns of coffins were placed, with markers at the front of each telling who was buried there. We placed flowers in the container attached to the front of her space."

"Are your parents buried there also?" asks Deb.

Cris shakes her head. "No, my mom and dad are now cremated with their ashes interred in the columbarium at Highland Presbyterian Church in Winston-Salem, North Carolina. The columbarium looks like a miniature version of the coffin condos, with stone walls to hold the urns and small markers with names and dates to mark who is interred below. Dad's ashes were originally interred in the First Presbyterian Church columbarium, but Mom got mad at them after he died so she moved her church membership and his ashes to Highland Presbyterian."

"So, I have to ask," says Deb hesitantly. "Do you visit your dad?"

"We still go by Highland occasionally, parking on the street and going in the side entrance. There are no places to put flowers so we don't – although some people bring fresh flowers and lay them next to, or on top of, the wall. Others have planted flowering plants in the ground nearby. We haven't. We don't bring flowers. We just come by to say hello. To say a prayer, send up a thought, to say hi to Mom and Dad," Cris responds thoughtfully.

How and why do the death rituals die? What are the tensions among the living and the dead that allow for the decreasing rates of traditional burials, increasing rates of cremations, and an abandonment of our dead buried in historic family, church, and town cemeteries? In part fostered by an increasing lack of access, population changes, laws and regulations, and shifts in cultural preferences (Basmajian & Courts, 2010; Beard & Burger, 2017; Davis, 1986; Hall, 2011; Hernandez, 1999; Kelly, 2012; Maples & East, 2013; Zelinsky, 1994), death, once so close, an intimate partner of life, is now physically far removed. Small church plots and family gravesites situated outside the kitchen window are now relegated to large corporate industrialized cemeteries, daunting in their breadth and depth, neat, manicured, clean. Death no longer sits Shivah in the living rooms of our homes. It is compartmentalized, sanitized, air conditioned. Death was once a family task. It is now medicalized, industrialized, and hidden from view. Death, like war, is now regulated – clean – its horror seemingly muted, diminished.

Deb walks to the kitchen to refill their beverages and remembers a cemetery visit with her cousin, Carole:

> *Carole swoops into the car with the grace of a bull in a china shop. Bony elbows askew, flailing arms and legs, she impatiently pulls at the car door handle, until I release the door lock with a grin. She tosses her head, scowls at me, and folds herself into the car, fumbling to pull a cigarette from a crumpled pack.*
>
> *"Forest Lawn first?" she asks, inhaling, then exhaling, deeply; cigarette smoke snakes up and out the open window.*
>
> *"Yeah," I reply, and turn the radio volume up. We both know why we'll visit Forest Lawn first; it's where most of our family now lives. Carole's mother, my Aunt Margaret Cotton; our grandparents, Nell Cotton and John Drummond Cunningham; our aunts and great-aunts, Daisy, Grace, and Honey; most of the Cottons and all of the Cunninghams lie buried in Forest Lawn Cemetery in Norfolk, Virginia. For Carole and me, visiting their graves isn't just about visiting the dead; it's about visiting with the living as well. It's our time together as much as it is our time with them. We are alive, they are dead, but our relationships with them allows us to continue to build this relationship with each other. We are familially, interpersonally, and relationally connected in this place because of these people. That's one of the things stories about the dead do; they strengthen and cement the stories of the living.*
>
> *Carole spreads a blanket over Nanny and Granddaddy's graves. I pull fried chicken and potato salad out of a bag. I lie down on the blanket, on top of my*

grandmother, and spread my arms out as if to hug her. Carole leans on grand-daddy's tombstone and lights another cigarette. Her long, crimson fingernails reflect the sunshine.

"Did you ever wonder why Granddaddy always called Nanny 'Dick?'" she asks.

I laugh. "Yeah, all the time. I knew why she called him Drummond, but never could understand why he called her Dick."

Carole sits down on granddaddy's grave, her back against his tombstone. She sweeps away some fallen leaves from the side of his grave. "Granddaddy had a boss at the shipyard who was a real tough guy, always giving orders. His name was Dick, but all the guys called him Sarge. Granddaddy started calling Nanny 'Sarge,' cuz' she gave the orders in the house, but eventually he just started calling her Dick." We both smile and remember.

I grab a drumstick, take a bite, and say, "Granddaddy always told me his hair was so gray because you spilled ashes on it when you were a baby, and the gray would never wash out."

Carole guffaws her loud harrumph and says, "He told me the same thing about you!" She takes a breast, bites into it, and says, "Not as good as Nanny's." We both nod and remember.

And so it goes. Each grave – more stories, more laughter, more memories. Each grave, each death, Carole and I are joined a little bit tighter, only second cousins, but in many ways sisters – sisters in family, sisters in life and death, sisters in the telling, sisters in the listening. These deaths, and the gravesite visits over the decades, join us, bond us, make us stronger.

We pack up our picnic, place flowers in front of our grandparents' tombstones, and walk two rows over to our aunts' and Carole's mother's gravesites. Carole starts placing flowers in front of the graves. I study the tombstones.

"You know, I never knew Aunt Honey's favorite flowers were yellow roses until her funeral," I observe as I look at Aunt Honey's tombstone.

"Well, they were," replies Carole, "but honey, here in the South, yellow roses are the funeral rose. All the Cottons knew that the funeral bespoke the woman. They believed that the more flowers at a funeral, the more beloved the deceased was. They fretted constantly that their funerals would be barren of flowers, so when they died I made sure there were lots of big flower arrangements at their funerals."

I never knew that. I lived in Florida during most of these deaths, and came to Virginia for the funerals. I never shared in the agony of watching the loved one die; I heard the reports through the safe and distant telephone, and then flew into town for their neat and sanitized funerals. I didn't hear the death rattles. I didn't stay to go through their things, to clean out their houses, to weed out the gardens of lives well lived.

I look over the cemetery. It's beautifully landscaped and undulating in the sunshine. I smell green grass, and in the distance, hear the muffled roar of a lawn mower. *I think about my Nanny mowing the grass, her face shaded by a wide brimmed hat. I think about my Granddaddy hoisting me up into a pony saddle, or gently, ever so gently, pulling my crab line in for me. I wish I could hear their voices again.*

"Go on, now," Carole says, watching me get teary eyed. I smile, and I realize I do hear their voices, in my cousin's voice, in my father's, in my own. I hear their voices in these shared stories, in these memories, in these visits between my cousin and me. I hear their voices in my nephews' voices, and I smile again.

Cemeteries as Historic Communication

"Cemeteries bind us to the past" (Hall, 2011, p. 317); they are, ironically, living histories in which death teaches us how people lived. Cemeteries are resting places for the dead, or, more accurately, storage places for the dead, places for disposal of corpses, but they are more than memorial gardens. Cemeteries "serve both functional and emotional purposes. They provide for disposal of corpses and, far more important, provide a place where the living can communicate with the dead. They are thus both sacred and profane" (Francaviglia, 1971, p. 501). So sacred and profane, that Francaviglia concludes that "they may bridge the nebulous gap between subconscious and conscious motivation in the manipulation of form and space" (p. 509). Wasserman (1998) calls them "places for ritual action," fulfilling social needs that "serve[s] intellectual, emotional, spiritual and communal functions" including spaces for "memory," "mourning," "reflection and healing," "ceremony," and "collective action" (p. 44). According to Levitt (2012), they are sites of both "mourning and celebration" (p. 22), transforming public space into social space.

Cemeteries construct particular histories that serve particular ends (Breede et al., 2016; Collier, 2003; Dunkley et al., 2010; Gatewood & Cameron, 2004; Hall, 2011; Hanks, 2015; Hernandez, 1999; Levitt, 2010, 2011; Maples & East, 2013). Their construction, layout, design, and use of symbolism "reflect historical eras" (Collier, 2003, p. 731), not only for culture writ large (i.e., "American culture") but for multiple co-cultures as well. They blend "personal memory and cultural memory" (Levitt, 2010, p. 69), providing "evidence of tradition" (Collier, 2003, p. 744) for individuals, communities and cultures. Operating not only on a "macro" level, they function on "micro" levels as well, serving to document, strengthen, preserve, and validate family claims, traditions, bonds, ruptures, and rituals (Collier, 2003; Maples & East, 2013), creating temporal legacies of sorts.

Furthermore, cemeteries socially construct a shared past and serve an important ideological function, especially for democracies. Hall (2011) suggests that they "temper the sovereignty of the present generation, limiting the progressivism inherent in democratic discourse" and, in doing so, "reflect a counter to the isolating individualism and cult of youth that capitalistic democracies foster" (p. 317), serving, in a sense, as a theoretical basis for cultural and historical tradition. They are "intergenerational" (p. 319), reminding us "that transmission of ideas, of principles, of right" (p. 320) take time. This historiographic function has allowed cemeteries – and by extension "historical heritage sites" that include cemeteries (Maples & East, 2013) – to become tourist attractions (Bowman & Pezzullo, 2010; Breede et al., 2016; Dunkley et al., 2010; Gatewood & Cameron, 2004; Hamm, 2015; Hanks, 2015; Levitt, 2010, 2012; Stone, 2006; Stone & Sharpley, 2008; Venbrux, 2010). Cemeteries are among some of the most visited tourism sites in the United States (Hamm, 2015) and represent a lucrative capital industry. Historically, in the United States, most people were buried, whereas most people neither paid for, published, nor were considered "worthy" enough for an obituary. Unlike obituaries, cemeteries, historically, have been a tableau for all, not just the nobility, and as such, are as appropriate for picnics as they are for burials, especially given their historical development in America. Deb reminisces:

> On a recent visit to my family home, my father observes, as he adjusts his favorite Lazyboy, "You never ask me about my family: my grandparents, my aunts ... have I ever told you any of the family stories?"
>
> I put down the newspaper I'm reading. I chuckle to myself. "Well, you never really told me many family stories, Dad, but everyone else did." I think back to warm afternoons huddled over sticky picture albums while my grandmother and grandfather recited names and argued over dates. I remember the evenings spent playing cards with my Aunt Margaret while she shuffled skillfully, dealing out the family's morality tales with the deftness of a southern preacher. I smile at the horrors shared by my Aunt Honey in the "ghost stories" I always begged for, the details so terrifying that I'd have nightmares afterward. I close my eyes, take a deep breath, and I can feel the heat and humidity of the attics I rummaged about in as a child; I can smell the faded newspaper clippings Carole pulled from the family tree she was compiling. My eyes fill with tears as I think about my cousin, dead now for almost ten years. I blink hard and fast, and pick the newspaper back up again.
>
> I try to get my brothers, my nephews, my dad – anyone – to go visit the gravesites with me. They won't go. They're too busy – too busy with the living – and I understand that. But I yearn for the closeness that's developed with the living in these shared moments with the dead, in these shared stories about the dead. I ask Dad if I can take some of his flower arrangements to the graves at Forest Lawn. He says, "Of course." Like always, the landscape is green and undulating. I put the flowers in front of the gravestones, and I wish my dad were with me.
>
> I save the last flower arrangement – this one of yellow roses – for Carole's grave.

Forest Lawn Cemeteries

It's no odd coincidence that the previous stories of cemetery visits all occur at "Forest Lawns." The creation of "Forest Lawn Cemetery," now a generic name almost synonymous with "the memorial park," transformed the funeral and cemetery industry and created the park-like standard in suburban cemeteries that many of us growing up in the 20th and 21st centuries picture as the quintessential graveyard. Characterized by an absence of large memorials blocking a park-like view, the modern forest lawns usually include botanical gardens, works of art, fountains, architectural marvels, wildlife displays, and other visitor features. Forest Lawn, Los Angeles, is considered to be the historic innovator of modern cemeteries.

Cris' family's Forest Lawn is one of the original Los Angeles Forest Lawn cemeteries. The city that became legendary for transforming the film industry is widely believed to be the site of a genesis of another sort, the transformation of American cemeteries. Established in 1906, the Forest Lawn Cemetery in Glendale, California (a suburb of Los Angeles) failed to succeed financially until, under the ownership of the American Security and Fidelity Company, Hubert Eaton became general manager in 1917. Private cemetery ownership by corporations was uncommon prior to this point in America, but motivated not only by economic gain but also by the immense popularity during the previous century of park-like cemeteries in New York and Boston. Forest Lawn revised the traditional graveyard landscape in three important ways: (1) Statuary, while not forbidden, are rare. All in-ground burials are marked by a flat bronze plaque creating an unobstructed view of the vista; (2) Thematic features, such as copies of Michelangelo's works and chapels constructed using the plans of famous European churches, create a historic and cultural experience; and (3) The cemetery's daily business includes activities outside of the death industry, now encompassing film premiers, rock concerts, and cultural celebrations (Atlas Obscura, 2015; Basmajian & Courts, 2010; Hamm, 2015; Levitt, 2010, 2012; Sloane, 2001). These innovations not only transformed America's death industries, but they also transformed the way many Americans experience death today.

Deb's Forest Lawn Norfolk, Virginia's Forest Lawn Cemetery, models Glendale's Forest Lawn tradition. Also established in 1906, Forest Lawn Norfolk includes historical attractions, an arboretum with over 70 species of trees, and a mausoleum designed by Chicago architect Sydney Lovell, with a skylight designed by Frank Lloyd Wright (City of Norfolk, 2017; Norfolk Society for Cemetery Conservation, 2017). It is neither owned by nor affiliated with Forest Lawn Memorial Park Association, the owner of multiple cemeteries and memorial parks in Southern California. These forest lawns are separate entities from the Forest Lawn Group, a privately held corporation founded in 1849, based in Buffalo, New York, which owns multiple cemeteries in upstate New York (Forest Lawn, 2017; Forest Lawn Group, 2017; Forest Lawn Memorial, 2017; Forest Lawn Memorial Park Association, 2017). As we previously observed, "Forest Lawn" is becoming as generic a descriptor as "the cemetery," in part, we suggest, due to Forest Lawn Glendale's early influences.

Disposal of Bodily Remains: To Dust You Shall Return

What we do with the bodies of our dead is an important cultural phenomenon – but, why? Why do we care what happens to a body after the person it belongs to, dies? As Diogenes the Cynic said, "What harm can the mangling of wild beasts do me if I am without consciousness?" (qtd in Laqueur, 2015, p. 3).

Yet, Laqueur says, the dead "define generations, demarcate the sacred and the profane and more ordinary spaces as well, are the guarantors of land and power and authority, mirror the living to themselves, and insist on our temporal limits. The dead are witnesses to mortality. They hear us and we speak to them even if we know that they, like all base matter, are deaf and dumb ....To treat a dead body as if it were ordinary organic matter ... is to deny its humanity. The corpse demands the attention of the living." (Laqueur, 2015, p. 4) Dead bodies do speak to us. Laqueur continues: "We endlessly invest the dead body with meaning because, through it, the human past somehow speaks to us" (p. 6).

"Forest lawns" aren't the only methods and places for burying or storing people when they're dead. Churchyards and farmlands, swamps and fields, oceans and rivers, columbaria and mausoleums, parks and battlefields – all serve as store yards for the dead. For most western funerals, however, as important as marking the life's end of a loved one is, modern funeral services can be very expensive, costing upwards of $11,000 for embalming, coffin, visitation, funeral, and burial, depending on various decisions and choices (Miller, 2016, para 13). The cost can be a burden for families; in 1998, average funeral costs were 25% more than the average annual income of a family on federal financial assistance (Banks, 1998). In light of the fact that social mores and survivors' guilt frequently compels loved ones to spend large sums of money on funeral and burial practices to represent and substitute for eternal love, the high cost to bury your loved one is problematic (Davis, 2008). Hard-handed sales tactics by funeral home staff are subjects of lore and investigative reporting (see, for instance, Davis, 2008; Mangla & Gibbs, 2012), and loved ones have to steel themselves against making unnecessary purchases. The following example of this comes from Davis (2010, pp. 87–88):

> *The morning after my dad's death, my mom and I are in the office of the funeral director. It is early, very early, for a morning after a night with very little sleep, but the funeral home guy last night insisted we come first thing in the morning. I really don't know why; he had some lame excuse that this was the only time he was free. What else did he have to do today? Mom didn't want to go alone, so I was elected to accompany her. We sit in chairs side by side, facing the funeral*

home guy across his desk, trying to focus on the business aspect of the transaction, trying to forget that we are sitting in a funeral home, a place with dead bodies, my dad's dead body. We read through papers, contracts, and disclaimers. My mom chokes on one of the disclaimers.

"This one is tough to read," she says as she hands it to me.

I read the fine print, reading about the cremation process and disclosure that one person's body parts may become mingled with another person's body parts in the cremation process. "Just sign it, and don't read anything," I advise. I am in professional mode, emotions detached, all business.

"Now, which urn will you be wanting?" The undertaker moves into sales mode. "We have a lovely brass urn that won't be destroyed by time or weather."

I jump in. "We've already discussed this with the church. Dad's ashes are going to be put into the church columbarium and we just need the smallest, cheapest urn you have because it will be protected inside the wall and it will never be seen. I understand that what we want is your $500 urn."

The man smiles ever so slightly. "Well, at First Presbyterian's columbarium, our $500 urn will not fit. You'll have to purchase our $1,500 urn instead."

Mom's face pales. She and Dad had always lived right at the edge of their means, and he had died with no savings or insurance. Not long before he died, Dad had sold his precious set of golf clubs for $500 to pay for his funeral costs. Mom and Dad had been assured by their minister that this would be the total cost. I look at Mom. She looks like she is going to burst out crying.

"What am I going to do?" she whispers to me. "I don't have that kind of money." I feel angry at the funeral home guy for making my mom cry. "Don't you worry, Mom," I pat her arm. "I'll pay for it." I don't know how, but I'll come up with it somehow.

The disposal of dead bodies has multiple purposes: public health purposes – to prevent the spread of disease; relational purposes – to show respect for loved ones; social purposes – to honor people who have died for a cause; and existential purposes – to prepare bodies for the afterlife. But, beyond that, the place and type of burial reflects social status and wealth and also reflects the culture of a group and its views about death.

As norms for disposing of our dead have changed over the course of time, space, and place so that death often seems far removed, it surrounds us still. The traditional American burial throughout the 20th century included embalming of the body, placement of the body in a wood or metal casket, viewing of the body at a funeral home, burial in a concrete or steel vault in a grave, and a tombstone marking the grave (Marsh, 2017). Today, bodies may be embalmed and buried, buried without embalming (green burials), or cremated (burned). Through the ages, there have been many ways to dispose of corpses.

In the 3–4 centuries BCE, in air or sky burials, bodies were left on mountaintops exposed for wild birds or animals to devour. In the 16th century, ritualistic cannibalism was practiced. Ancient Egyptians mummified their dead, removing all the organs and stuffing the body with dry materials and wrapping it in linens. Bodies have been burned in funeral pyres or crematoriums; or buried at sea, buried in caves, buried in trees, and buried in the ground. The forest lawn cemetery traditions, rituals, norms, and layouts were not typical early in America's history. As Beard and Burger (2017) observe, "In early American society, the death rituals were simple" (p. 47). Most funerals among the early colonies' population, religious in nature, were either austere or formalized, depending on the prevailing religious doctrine of the decedent, but the process for preparing a body for burial, regardless of faith, was almost always performed by family members, usually women. Depending on custom and geography, the women of the family may have been assisted by the enslaved or indentured population. By the end of the 17th century in the American colonies, the emergence of the before burial home visit, processional to the burial site, and sometimes lavish feasts became more common. The growth of economically viable American cities fostered an increasing visibility of class distinctions, which in turn became noticeable within burial practices, allowing for ornate grave markers and extended parades to city cemeteries for the wealthy, and fostering the continuance of burials in small family plots or churchyards with more modest grave markers for the less affluent.

As the 18th century progressed, American culture became more geographically distanced, life spans increased, death became less frequent, and burials in cemeteries reflected these changing demographics, extending the funereal practices and lavish feasts to accommodate traveling family. Finally, by end of the 19th century, the Industrial Revolution had enabled manufacturing advances that allowed for better casket construction, the rediscovery of the art of embalming, and the subsequent creation of new occupations (i.e., casket makers, embalmers, funeral directors, mortuary schools). Continuing prosperity created status displays that were evident in not only the type of casket one might purchase, but also fostered the beautification of the body and its associated viewing that included displays of wealth such as jewelry, flowers, and ornate headstones. The emergence of local, state, and federal laws regulating the disposal of the dead in the 19th and 20th centuries and the growing death industry itself dictated and enabled our modern forest lawns (Basmajian & Courts, 2010; Beard & Burger, 2017; Kelly, 2012; Maples & East, 2013; Tarpley, 2006).

Today, in addition to cemeteries, bodies can be buried at home in most states. Cremains can be buried in a grave, stored in an urn, scattered on the ground, or interred in a columbarium (stone wall) (Marsh, 2017). You can even have your loved one's cremains turned into a diamond or a bead, glass paperweight, or vinyl record, thrown into a work of pottery, or scattered out of an airplane (Green, 2014; Marsh, 2017). Your body can be cryogenically frozen so it will come back to life someday; your ashes can be shot into outer space. You can have a floating ceremony in which your loved ones can purchase a water-soluble urn which will float for a few minutes before sinking below the surface to biodegrade naturally, or a ceremony in which your ashes are raked into the ground or placed in a trench around a tree or shrub. Instead of being cremated by fire, you can have a more environmentally friendly water cremation in which the funeral home uses a water and salt-based solution in a process called alkaline hydrolysis to dissolve the body (Marsh, 2017), or you can have a bio-cremation in which your tissues are dissolved with a potassium hydroxide solution. Your cremains can be mixed with an ink solution and tattooed onto a loved one's skin. Your casket can be personalized with sports emblems (Green, 2014). You can choose a bio-degradable casket or wrap the body in a simple shroud for a green burial (Green, 2014; Marsh, 2017). Finally, you can put QR codes on your gravestone for an interactive headstone, or on a cremains urn – visitors can scan the code with their mobile phones to open a website with information about the deceased, including a photo, biography, profile, videos, and tributes from loved ones (https://www.thesun.co.uk/archives/news/894713/grave-stone-qr-codes-allow-people-to-connect-with-the-dead/).

Modern mortuary practices of embalming and preparing the body can be controversial. Embalming practices raise environmental concerns, and beautification of the corpse that incudes dressing the deceased's body in street clothes, applying makeup, and styling hair is considered by some to be a waste of time and perpetuation of the denial of death. As an interview participant quoted by Davis (2008, p. 413) stated:

> You're spending $15,000 for a funeral director to perpetuate the denial, which is basically what we're doing. The makeup and everything. It doesn't look like they're dead. I mean, that's the first thing you hear people saying: 'She looked so good.'

A trend that seems to be catching on is the home burial movement, in which families participate in preparing the body for burial (Green, 2014).

Since funeral practices and cemeteries reflect and reify cultural norms, then cemeteries, like American history itself, are racialized, classed, gendered, and disparate in multiple ways (Abel, 2008; Basmajian & Courts, 2010; Breede et al., 2016; Brooks, 2011; Davis, 1986; Hernandez, 1999; Kelly, 2012; Maples & East, 2013; Tarpley, 2006; Zelinsky, 1994). Like many graveyards across America, the original Forest Lawn was segregated, resisting growing calls to desegregate until forced by law, and while now desegregated, like many cemeteries, forest lawns nowadays include a separate Jewish section (Forest Lawn, 2017; Forest Lawn Memorial, 2017; Forest Lawn Memorial Park Association, 2017; Sloane, 2001). Within few places are these discrepancies more noticeable than in the historic graveyards and cemeteries of the American South.

Historic Exclusively Minority Cemeteries

Juxtaposed against the cultural backdrop of manicured forest lawns, cremains as diamonds, and space burials, are historic small town, rural, and plantation cemeteries primarily holding the remains of formerly enslaved Africans. Cris and Deb and colleague Jan Warren-Findlow[1] spent several years visiting and researching historical cemeteries within North and South Carolina in which were buried enslaved and formerly enslaved Africans and their descendants, including Old Westview Cemetery in Wadesboro, North Carolina; and Alderly, Bellefield, Fraser's Point, Marietta, and Strawberry Hill cemeteries at Hobcaw Barony, the site of South Carolina's sixteen original land grant plantations; and the Sam Hill Cemetery at Hampton Plantation; all located in coastal South Carolina; to better understand how life and death were constructed, and how power is constructed, maintained, reified, and experienced within the constraints of race and class in exclusively minority cemeteries. Here is a description of one of the cemeteries:

> *Memories of long ago cemetery visits haunt me as I swat at something, hoping it's a gnat and not a mosquito. I wipe sweat off my forehead and the steamy air sticks against my skin. I glance at the trash and weeds at my feet. I had been warned of the condition of the 160-year old cemetery, but the extent of the cemetery's disorder defies description. The gravel parking area becomes red clay, sprouts into overgrown weeds, then blends into ancient grave markers, broken, half buried under what looks like trash. I know a sign marks the entrance, but its unobtrusive placement farther down on the side of the road renders it invisible. In this section, the graves hold the remains of mid-19th century formerly enslaved Africans, but glancing around, it just looks like a vacant lot or a dumping ground.*
>
> *Weeds and brush cover widespread acres and only ongoing maintenance can hope to keep it orderly. The only visible life comes primarily through the wild efforts of Mother Nature as she tries to reclaim it, decompose it, bury it under an encroaching jungle. As I look more closely, I see signs of the decay of more recent lives scattered among the weeds and broken shards that mark burial places: empty condom wrappers, empty beer cans, liquor bottles. I look around and see nature, unkempt and out of control.*
>
> *I briskly walk down the asphalt road. Still strewn with trash and weeds, large open expanses of overgrown crabgrass and plots of land clearly delineated with a mounded appearance and, in some cases, small foot-high fences, characterize this area. Many of these plots – family plots, I later learn – have large expensive-looking elaborate marble grave markers; many are several feet wide and high. A row of dilapidated country houses sit next to the cemetery, one no more than five feet from a grave stone. They look abandoned, although I notice late model cars parked in front of several of them and a basketball hoop attached to another. Despite their appearance, there must be life in them.*

Miller and Rivera (2006) note in their analysis of New Orleans' cemeteries the integration of slave-era cemeteries in that city – they report slave owners and those enslaved entombed close to each other, or on occasion, together. In other U.S. cities – in both the north and the south, however, scholars report discovering long forgotten and unmarked African American burials hidden under city streets and buildings (Wright, 2005), and finding many slave-era cemeteries for enslaved Africans in "unwanted places" (p. 64).

Many tensions in understanding these historic cemeteries lie in the ancient African burial and homegoing customs at the time of slavery and post-reconstruction. Memorializing the dead did not seem to be a goal of African burials, but maintaining African cultural and religious rituals was. Many among the enslaved population in South Carolina attempted to return to Africa, and slave narratives frequently recounted such attempts, both real and imagined. Often prevented from resisting their enslavement physically, Africans resisted culturally by maintaining Muslim and African practices and beliefs, and southern African and African American burial customs during the colonial, antebellum, and post-reconstruction era were influenced by Christian, Muslim, and African heritage, and by the experience of being a former, or sometimes newly freed, slave. The death of a slave was viewed by other enslaved as a cause for celebration, an escape to a more positive life, a final opportunity to be reunited with loved ones separated by slavery – a homegoing (Bell, 2010).

African and African American cemeteries were often located on marginal land. They rarely had formal grave markers. Funerals and burials were some of the few instances for which the enslaved population of a plantation were allowed freedom of movement, and they reportedly were able to observe the burial traditions as they wished, but they had no resources for formal gravestones, and marking their graves with names might have been problematic – enslaved Africans frequently had multiple names (plantation names and private names) (Bell, 2010; Brooks, 2011).

Africans, and later, enslaved Africans, (and African Americans today in parts of the Carolinas) denoted their graves with items that now, hundreds of years later, look like trash – broken stones, broken pottery, shells, glassware, and personal items related to the deceased. Many of the graves were marked by white pipes, serving as speaking tubes – a communication channel between the living and the dead. Some artifacts were chosen as representations of water (signifying their return to Africa by boat), others to confuse and frighten evil spirits. Pottery was broken to render them useless to robbers and to break the "chains" of death, or the bonds of slavery. Other items were chosen because they might need them in their next life, or they would be of use to the deceased in their journey to the world of the dead. Following African customs, graves marked with broken pottery were interspersed with organic matter and personal affects. Because many of the older markers in these cemeteries consist of organic matter, they continue in varying stages of decay.

Enslaved Africans were often buried facing east, toward Mecca, and facing the ocean from which so many of them arrived (Bell, 2010; Brooks, 2011; Jamieson, 1995). In southern African slave burials, it was traditional to plant a Sia tree upon the grave to provide shade and to symbolize eternity of the soul.

Cemeteries are a communication genre subject to cultural norms for burial, a site of communication with rules and expectations. With symbols of both life and death, cemeteries create a liminal space in which the living come to visit the dead in an attempt to bring them back to life – and in which life is constructed in a place of death. All cemeteries represent the mythic arguments of life and death, light and dark, good and evil, rebirth and decay, absence and presence, but the tensions stand out in these marginalized spaces.

Cemeteries as a rule hold the characteristic of stasis – gravestones remaining in place long after loved ones bury their dead, and families finding their place (into eternity) in family plots. In fact, "perpetual care" cemeteries offer continual maintenance indefinitely of the graves and grounds. Of course, care in the future requires resources from the past, and even perpetual care has a specific social and financial meaning – people with money have the ability to have their gravestones maintained throughout time, while those without sufficient funds do not. These minority and plantation cemeteries, despite their historic nature, evolved as they age, yet resist bridging the past, present, and future as in other cemeteries.

Most western cemeteries contain symbols of order and control – graves lined in neat rows, often in a checkerboard pattern, neatly mown grass, maintained foliage, fresh (or fresh looking) cut flowers. It's through this symbolic control that we construct an illusion of control over death. However, the visuals in these historic minority cemeteries don't convey order. Even its foliage is uncontrolled, transgressive. Compared to the cemeteries "on the other side of town" which are nicer, better kept, tidier, these spaces grow native. These cemeteries speak a rhetoric of decay – a hint perhaps of the urban decay that threatens this side of town.

It's easy for the western onlooker to assume that characteristics of wild, unkempt, and out of control have unpleasant or negative connotations. But perhaps this freedom of growth could be read as an unfettered, natural, reversion of the enslaved to a free person in death. Maybe the wildness in these cemeteries do not contradict – maybe to the enslaved person, resistance *does* represent freedom. Yet – contradictorily – there's a need for the people buried here and their descendants to be considered, respected, and included. This ground enfolds the final resting place of *people* – people about whom other people care, who lived and died with dignity and deserve dignity in their death. Rescuing the fragments of enslavement, marginalization, and disempowerment from permanent decomposition enacts resistance and gives the dead back their voices.

We construct identity through symbols (Leeds-Hurwitz, 1993), and cemeteries in general – and these historic cemeteries specifically – construct identity. Wright (2003) suggests that gravestones and their epitaphs "act as physical storehouses of memory" (p. 28). We add that cemeteries hold both historical and personal memories. In these cemeteries, however, the repository is more symbolic than overt, as much in the absences as in the presences. Most of the grave markers in these cemeteries have no writing at all – no way of knowing whose body the grave holds or when the burial took place. The concept of representation is a salient as we consider the critical construction of identity for people whose existence is not represented or marked. Gatens (1997) suggests that "slaves, foreigners, women, the conquered, children, the working classes, have all been excluded from political participation, at one time or another, by their bodily specificity" (p. 83). It is especially poignant to think that people excluded from representation because of their very embodiment are excluded from memory due to this lack of representation. The body politic represents the voices of both the living and the dead.

In many ways, death shifts the representation from the individual to the social (Cannon, 2002), and cemeteries bridge both private and public spaces (Wright, 2005), ones that juxtapose individual and collective identity (Chesson, 2001). Contemporary cemeteries construct the dead through their individual identities (with clearly marked grave markers with legibly inscribed names and dates of birth and death), as well as their family identities (with family plots, relational information inscribed on the grave markers), and cultural identities (with affiliative symbols on monuments and inscriptions).

However, it is in the older minority cemeteries where the anonymous collective identity is unique: the unmarked graves of people notable because of their communal characteristics – formerly enslaved Africans and their descendants; survivors of slavery, marginalization, and poverty; people who work to make better lives in their world. The unmarked graves remain one of the greatest tragedies embodied in these cemeteries – after we die, what is more important than we "were"? Symbolic markings depicting our identity as group members form our cultural value. If we're not remembered, did our existence matter? Did we even exist at all? And if our existence didn't matter, will the existence of our descendants matter either? Perhaps mattering in this context tends toward the more collective than individual. In the process of decomposition, organic material breaks down and collapses into the collective. As the organic markers denoting the individual graves collapse and coalesce, the historical – collective – significance of this sacred site of bravery and hardship intensifies.

Some cemetery scholars (see Wright, 2005) argue that cemeteries as a genre represent inclusive spaces, making room for people otherwise marginalized, for inclusion and collection of memories. We suggest that cemeteries like these represent exceptions – places of segregation, places set aside for people marginalized in the South and in other rural U.S. towns, places of people being dismissed and forgotten.

Conclusion

From historically segregated cemeteries across the American South to the small mountain cemeteries in Appalachia, from Hispanic cemeteries buried deep in the heart of Texas to small grave plots framing the farmhouses along the mid-western plains, cemeteries throughout the United States reflect the histories, cultures, norms, traditions, and realities of those who buried people there over the course of the last four hundred years. Like most of our traditions in the United States, funereal and cemetery traditions today result from histories of inclusion and seclusion; conquest and surrender; religion and superstition; immigration and migration, free and forced; and quests for commercial and economic profit. Our social construction of death reflects not only our psychological fear of and fascination with death but also the shifting sociologies of America. As Francaviglia (1971) asserts, "in the cemetery, architecture 'town' planning, display of social status, and racial segregation all mirror the living, not the dead. Cemeteries, as the visual and spatial expression of death, may tell us a great deal about the living people who created them" (p. 509).

If death marks the line of battle between community and solitude, fertility and barrenness, good and evil, life and death, cemeteries represent the site of that battle. Cemeteries denote where the living meet the dead, where the rhetoric of decay meets the rhetoric of rebirth. They epitomize the liminal space where these ideas meet, where we can go to be reminded of our identity, our history, and our future. Places where the living come to bury the dead, cemeteries manifest the present visiting the past, and the remnants awaiting the future.

References

Abel, E. L. (2008). Changes in gender discrimination after death: Evidence from a cemetery. Omega – Journal of Death and Dying, 58(2), 147–152. doi: 10.2190/OM.58.2.d
Atlas Obscura. (2015). Obscura Society LA: The Disneyland of Death. Downloaded June 28, 2017 from http://www.atlasobscura.com/events/obscura-society-la-the-disneyland-of-death
Banks, D. A. (1998). The economics of death? A descriptive study of the impact of funeral and cremation costs on U.S. households. Death Studies, 22(3), 269–285.
Basmajian, C., & Courts, C. (2010). Planning for the disposal of the dead. Journal of the American Planning Association, 7(3), 305–317.
Beard, V. R., & Burger, W. C. (2017). Change and innovation in the funeral industry: A typology of motivations. Omega – Journal of Death and Dying, 75(1), 47–68. doi: 10.1177/003022815612405.

Bell, K. B. (2010). Rice, resistance, and forced transatlantic communities: (Re)envisioning the African diaspora in Low Country Georgia, 1750–1800. Journal of African American History, 95(2), 157–182.

Bowman, M. S., & Pezzullo, P. (2010). What's so "dark" about "dark tourism"?: Death, tours, and performance. Tourist Studies, 9(3), 187–202. doi: 10.1177/1468797610382699.

Breede, D. C.; Davis, C. S.; & Warren-Findlow, J. (2016). Absence, revision, and the Other: Rhetorics of South Carolina antebellum tourism sites. Journal of Hate Studies 13(1), 17–42.

Brooks, C. (2011). Enclosing their immortal souls: A survey of two African American cemeteries in Georgetown, South Carolina. Southeastern Archaeology, 30(1), 176–186.

Cannon, A. (2002). Spatial narratives of death, memory and transcendence. Archeological Papers of the American Anthropological Association. Special Issue: The Place and Space of Death. pp. 191–199.

Chesson, M. S. (2001). Social memory, identity, and death: An introduction. Archeological Papers of the American Anthropological Association. Special Issue: Social Memory, Identity, and Death: Anthropological Perspectives on Mortuary Rituals. pp. 1–10.

City of Norfolk. (2017). City of Norfolk, Virginia – Official Website. Facilities. Forest Lawn Cemetery. Downloaded on June 28, 2017 from https://www.norfolk.gov/facilities/facility/details/48

Collier, C. D. A. (2003). Tradition, modernity, and postmodernity in symbolism of death. The Sociological Quarterly, 44, (4), 727–749.

Davis, C. S. (2008). A funeral liturgy: Death rituals as symbolic communication. Journal of Loss and Trauma, 13(5), 406–452.

Davis, C. S. (2010). Death: The beginning of a relationship. Cresskill, NJ: Hampton Press.

Davis, H. A. (1986). Public archaeology forum. Journal of Field Archaeology, 13(3), 339–345.

Dunkley, R.; Morgan, N., & Westwood, S. (2010). Visting the trenches: Exploring meanings and motivations in battlefield tourism. Tourism Management, 32, 860–868. doi: 10.1016/j.tourman.201007.011.

Forest Lawn Group. (2017). Company Overview. Private Company Information. Bloomberg. Downloaded June 28, 2017 from https://www.bloomberg.com/research/stocks/private/snapshot.asp?privcapId=49680105.

Forest Lawn Memorial Park Association. (2017). Company Overview. Private Company Information. Bloomberg. Downloaded June 28, 2017 from https://www.bloomberg.com/research/stocks/private/snapshot.asp?privcapId=428189

Forest Lawn Memorial Parks & Mortuaries. (2017). Official Website. FAQ. Downloaded June 28, 2017 from http://forestlawn.com/faq/

Francaviglia, R. V. (1971). The cemetery as evolving cultural landscape. Annals of the Association of American Geographers, 61(3), 501–509.

Gatens, M. (1997). Corporeal representation in/and the body politic. In Conboy, K., Medina, N., & Stanbury, S. (Eds.). Writing on the body: Female embodiment and feminist theory. pp. 80–89. New York, NY: Columbia University Press.

Gatewood, J. B., & Cameron, C. M. (2004). Battlefield pilgrims at Gettysburg National Military Park. Ethnology, 43(3), 193–216.

Green, E. (2014, August 19). Burying your dead without religion. The Atlantic. Retrieved from https://theatlantic.com

Hall, L. K. (2011). The political significance of burial and remembrance. Social Science and Public Policy, 48, 316–322. doi: 10.1007.s12115-12011-9444-9445.

Hamm, C. (2015). 10 cemeteries you'll never regret visiting. Downloaded June 28, 2017 from http://www.latimes.com/travel/la-tr-10-cemeteries-to-visit-20150520-htmistory.html

Hanks, M. (2015). Haunted heritage: The cultural politics of ghost tourism, populism, and the past. Walnut Creek, CA: Left Coast Press.

Hernandez, M. T. (1999). Reconditioning history: Adapting knowledge from the past into realities of the present. Rethinking History, 3(3), 289–307.

Jamieson, R. W. (1995). Material culture and social death: African-American burial practices. Historical Archaeology, 29(4), 39–58.

Kelly, S. (2012). Dead bodies that matter: Toward a new ecology of human death in American culture. The Journal of American Culture, 35(1), 37–51.

Laqueur, T. W. (2015). The work of the dead: A cultural history of mortal remains. Princeton, NJ: Princeton University Press.

Leeds-Hurwitz, W. (1993). Semiotics and communication: Signs, codes, cultures. Hillsdale, NJ: Lawrence Erlbaum.

Levitt, L. (2010). Death on display: Reifying stardom through Hollywood's dark tourism. The Velvet Light Trap, 65, 63–70.

Levitt, L. (2011). Speaking memory, building history. Radical History Review, 111, 65–78. doi: 10.1215/01636545–1268704.

Levitt, L. (2012). Solemnity and celebration: Dark tourism experiences at Hollywood Forever Cemetery. Journal of Unconventional Parks, Tourism, & Recreation Research, 4(1), 20–25.

Mangla, I. S., & Gibbs, L. (2012 November 9). When putting a loved one to rest, avoid these misleading sales tactics. Time.com. Retrieved from: http://time.com/money/2793582/avoid-misleading-funeral-and-cemetery-sales-tactics/

Maples, J. N., & East, E. A. (2013). Destroying mountains, destroying cemeteries: Historic mountain cemeteries on the coalfields of Boone, Kanawha, and Raleigh Counties, West Virginia. Journal of Appalachian Studies, 19(1/2), 7–26.

Marsh, T. D. (2017, October 27). Life after death: Americans are embracing new ways to leave their remains. The Conversation. Retrieved from https://theconversation.com

Miller, J. T. (2016 October 17). This is how much an average funeral costs. Huffington Post. Retrieved from: https://www.huffingtonpost.com/entry/how-much-does-a-funeral-cost_us_5804c784e4b0f42ad3d264de

Miller, D. S., & Rivera, J. D. (2006). Hallowed ground, place, and culture: The cemetery and the creation of place. Space and Culture, 9(4), 334–350.

Norfolk Society for Cemetery Conservation. (2017). Norfolk Society for Cemetery Conservation. Forest Lawn. Downloaded June 28, 2017 from http://www.norfolksocietyforcemeteryconservation.org/forest-lawn-cemetery

Perlmutt, D. (2010 January 18). Neglected black cemetery a trove of fading history. WCNC News. Retrieved from http://www.wcnc.com/news/

Sloane, D. C. (2001). Selling eternity in 1920's Los Angeles. In Sitton, T., & Deverell, W. F., (Eds.), Metropolis in the Making: Los Angeles in the 1920s. pp. 341–360. Berkeley/Los Angeles: University of California Press.

Stone, P. R. (2006). A dark tourism spectrum: Towards a typology of death and macabre related tourist sites, attractions and exhibitions. Tourism, 54(2), 145–160.

Stone, P. R., & Sharpley, R. (2008). Consuming dark tourism: A thanatological perspective. Annals of Tourism Research, 35(2), 574–595. doi: 10.1016/j.annals.2008.02.003.

Tarpley, F. (2006). Naming America's graveyards, cemeteries, memorial parks, and gardens of memories. Names, 54(2), 91–101.

Venbrux, E. (2010). Cemetery tourism: Coming to terms with death? La ricerca Folklorica, 61, 41–49.

Wasserman, J. R. (1998). To trace the shifting sands: Community, ritual, and the memorial landscape. Landscape Journal, 17(1), 42–61.

Wikipedia. (2017) Forest Lawn Memorial Parks & Mortuaries. Downloaded June 28, 2017 from https://en.wikipedia.org/wiki/forest_lawn_memorial-parks_%26_mortuaries.

Wright, E. (2003). Reading the cemetery. "Lieu de Mémoire par Excellance." Rhetoric Society Quarterly, 33(2), 27–44.

Wright, E. (2005). Rhetorical spaces in memorial places: The cemetery as a rhetorical memory place/space. Rhetoric Society Quarterly, 35(4), 51–81.

Zelinsky, W. (1994). Gathering places for America's dead: How many, where, and why? Professional Geographer, 46(1), 29–38.

10

THE FINAL WORD: COMMUNICATING ABOUT DEATH IN EPITAPHS

Cris yawns and stretches out her arms. "I'm used to staying up late, but this has got to be past your bedtime," she says.

Deb smiles a sleepy smile. "Yeah, but I'm enjoying reminiscing with you," she says. "How long as it been since you, Jan, and I did all those cemetery visits? It was research, but we had fun times!"

"Yes," Cris says, laughing, "traipsing through those plantation ruins, in the swamps, swatting giant zombie mosquitos! Good times indeed!"

"But we learned a lot," says Deb. "And besides, it wasn't all in the swamps. We also went to Conway Presbyterian Church cemetery; the Routledge cemetery at Hampton Plantation; and St. John's Unitarian, St. Michael's Episcopal and St. Philip's Episcopal Churches cemeteries and Charles Towne Landing Historical site cemeteries in Charleston."

"We certainly saw the two extremes of historic cemeteries," says Cris. "I enjoyed our time in Charleston. It was steamy there too, though."

Deb sighs as she remembers the time they spent traveling, researching, and writing.

> *The air sings of church bells. The air smells of early June – honeysuckle, the rich fecund salt of the rivers and ocean, car exhaust. The air drips water – beading on our foreheads, under our noses, beneath our breasts. The air lives and breathes. We sit on a black, wrought iron bench on a cobblestoned street near a church, listening to the bells, smelling the honeysuckle. The same street, the same church, the same bells have called the fast and faithful to worship for over three hundred years – nothing in time – everything in history. We are here in the "Holy City," Charleston, South Carolina, so nick-named because of its number and diversity of churches throughout the centuries: white steepled Anglican, Presbyterian, and Methodist churches surrounded by brick walls and lined with crumbling tombstones; old stone*

Congregational and Unitarian churches with rich, green, overgrown graveyards — deep in story and grass; pink French Huegenot and AME churches, doors and hearts wide open. Around every corner, along every street, are churches surrounded by their dead. It's an ideal place to remember — privately and publicly.

We walk through the graveyard at St. Michael's, one of the oldest churches, and graveyards, in America. Like many of the church cemeteries in the historic area, this graveyard is walled, with walkways delineated by gray stones. Everything's old: many of the tombstones are too old to read; whole sections of grave markers have been moved and/or replaced — everything from earthquakes to floods to war erasing the past; newer sections of the cemetery — mostly holding cremains with initials and dates — stand out. We're busy reading epitaphs, writing down descriptions, sketching representations. Cris pauses from dictating oral field notes into her cellphone, and says, "These older gravestones are so much more descriptive than some modern ones. They're the Twitter version of the deceased's life, an autobiography in 140 characters or less!" She grins under her reddish curls. Her nose is pink, and her eyes are bright.

Deb giggles and nods. "Yeah. Epitaphs and obituaries seems to be our last "hurrah," don't they? A final chance to story ourselves and others, and perhaps to begin to construct memories based on our stories and identities."

"Sometimes idealized identities," Cris observes, pointing to an etching on a tombstone of a Madonna-like figure attended by angels.

"Yes, and sometimes very traditional and rigid identities," Deb walks toward another tombstone:

Sacred to the memory of Henry W. Conner
Born Mecklenburg, NC – March 4 1797
Died in Charleston – January 11 1861
Possessed of high talents rare energy
And unswerving integrity He discharged the offices of private friendship And
Public duty .... As a memorial of his virtues and their loss

Cris has begun writing notes. She pauses and looks up. "I wonder how epitaphs and tombstones do that? As the 'Twitter' version of a life story, space and money dictate a pretty short narrative."

Deb lowers her camera and joins Cris. "Yeah," she says, gazing at the tombstone. "And some of these are really long. That costs a lot of money, just like long obituaries in the newspaper do."

"There's quite a bit of literature that talks about how public remembrances and characterizations of men and women are rather gendered and traditional, especially historic depictions," murmurs Cris, "but I wonder what types of deviations from traditional representations might have occurred, especially in a place like Charleston, which, interestingly enough, is noted for some pretty progressive notions about religion, race, and gender, no matter how subversive that might sound."

"Yes!" Deb's excitement is palpable. "We know that Charleston was unusual for the religious freedoms afforded, first in the colony and then the city! Quakers, French Huguenots, even Catholics practiced their religion relatively freely in Charleston. In this very graveyard, there's no segregation among Jewish and Christian burials, unlike some of the historic cemeteries in other southern British colonies, such as Virginia!"

"And we know that unlike many of the slaveholders in the early colonies, South Carolinian plantation mistresses often taught their slaves to read and write, in violation of state law (Horry, 1793; Marshall, 2014; Pinckney 1997)." Cris has taken a seat on a nearby bench and is scribbling notes frantically now.

"Carolina plantation mistresses!" Deb exclaims. "We also know that women deviated from subservient and traditional gender roles in lots of ways in the early plantation system. They were often the ones running things while the men were off fighting wars … "

"Or in the Paris salons …" Cris interrupts.

"Yes," agrees Deb. "I wonder if their epitaphs recall any of that, if they reflect and sustain those traditional gender roles or deviate …"

"Much like some of the women of early Charleston did!" Cris finishes the sentence. The two researchers gaze at the tombstone. The church bells chime in the distance.

Historic tombstones and the gendered notions contained within those epitaphs constructed and sustained traditional and subversive gendered and racialized identities, and continue to do so, especially among women, in the South. While, at first examination, epitaphs and obituaries seem to construct and sustain very traditional gender identities, there is an underlying subversion of these constructs within these texts that suggest that gender constructions, and the resulting "Twitter" versions of life stories that emerge from these constructions, are complex, powerful, progressive, and often overshadowed by other socially constructed standpoints such as religion and class.

Scholars from a variety of disciplines have documented the differences in representations of men and women in historical remembrances (Abel, 2008; Marshall, 2014) as well as the gendered differences inherent and extant within these descriptions. Men in our culture have been socially constructed as aggressive, ambitious, strong, sexual beings – "sturdy oaks" as Wood (2016) suggests; for women, appearance is often noted (Marshall, 2014), as are qualities such as nurturing, supportive, relational, and caring (Wood, 2016). Increasingly, these relatively rigid, traditional, and predictable constructions are becoming more complex, androgynous, and contextual. Historical representations of sex and gender are quite different. Saturated with overt religious references, especially within the church graveyards we often analyzed, nuanced by flowery, metaphorical language, and fixed in time and place, it is unsurprising that gravestone epitaphs in historic southern churchyards construct gender roles, performances, and agencies quite traditionally. However, there are interesting deviances, especially via socially constructed metaphor, that are noteworthy. In addition, especially in the South, race, religion, and class become important socially constructed influences as well.

Jackson (1999) suggests that no matter how much we may try to remove ourselves from the constraints of social constructions of self/selves – regardless of standpoint – "these terrains are still observed as socially constructed residences. Although the space may have been temporarily vacated, the social expectation presupposes these spaces are where we live" (p. 38). He goes on to assert that, of course, these spaces "fail to account for both those who do not intend to return to their assigned homes once they have left and those who have never lived in these spaces" (p. 38). While history facilitates these critiques, and while these spaces are always present, absences from these socially constructed spaces – especially within gender, race, religion, and class remain present, albeit ephemerally, fleetingly. "The imaginative and rhetorical possibilities of past traces" (Katriel, 1993, p. 69) is a relevant concept to explore "the triple burden of race, gender and class" (Jordan, 2005, p. 218) within our "final word" texts: epitaphs and gravesites.

Heritage sites, including historic churches, graveyards, and cemeteries, serve as engaging texts within which to understand cultural, ideological, and historical frameworks, importances, and messages (Aden, 2012; Anderson, 1991; Bergman, 2013; Bowman & Pezzullo, 2010; Brooks, 2011; Gatewood & Cameron, 2004; Hanks, 2015; Iles, 2006; Katriel, 1993; Maurantonio, 2015; Miller, 2005; Roach, 1996; Wallace, 1981). Rich in both the obvious and the nuanced, these sites, among others such as museums, plantations, monuments, and memorials, communicate not only the history and histories of a culture via that which is important, but they often serve as sites within which we can examine and critique our taken for granted assumptions about our social constructions. They create and sustain imagined communities, public memory, and notions of nationalism and patriotism. In addition to being institutionally and popularly sanctioned and endorsed, they are also widely visited and disseminated, often entertaining as well as edifying, and contain associated other pleasures for the senses, the body, and the mind.

Obituaries, as we observe in Chapter 7, are a bit different. Obituaries are found in newspapers and online, via only the mediated as opposed to the live, and therefore the performances and functions of the texts are more rigidly purposeful than of those of epitaphs and often more fleeting. Obituaries are sought after, consumed with great purpose. Generally, people read obituaries to find out if someone they know or love has died. People do visit historic graveyards and read epitaphs for those purposes, but visiting graveyards is a pastime that is much more situated, contextual, and recreational than reading obituaries. Visitors can be seen exploring, strolling, visiting, consuming, relaxing, burying, grieving, and touring; they are not merely seeking specific information. Quite the opposite, they are often adventuring. Obituaries are micro in orientation; epitaphs are the macro version. This leads to interesting cultural, ideological, and interpretive ramifications. Epitaphs can be enjoyed; they entertain as well as inform. Obituaries inform – while they are sometimes grand narrative adventures, they are generally utilitarian in nature and purpose – and often consumed sadly, and fairly quickly.

Hampton Plantation Cemeteries, McClellanville, South Carolina

Hampton Plantation was the home of Daniel Huger Horry and Harriot Pinckney Horry during the Revolutionary War period. Both were from prominent plantation families. Eliza Lucas Pinckney, Harriot's mother, arrived in the British colony of Carolina from her home in the West Indies to manage her father's multiple plantations when he was deployed for military service. She was 16 years old. After creating a haven at Hampton for revolutionaries during the war, Harriot and her mother managed the extensive rice plantation during the post-war period; continued their experiments in botany, agriculture, and forestry; designed and built the first "Adam" style portico in the Carolina Low Country onto the house; and travelled to Philadelphia together to seek treatment for what was widely thought to be Eliza's breast cancer. George Washington was one of Eliza's pall bearers; to this day, she remains the only woman in South Carolina history to be inducted into the South Carolina Agricultural Hall of Fame. Harriot's daughter married into the Rutledge family, another prominent plantation family at the time, inherited Hampton Plantation, and continued to manage it until her death. Hampton Plantation remained in the Rutledge family until they gifted it to the State of South Carolina in 1971 (South Carolina State Parks, 2016).

On the day we visit:

> *as is typical in the low country of South Carolina, especially in the summer in the dense swamps and low-lying forests along the rivers, it is steamy. Our sunglasses fog as we get out of the air-conditioned car; it is still and quiet. Buzzing insects are the only sound. We walk around the house exploring and taking field notes. We're looking for graves. Cris begins reading one of the epitaphs:*

> RIP in memory of John Henry Rutledge
> Son of Frederick and Harriott (Harry Rutledge) who departed this life on the 5th of March 1830 aged 21 years – he was distinguished for fortitude and firmness – the goodness and the magnanimity that he showed even in the agonies of painful death made an indelible impression upon all who witnessed it. He died in peace with all men and on the full confidence that his maker would receive his soul with that mercy and forgiveness who is the hope and solace of the penitent in his approach to the throne if the eternal [sic].
> *Rutledge epitaph*

> *The stone is white marble. The little cemetery is gated. Small wrens hop about brown, dry leaves covering the ground. Water is everywhere – filling our noses, condensing on the stone, pooling in the fields, collecting in the paths.*
>
> *Cris remarks, "I'm surprised the only mention of the Pinckney/Horry women is on the one or two plaques on the house and on the tree that George Washington visited."*

"*Sort of goes along with the traditional gendered expectations for women of hostess, wife, and mother, yes? Very domesticated, very located within the home, within the familiar, within the safe. Interesting that what little text we can read is very intent on that 'beloved wife/beloved home by the river,'*" Deb grunts as she bends down and reads one of the epitaphs. She grunts again as she stands. "*It's so incongruous given their contributions to so many fields of science.*"

"*And their contributions to the cause of America!*" Cris exclaims. "*It seems so unfair that there is so little evidence of them here – all they did seems to be absent. And it's just outrageous to me that Eliza Lucas Pinckney, the mother of a signer of the Declaration of Independence, has no memorial here!*"

"*Well, neither do many of the men,*" Deb responds wryly.

"*True, but they were dead, fighting wars, or had taken off to Europe!*" Cris's outrage is palpable. She lifts her camera and continues taking pictures.

As we walk further and further back into the swamps, further and further away from the manicured lawns of Hampton, we come to Sam Hill Cemetery, an African American cemetery that is thought to have recent burials on top of long ago slave remains. Some gravesites are swept clean, a tradition among the descendants of West Africans here in the low country; some are surrounded by little white picket fences. The tombstones are smaller, less ornate, and often absent. While we write descriptions in our black and white composition books, Cris murmurs, "*So many family members all together.*"

"*Yes,*" Deb replies. "*Notice how one of the only descriptors or roles is 'Wife.' It highlights again the importance of the domestic in these epitaphs.*"

"*True,*" Cris pauses thoughtfully. "*But look at this one …*" Cris points to a stainless steel, shiny grave marker with a faded color photograph inside it. A handsome young black man smiles through the years, his uniform signifying Army. She reads, "*You've gone to be with the Lord, and a part of us went along with you. Rest in peace. Loving you forever in our hearts.*" She points to another family plot; here, there are no gravestones, just sticks tied together to make a cross with a handmade tattered pink bow holding it together. It reads, "*RIP. Maurice. MA.*"

We pick our way through half buried stones. The mosquitos buzz angrily.

A loving mother wife and grandmother.
Barianne B. Deas, 1952–2009. Beloved wife. Sleep on sweet wife and mother and take thy rest. God called thee home. He thought it best.
PFC US Army Korea. In loving memory of Willie Alston, a beloved friend and uncle we love you.
Rena B. Singleton, 1943–2004, a caring and loving wife "Christ is the Answer"
Gerald Lee Garnett, 1944–1993. He is next to Mary Garnett, 1908–1997.

Cris remarks, "You know, Deb, it's not just the women who are characterized and constructed relationally, according to their roles as wife, mother, and grandmother. Some of the men are too."

"You're right," Deb agrees. "It seems as though family, relationships, and the successful performance of prescribed gender roles within those families were important identifiers for everyone, not just for women. Sure you see mention of Army service, but even when folks don't have money or means for a large, well chiseled tombstone, they're writing in the epitaphs what's most important to them – whether they're men or women – their families."

"And so many religious references!" exclaims Cris. "Of course, in Christian cemeteries you'd expect an invocation of the divine, but even when there's little else on the marker, there's often a religious note."

"It'll be interesting to see how these themes plays out in other cemeteries we're visiting." Deb swats at another mosquito.

St. Michael's Episcopal Church Graveyard, Charleston, South Carolina

St. Michael's Episcopal Church is the oldest church in Charleston. Founded in 1751, it served as the center of organized activity against the English early in the revolutionary fervor of the 1760s and 1770s and was a focal point of secessionist rhetoric and outright rebellion during the 1850s and 1860s. It has a fiery history, literally and figuratively, having survived British and American bombardment; natural disasters including hurricanes, earthquakes, floods, a cyclone and a fire (St. Michael's Episcopal Church, 2016). Its Sunday morning services are still well attended.

None of this subversive or riotous behavior is evident when we visit:

Magnolia leaves crunch under foot; mosquitos buzz about the vibrant colors of the azalea bushes; and it is quiet except for the diesel braking and accelerating of tour busses stopping in the street next to the cemetery. We can hear the tour guides' crackly voices deliver the spiel through their microphones, "… and buried here are lots of famous South Carolinians – and Americans."

"Including Pinckneys," Cris chuckles as she looks down at the cemetery map. Family plots are noted and numbered; we are cautioned not to take etchings from the dry, crumbling tombstones. Tourists dot the paths through the graveyard; they are also consulting pamphlets. Like us, they have cameras looped around their necks. Their sunglasses reflect the epitaphs as they cruise the graves

"And Middletons and Rutledges and …." We both smile. The prominent families of the area are well represented, and the records of their intermarriages highly visible, as we wind our way through small, faded, half buried stones, smooth and shiny from the centuries; well-marked, well-groomed family plots; slabs of marble lying down and slabs of marble sitting upright. We come to the Pinckney family plot. Cris begins to read:

Sacred to the memory of Harriett Pinckney daughter of General Charles Cotesworth Pinckney. She was born on the 17th of December in the year 1776 in the dawn of the national glory and died 15th March 1866 at the close of the new revolution. It had been for the blessing of many God accorded her length of days and the prosperity of her long and beautiful life she would have included all her friends. They loved her for her warm heart, her sunny temper, her unfailing sympathy. They loved her for her happy nature in which there was much of heaven. "Nearer to God" [sic].

Horry epitaph

Deb joins her and reads another memorial:

The earthly remains of Charles Cotesworth Pinckney son of Charles Pinckney and Eliza Lucas born 20th of February 17, 1716 died 16 august 1825 ... to the memory of General Charles Cotesworth Pinckney one of the founders of the American Republican war.

"Oh my, this is like this guy's whole biography!" Deb leans her face in close to the monument. She continues to read silently.

He was the companion of arms and the friend of Washington. In Washington. In peace he enjoyed his unchanging confidence and maintained with enlightened zeal the principles of his administration and of the constitution. As a statesman he bequeathed to his country the sentiment "millions for defense not a cent for tribute." As a lawyer his learning was various and profound. His principles pure his practice liberal. With all the accomplishments of the gentleman he combined the virtues of the patriot and the piety of the Christian. His name is recorded in the history of his country inscribed on the charter of her liberties and cherished in the affections of her citizens. Placed by his descendants, The society of colonial wars in the State of South Carolina, The William Moultrie chapter sons of the American Revolution, The Rebecca Mott chapter daughters of the American Revolution 2010 [sic].

Pinckney epitaph

"Look over here!" Cris motions into another section of the graveyard. She points to a raised pedestal, with a flat top about the length of a large tombstone. There's a coat of arms on one end of it and on the side it says:

Sacred to the memory of Mrs. Maria Simons neigh Vanderhorst, consort of dr. B. B.Simons. Born November 2 [looks like] 1770 died April 4th 1845. The Lord our righteousness in our hands no price I bring simply to thy cross I cling [sic].

"And I'm sure interested in the word consort!"

"Look," observes Deb, walking over to the other side of the grave. "It says,

'Sacred to the memory of Benjamin B. Simons MD. Born December 5th 1776 died' ... [looks like] September, [maybe] 1844. As a physician he was eminent as a surgeon he had no sufferers in the United States. As a man he was serious just with stern integrity and uncompromising honor he was distinguished in his day and generation [sic]."

Simons epitaph

"This one's interesting," murmurs Deb as she reads the sunlit and shadowed dappled tombstone and pedestal underneath it:

Sacred to the memory of John Julius Pringle Esquire ... was committed to the earth all that is mortal and perishable of Susannah 47 years. The very amiable and excellent wife of John Joyous Pringle Esquire. She was born 14th December 1768 and died 7th February 1831. She was liberally endowed with the qualities of the head, heart and person which most adorn and endear the loveliest of her sex. These were rendered the more estimable by her discreet, moral and pious conduct in her life she was therefore much beloved and at her death much lamented. But her afflicted husband and children survived not as those without hope for they were by this hope consoled. That God had will to translate her from this frail and fleeting distance to one of everlasting bliss and that by his grace they may so live and hear as to be reconciled rendered to her hereafter [sic].

Pringle epitaphs

Cris bends down to read the inscription for herself. "The gravestones and the memorial stones are so different. The memorials were clearly placed here after the grave markers and contain so much more information than initials, names, and/ or dates of death. Women are always referred to as 'wife of,' whereas the men are rarely referred to as 'husband of.'" Cris walks over to another nearby rather large marker. "And Capt. Peter Smith's family doesn't even get a listing of their names, even though the stone is certainly large enough," notes Cris.

"Yes, but isn't is interesting how many of the gravestones are complimentary, not only in what they say but in the size and shape?" Deb brushes black debris and old brown acorns off a grave, squinting to read the engravings. "You know, though, since most of the stones were destroyed in the earthquake of 1886 and replaced in 1923, we really don't know how faithful the replacement stones were to the originals. We might be looking at the social conventions of the early 20th century rather than those of the 19th and 18th centuries."

"There are still so many interesting differences. Even though women clearly lived longer than men, according to most of these tombstones, men often are the

ones warranting an upright stone." Cris points to a nearby pair of graves. "There are some interesting gender constructions, though, especially if you know some of the stories surrounding the people buried here — remember we read about 'Sue,' who wrote those scandalous novels (Gabriel and Miller, 2005):

> Susan Dupont Petigru King Bowen
> 1824–1875
> Undismayed. Unshaken [sic]. "

"Oh, yeah, even though she converted to Roman Catholicism, she's still buried here," Deb straightens up from peering at the epitaphs. "But what does all this have to say about socially constructed norms?" The tour guide's scratchy voice sounds far away. The church bells ring.

Hobcaw Barony Cemeteries, Georgetown, South Carolina

Hobcaw Barony, the site of the original 1718 King's land grant of South Carolina as reward for faithful military and/or political service to distinguished sons of prominent families, is the home of dozens of former plantations. Originally granted as sixteen separate tracts, it was sold and subdivided, combined and merged over the centuries until it was bought in its entirety by wealthy New York financier Bernard Baruch in 1905 (Hobcaw Barony, 2016). Much like its history of division and separation, integration and segregation, it is the site of hundreds of documentable gravesites and probably thousands of black and white burials over its almost 300-year history of mostly European and African burials, and prior to that, Native American habitation. There are multiple cemeteries, including white owners' well-marked family plots, as well as former slaves and their descendants' gravesites, at what are theorized to have at one time been mass slave graves and are now familial burial sites dating back generations. Dug within ground almost as permeable as the air, surrounded by water, most have long ago decayed, disintegrated, and returned to the ocean which, for many of the dead buried in this place, brought them here.

Alderly and Marietta Cemeteries in Hobcaw Barony

The day we visit, we find few markers save wooden signs, rough dirt roads, and mounds of dirt marking boundaries. Otherwise, the places where thousands of dead Africans (Brooks, 2011), and more recent African Americans, are buried in the swamp are indistinguishable from the woods surrounding them.

Cris pauses from dictating field notes to remark, "I'm not sure how the archaeologists even determined this was a cemetery, perhaps they just knew from the surveys, plaques, maps, because there is no indication of anything back here." She shivers. "My toes are cold." It's late fall. We're standing in wet, black, rich soil, blanketed with layers of dead leaves. Sunlight peeks through the trees. There's nothing that looks like a grave, not even remnants like we've seen before: broken shells, carved wood, trash.

"Look!" Deb points about eight feet away at an old marker, the kind that funeral homes used to use. Nearby it is a marble stone that says, "James Simmons, South Carolina." Above the stone is a cross that says:

James Simmons, South Carolina, Private PVT, served BN.OMC. 339, FCRV.BN.OMC. January 30, 1943 [sic].

The ground is pocketed and indented. "Look!" Cris stands still and gasps. "We're surrounded by graves."

Edward Kennedy October 6, 1909 March 9, 1929
He was the sunshine of our home [sic].

Many of the stones are covered in moss and unreadable. Many of the stones look hand carved; some have rotting, wooden markers that are roughly etched. Many have seashells in front of them, around them, piled on top of them.

Megan T. Rolin August 16, 1910 March 9, 1929
Louis Capri New York, Private, 304 pioneer infantry January 6 1941
Jack Jenkins October 1959 [sic].

A concrete stone lies flat on the ground. It's got a rusted metal name plate on it, with an engraved wreath:

Reverend Abraham Wright, 1866–1939

Nearby is another stone, about three inches wide from back to front, about three feet tall from top to bottom, about eighteen inches wide from left to right. It's peaked – diamond shaped – and there's a real picture:

Christopher E. Sands, 1870–1930, gone but not forgotten.

There are dozens of stones all around us: some broken, some whole; some with faded engraving, some worn clean; some small, some large; some concrete, some marble. A standing stone, concrete, with a dove surrounded by flowers at its top:

Annie S. Crate, died June 8, 1939. At rest.

A standing stone, marble, about two feet tall, about a foot wide, with a cross:

Alfred Sams, South Carolina, Private (PVT) 345, October 11, 1918

"They don't seem to be placed in any uniform order – this one's catty corner to that one," Cris observes as she points to several graves, "but they're all facing the same way."

"Always east," Deb replies.

"Always east," Cris repeats, "toward the sea, toward Africa."

"Toward home," Deb responds like a refrain. They continue documenting the gravesites, their sodden sneakers sinking in the rich, black mud.

Fraser's Point and Strawberry Hill Cemeteries in Hobcaw Barony

"These are white people's cemeteries," observes Cris. The small family cemetery is on a small incline – fenced, landscaped and well maintained. There is a sprawling live oak tree at the top of the hill; the Spanish moss hanging from its massive branches caresses the old tombstones ever so gently. The graves are neat, bounded, and marked by marble stones:

Jane Huskins, 1873–1944
Sarah Eakins, 1865–1940
R. J. King, October 17, 1873 – May 25, 1923

Behind those graves stands what appears to be an old chimney or hearth. It's solid brick and crumbling. There are more markers behind it:

In memory of Mrs. Lydia Coachman, wife of John Coachman, daughter of Joseph Towner, and Lydia his wife, died March 1798, aged 19 years, two months, 28 days, my wife, my only friend, my happiness, I'm lost without you [sic].

Crumbling stones dot the hill crest. Many are unreadable; some are legible:

1907, Avril L., daughter of Richard R. and Mary E. Caines

A large triangular shaped stone says:

Mary E., wife of Richard R. Caines, April 28 1882–February 27 1926

A smaller stone stands next to it:

Richard Randolph Caines, October 12, 1859 – May 18

An even smaller stone:

In memory Gabriel Aaron, son of RNSB born December 5, 1873 died May 23, 1885

Pieces of stones lie scattered about, and several look as though someone has tried to piece them together. They are fitted together like puzzles, their edges gray and molded. Others still stand, three feet or more, with matching footstones at each end:

In memoriam, Richard, C. Caines, born March 28, 1812, died June 4, 1881, may his soul rest in peace.
In memory of Louisa Elizabeth Caines, who died May 7, 1854, aged 29 years, two months and five days; leaving an affectionate husband and six children [sic].

The remains of a crumbling red brick wall bound the cemetery, and beyond lies Strawberry Swamp, its trees silvery in the sunlight. Small yellow and white butterflies flit in the shimmering rays. Another old family cemetery, with traditional, upright marble stones:

John Thompson, who was born November 7, 1774 and died May 26, 1833
Sarah Myers, his wife, was born October 10, 1777 and died January 26, 1823
Isaac Thompson, his brother was born November 17, 1772 and died January 23, 1823
Blessed are the dead that die in the Lord
In memory of the daughter of James and Sarah Bryan, born January 18, 1850, died
January 31st, 1850 [sic]

There's a monument up on a hill, about five feet tall with a cathedral point at the top:

In memory of James Albert Donaldson, his loving wife and two sons
A loving husband; affectionate father and a true friend.
Born in Amagh Ireland 1836
Died in Georgetown, South Carolina, November 21st, 1884. [sic]

Cris reads aloud, "A loving husband, affectionate father ..."
Deb interrupts, "... and a true friend. And this was his, his wife and the children ... "
But the comment was about him! 'Loving and affectionate' is a kind of virtue you would expect to see on a woman's grave!"
"We've seen that at Hampton and St. Michaels, too," Deb and Cris look at each other quizzically. "I get the flowery language of the past, but those types of gender constructions on a man's tombstone are really interesting! Socially constructed gender, especially on these old epitaphs, seems much more complex and androgynous than we expected."

Like today, gender constructions from the past, as summarized in the final words of epitaphs, are often complex, contradictory, and contested. They remain influenced and mediated by other standpoints such as class, race, religion, and multiple other standpoints that we all wear like clothing. Davis (1991) uses the metaphor of a salad to describe gendered performances; the description seems apt as we examine socially constructed standpoints as articulated in the final word: epitaphs and obituaries. Individual identities assumed and worn like vegetables added and omitted in preparation, displayed via dazzling dressings, spiced by various seasonings – crisp and tangy, acidic and cool – diverse in their tastes. Such are both current and historical gender constructions.

In our analysis of epitaphs, grave markers, plaques, and memorials located at cemeteries across the south and northeastern Carolinas, we note interesting similarities and differences among gender constructions for men and women. Class, of course, is not only reflected in the size, expense, and type of thanatological items located at the graves – whether found in ordered, affluent, primarily white churchyards or in nearly un-locatable black or white family graveyards now swamped and overgrown or neatly fenced – the location, markers, decoratives, upkeep, and artifacts at and around the graves certainly reflected the class of the deceased and their families. Length, type, and surfaces for epitaphs ranged from simple, hand-carved pieces of wood to blocks of concrete to ornately and lengthily engraved stone. Faded pink handmade bows, tied carefully around sticks in one graveyard contrasted with the curved angels etched in imported marble by some of the most famous artisans in the "new" and "old" worlds that we found in other graveyards. None of this was surprising to us.

Of course, the spiritual, cultural and religious conventions of the dead inform and influence these socially constructed choices, as they do the spatial, architectural, and aesthetic designs we found in the grave yards. For the white, primarily Christian elite, Bible quotations, theological references, and related iconography on gravestones marking trimmed, identifiable graves were the norm. The West African slaves and their descendants who were largely Christianized often adopted creolized religious customs, much as they did with other cultural ways of being, including language, family life, and cultural rituals. Their graves were marked with frequent Christian references in epitaph as well as in iconography ("closer to God," "God called him home," crosses, crucifixes, angels, etc.), yet much of the material culture at the gravesites was more typical of West African burial traditions. As we noted in Chapter 9, conch shells, glassware and pottery, both whole and broken, and personal items such as combs, brushes, and mirrors are scattered among these gravesites, in keeping with the "home going" traditions of the Ibo, Bakongo, and other tribes inhabiting the coast of mid-western Africa (Babson, 1990; Bell, 2010; Fairbanks, 1984; Fennell, 2011; Ferguson, 1992; Goodwine, 1998; Handler, 1996; Handler & Corruccini, 1983; Mufwene, 1998; Russell, 1997; Schuyler, 1980; Wilkie, 1997; Young, 1996).

We were also unsurprised by the long listings of accomplishments for the favored sons of South Carolina or by the relatively brief traditional constructions on the tombstones of equally influential women in the post-colonial and antebellum south; we also found the generally traditional gender constructions unremarkable. As expected, men were often characterized as "sturdy oaks" (Wood, 2016):

He was distinguished for fortitude and firmness (Rutledge epitaph, St. Michael's)
He was serious just with stern integrity and uncompromising honor (Simons epitaph, St. Michaels)

Women, on the other hand, were more noted for beauty and sensitivity:

They loved her for her warm heart, her sunny temper, her unfailing sympathy. They loved her for her happy nature in which there was much of heaven

(Horry epitaph)

We were surprised, however, by the focus on family and relational interpersonal roles, functions, performances, values, and losses as articulated in epitaphs at all of the locations. Whether flowery, Victorian-style poetry inscribed on imported Italian marble or whether meticulously carved lettering, sealed and burnt, etched into now rotting wood, the relational importance of the dead to the living was striking. While we expected descriptions of women as "friend to all" or "beloved in countenance and action," we did not expect such domesticated constructions of gender on the grave markers of men, or for the loss, especially of women, to be expressed in such anguished ways. We were also struck by how frequently we documented these findings at both black and white, rich and poor cemeteries. The importance and necessity of tightly bound nuclear and extended family is of course important today as it was in the past, but its necessity for marital, social, economic, and emotional success in the past cannot be overstated – for white and for black travelers to the Americas – whether forced or voluntary. The loss of a young mother or father to a large family had repercussions that were keenly felt, whether the mother was white or black, rich or poor, slave or free. For both men and women, these losses were recorded on the deceased's grave marker in heart wrenching ways.

Katriel's (1993) notion of "consensual and oppositional narrative dialogues" (p. 71) seems particularly applicable here. We apply this idea to epitaphs. There are "consensual narrative dialogues" those that are complicit in our gendered conceptualizations, but there are also "oppositional narrative dialogues," those that resist and reify rigid gendered constructions. Similar to some of our developing ideas regarding the hegemonic and subversive narratives told and imagined, explicit and covert, surrounding the rhetorics at national memorials and monuments, these public and publicized narratives are socially constructed and therefore interpretive and interpreted differently (Breede et al., 2016).

These are not new ideas. The tensions among intent and interpretation within public space are fraught with multiple discourses and are usually highly contested (Aden 2012; Bruner & Kirshenblatt-Gimblett, 2004; Butler et al., 2008; Carter et al., 2011; Iles, 2006; Maurantonio, 2015; Mitchell, 2011; Noy, 2008). As Hanks (2015) contends, we are often confronted with "multiple versions of an unknown past" (p. 170) that frequently tend to "offer new and sometimes contradictory visions of the past" (p. 172).

Hanks (2015) argues that "scholars who focus on issues of historical memory and social transformation deploy the rhetoric of hauntings, ghosts and specters to signify the present absences they seek to illuminate, particularly in the areas of post-colonialism, displaced cultural identity, and racial memory" (p. 20). Her notion of "ghost as metaphor" (p. 21) therefore becomes particularly useful as we consider the origins and presences of a people who were transplanted, whether from Europe or from Africa; whose pasts are intertwined as oppressors and oppressed; whose cultures are simultaneously integrated and segregated; and whose collective and familial social memories reflect these and other realities. It allows us to consider "group specific understandings of the past" (p. 30) especially as they shape present understandings. We suggest such "ghost metaphors" at work account for some of the dizzying complexities and contradictions as we examine gender constructions both past and present.

The idea of "ghost as metaphor" is particularly applicable given some of the absences we note in this research. Women who are considered some of the most influential founders of our country are often just as absent from these cultural and rhetorical texts as many other women are. Eliza Lucas Pinckney – the mother of some of our most historically important early patriots, the creator of agricultural innovations including the process for extracting dye from indigo plants and the early experiments preventing genetic disease in rice, the only woman in the South Carolina Agricultural Hall of Fame – lacks a formal memorial at either the plantation she helped save from the British or at the cemetery where most of her family is buried. Her absence is a ghostly afterthought, even in places that seek to honor and preserve the memories of the dead.

Conclusion

Silence and absence are powerful rhetorics, and revelation and concealment cannot exist without each other (Holdstein, 2011; Landau, 2011; Scott, 1993). Both withhold and fulfill (Scott 1993). Written epitaphs on gravestones in family cemeteries and churchyards communicate institutional authority and help create collective public memory. Their absences may not be as sanctioned, but they are just as powerful as utterances. They are invisible, but just as real as air or gravity and equally elusive. They punctuate (Scott, 1993) and italicize the stated. Their constructions, like human identities themselves, are rich, complex, contradictory, and nuanced. While individual human agents can never be reduced to the Twitter version of their lives as inscribed as epitaph, their epitaphs, and that which we know but remains unsaid, can help us understand human narratives, and the socially constructed standpoints that comprise and anchor them.

References

Abel, E. L. (2008). Changes in gender discrimination after death: Evidence from a cemetery. Omega – Journal of Death and Dying, 58(2), 147–152. doi: 10.2190/OM.58.2.d.

Aden, R. C. (2012). When memories and discourses collide: The president's house and places of public memory. Communication Monographs, 79(1), 72–92.

Anderson, P. (1991). Imagined communities: Reflections on the origin and spread of Nationalism. London: Verso.

Babson, D. (1990). The archaeology of racism and ethnicity on southern plantations. Historical Archaeology, 24(4), 20–28.

Bell, K. B. (2010). Rice, resistance, and forced transatlantic communities: (Re)envisioning the African Diaspora in Lowcountry Georgia, 1750–1800. The Journal of African American History, 95(2), 157–182.

Berger, A. A. (2013). Theorizing tourism: Analyzing iconic destinations. Walnut Creek, CA: Left Coast Press.

Bergman, T. (2013). Exhibiting patriotism: Creating and contesting interpretations of American historic sites. Walnut Creek, CA: Left Coast Press.

Bowman, M. S., & Pezzullo, P. C. (2010). What's so dark about "dark tourism"?: Death, tours and performance. Tourist Studies, 9(3), 187–202. doi: 101177/1468797610382699.

Breede, D. C.; Davis, C. S.; & Warren-Findlow, J. (2016). Absence, revision, and the Other: Rhetorics of South Carolina antebellum tourism sites. Journal of Hate Studies, 13(1), 17–42.

Brooks, C. (2011). Enclosing their immortal souls: A survey of two African American cemeteries in Georgetown, South Carolina. Southeastern Archaeology, 30(1), 176–186.

Bruner, E. M., & Kirshenblatt-Gimblett, B. (2004). Maasai on the lawn: Tourist realism in East Africa. In Bruner, E. M. (Ed.), Culture on tour: Ethnographies of travel, pp. 33–70. Chicago: University of Chicago.

Butler, D. L.; Carter, P. L.; & Dwyer, O. J. (2008). Imagining plantations: Slavery, dominant narratives, and the foreign born. Southeastern Geographer, 48(3), 288–302.

Carter, Butler, P. L., D. L.; & Dwyer, O. J. (2011). Defetishizing the plantation: African Americans in the memorialized south. Historical Geography, 39, 128–146.

Davis, F. (1991). Moving the mountain: The women's movement in America since 1960. New York: Simon and Schuster.

Fairbanks, C. H. (1984). The plantation archeology of the Southeast coast. Historical Archaeology, 18(1), 1–14.

Fennell, C. C. (2011). Early African America: Archeological studies of significance and diversity. Journal of Archeological Research, 19(1), 1–49.

Ferguson, L. (1992.) Uncommon ground: Archeology and early African America, 1650–1800. Washington, D.C.: Smithsonian Institution.

Gabriel, P. D., & Miller, R. M. (2005). Touring the tombstones: A guide to Charleston's historic churchyards. Pamphlet Vol 1. Charleston, South Carolina.

Gatewood, J. B., & Cameron, C. M. (2004). Battlefield pilgrims at Gettysburg National Military Park. Ethnology, 43(3), 193–216.

Goodwine, M. L. (1998). "Holdin' pun we gulcha": Sites, individuals and organizations preserving the Gullah and Geechee heritage. In Goodwine, M. L. (Ed.), The legacy of Ibo Landing: Gullah roots of African American culture: The Clarity Press Gullah Project, pp. 184–197. Atlanta, GA: Clarity Press.

Goodwine, M. L., & The Clarity Press Gullah Project (Eds) (1998). The legacy of Ibo Landing: Gullah roots of African American culture. Atlanta: Clarity Press.

Handler, J. S. (1996). A prone burial from a plantation slave cemetery in Barbados, West Indies: Possible evidence for an African-type witch or other negatively viewed person. Historical Archaeology, 30(3), 76–86.

Handler, J. S., & Corruccini, R. S. (1983). Plantation slave life in Barbados: A physical anthropological analysis. Journal of Interdisciplinary History, 14(1), 65–90.

Hanks, M. (2015). Haunted heritage: The cultural politics of ghost tourism, populism, and the past. Walnut Creek, CA: Left Coast Press.

Hobcaw Barony. (2016). History of Hobcaw Barony. Available at: http://hobcawbarony.org/about-hobcaw/history/.

Holdstein, D. H. (2011). Rhetorical silence, scholarly absence, and tradition rethought. Pedagogy: Critical approaches to teaching literature, language, composition, and culture, 11(3), 451–464. doi: 10.1215/1531–4200–1302714.

Horry, H. P. (1793–1794). Diary of Harriot Pinckney Horry 1793–1794. Typewritten transcript of handwritten diary. Horry-Pinckney Family Papers. Charleston SC: South Carolina Historical Society.

Iles, J. (2006). Recalling the ghosts of war: Performing tourism on the battlefields of the Western Front. Text and Performance Quarterly, 26(2), 162–180. doi: 10.1080/10462930500519374.

Jackson, R. L., II. (1999). White space, white privilege: Mapping discursive inquiry into the self. Quarterly Journal of Speec, 85, 38–54.

Jordan, E. G. (2005). "Unrelenting toil": Expanding archeological interpretations of the female slave experience. Slavery and Abolition, 26, 217–232. doi: 10.1080/01440390500176350.

Katriel, T. (1993.) "Our future is where our past is": Studying heritage museums as ideological and performative arenas. Communication Monographs, 60, 69–75.

Landau, J. (2011). Women will get cancer: Visual and verbal presence (and absence) in a pharmaceutical advertising campaign about HPV. Argumentation and Advocacy, 48, 39–54.

Marshall, A. T. (2014). "They are supposed to be lurking about the city": Enslaved women runaways in antebellum Charleston. The South Carolina Historical Magazine, 115(3), 188–202.

Maurantonio, N. (2015). Material rhetoric, public memory, and the Post-It Note. Southern Communication Journal, 80(2), 83–101. doi: 10.180/1041794X.2015.1011344.

Miller, J. B. (2005). Coyote's tale on the Old Oregon Trail: Challenging cultural memory through narrative at the Tamastslikt Cultural Institute. Text and Performance Quarterly, 25(3), 220–238. doi: 10.1080/10462930500271786.

Mitchell, T. (2011). New Deal, new landscape: The Civilian Conservation Corps and South Carolina's state parks. Columbia, SC: University of South Carolina Press.

Mufwene, S. S. (1998). The ecology of Gullah's survival. In Goodwine, M. L., & The Clarity Press Gullah Project (Eds.) The legacy of Ibo Landing: Gullah roots of African American culture. pp. 175–183. Atlanta: Clarity Press.

Noy, C. (2008). Pages as stages: A performance approach to visitor books. Annals of Tourism Research, 35(2), 509–528.

Pinckney, E. (Ed.) (1997). The letterbook of Eliza Lucas Pinckney. Columbia SC: University of South Carolina Press.

Roach, J. (1996). Introduction: History, memory and performance. In Roach, J. (Ed.), Cities of the dead: Circum-Atlantic performance. pp. 1–31. New York, NY: Columbia University Press.

Russell, A. E. (1997). Material culture and African-American spirituality at the Hermitage. Historical Archaeology, 31(2), 63–80.

Schuyler, R. L. (Ed.) (1980). Archeological perspectives on ethnicity in America. Farmingdale, NY: Baywood Publishing Company.

Scott, R. L. (1993). Dialectical tensions of speaking and silence. Quarterly Journal of Speech, 79(1), 1–18.

South Carolina Department of Parks, Recreation and Tourism. (2009). South Carolina's Hampton Plantation State Historic Site. Columbia: State of South Carolina.

South Carolina Historical Society. (2013). Library and archives. Fireproof Building. Charleston, South Carolina. Available: http://schistory.org/

South Carolina State Parks. (2016.) Hampton Plantation. Accessed http://south-carolina-plantations.com/charleston/hampton.html

St. Michael's Episcopal Church. (2016). Available at: http://www.nps.gov/nr/travel/charleston/smi.htm

Wallace, M. (1981). Visiting the past: History museums in the United States. Radical History Review, 25, 63–96.

Wilkie, L. A. (1997). Secret and sacred: Contextualizing the artifacts of African-American magic and religion. Historical Archaeology, 31(4), 81–106.

Wood, J. (2016). Gendered Lives: Communication, Gender and Culture. (12th Edition). Belmont, CA: Wadsworth.

Young, A. L. (1996). Archeological evidence of African-style ritual and healing practices in the Upland South. Tennessee Anthropologist, 21(2), 131–155.

11

WORTH DYING FOR: COMMUNICATING ABOUT DEATH IN MONUMENTS AND MEMORIALS

"How's Robin doing?" Deb asks as she stifles a yawn.

"I'm seeing her and Jonah next week in D.C.," Cris says. "I'm Nana-sitting while she's at a conference."

"You gonna' do any sightseeing while you're there?" Deb asks.

"Maybe a little bit," Cris answers. "I love to sightsee in D.C. The last time Jerry and I went up there, we had a death and dying vacation." Cris laughs. "We visited all the cemeteries, monuments, memorials, and museums in the area that commemorate people who have died."

"Where did you go?"

"Oh my gosh," Cris says, thinking back as she ticks the list on her fingers. "We went to the Holocaust Museum, the Martin Luther King Memorial, the World War II, Korean War, and Vietnam War Memorials; the Washington, Jefferson, and Lincoln Monuments; Arlington National Cemetery; and the Pentagon 911 Memorial."

"I love to visit the monuments and memorials around D.C.," Deb comments. "Those are all powerful cultural sites of commemoration and loss."

Cris nods. "The Korean War Memorial is my favorite. It's haunting. What's your favorite?"

"Arlington National Cemetery," Deb answers.

"I always get really emotional when I visit the memorials," Cris says. "When I was there last, it was really clear to me how these sites are all memorials to death, and they all serve to transmit the national and cultural values of what is worth dying for."

Vietnam Veteran's Memorial Wall

Cris remembers her last visit to the Vietnam Memorial:

> *When you walk up to the Vietnam Veteran's Memorial Wall, the park-like set-ting of the tree-lined walkway belies the memorial hidden behind the grassy hill. Only the somber faces of the people leaving give a hint to where you are heading. Before you see the arched wall, you see the people kneeling, bent down, on ladders, touching, reading, tracing, praying, standing, leaving flowers on the brick-lined base, tracing etchings of the name of a loved one. Their reflections are mirrored back to them, to us, in the black granite, so that they emerge from the names, as if from the wall itself. The living from the dead, reflections of the living tracing memories of the dead, long gone but yet remembered in the name. We see ourselves in them and perhaps they see themselves in us.*
>
> *It strikes me that the Vietnam Memorial is unlike other war memorials here in Washington, D.C. It is a not a memorial to victory or valor; it is a memorial to defeat, waste, and loss. It is a memorial of sadness.*
>
> *Jerry finds the name in the directory and walks to its place on the wall. He touches his hand to the engraving, feeling the letters under his fingers, feeling the rough carving next to the smooth granite. Memories at the wall are tactile, recol-lection through touch, a caress, hand to stone. Jerry wipes a tear from the corner of his eye. "I knew Pete from high school," he says. "He went over about the same time I did. Both drafted." I've heard this story many times before, but I listen silently, letting him bear witness to his personal experience of our country's history. "I was drafted on my 19th birthday. I didn't want to go but my country called."*

Blair and Michel (2007) note the radical democracy of this wall. Unlike pre-vious war memorials, the names on the wall of each of the soldiers killed or missing in action are listed as equals – no names, ranks, or service branches are included. In addition, the practice of placing flowers and other material items at the wall, mentioned by Blair and Michel (2007) as an ongoing alteration of the rhetoric of the memorial, is another way in which the memorial is under creative democratic control. Yet, Blair and Michel also point out the hegem-onic importance of including this memorial on the National Mall, and adding two realistic sculptures, one of soldiers and one of servicewomen. The fact that this memorial is a "veterans" memorial and not a "war" memorial (p. 601); that, unlike previous war memorials, it foregrounds individual loss instead of military victory (Sturken, 1991), is a significant attempt to rehistoricize the Vietnam War (Sturken, 1991), to valorize servicemen and women with-out sanctioning the war. The emphasis on names, suggests Blair and Michel (2007), "marks a general relationship between individual and collective"

(p. 605). These distinctions underscore the extent to which this memorial is a testament to the decades-long ambivalence Americans have had with this conflict – starting with the widespread anti-war demonstrations and protests, the Kent State killings, death and carnage on the nightly news, draft dodgers fleeing to Canada; through President Johnson's escalation of troops, Nixon's secret bombing of Cambodia, the Mai Lai Massacre; with over 50,000 Americans dead, over 150,000 wounded, and 10,000 missing; to the fall of Saigon and spitting on our soldiers when they returned home, and the later pardoning of the draft dodgers who were then welcomed home from Canada by President Carter. Known as the only war America lost, Vietnam is to some a symbol of national shame and regret.

> *I stand watching the visitors making tracing etchings – touching, leaning, reflecting in and from the mirrored wall, carrying home all that is left of their loved one – their name. This is a place of bodily experience, embodied remembering, witnessing for those who gave their bodies in the ultimate sacrifice, remembering them through our bodies as we reach out the remnant of their short lives. Jerry and I walk back to the car in silence. This place calls for silence.*

Construction of National Identity

Our national identity is constructed by and reflected in the commemorative monuments, memorials, and museums in and near Washington, D.C. Collectively, our country's identity is multivocal and polysemic, and both hegemony and resistance co-exist in our commemorative sites. We are a country of both nationalists and revolutionaries; anarchists and activists, and our national commemorative sites construct and reflect this prism of ideas, beliefs, meanings, and narratives.

Many of the sites at the National Mall – the Vietnam Veteran's Memorial Wall, the World War II Veteran's Memorial, the Korean War Veteran's Memorial; and the Holocaust Museum, which touches on American identity in a more indirect manner; were recently (in the past four decades) built, and represent a "groundswell … of public memorializing" (Blair & Michel, 2007, p. 597) that is both rhetorically and politically notable. Given the sites' collective – and canonical – focus on remembering and memorializing national deaths, it's important to consider how these sites construct the idea of what's worth dying for, and – by extension – our collective identity of voices and values. Space is a place with constituted meaning which is constructed and formed through discourse (Foucault, 1972). Rhetoric, place, and memory are inexorably entangled (Blair et al., 2010). Sites such as these are themselves performances, suggests Sather-Wagstaff (2011), and it is through the interactions between site and tourist, ideology and experience, that constitutes their meaning.

Cultural Authenticity, Memory, and Sacrilization

While personal memorials and memorial rituals are constructed as a form of and search for social support, to commemorate and remember our deceased loved ones, and to continue the bonds with our deceased loved ones (Klaassens & Bijlsma, 2014; Neimeyer et al., 2002), public historical sites are part of a national presentation of history (Blair & Michel, 2007), and, as such, have additional, and sometimes different and competing purposes. Public commemoration sites construct cultural identity (Blair et al., 2010; Sturken, 1997) and repair conflicted memory (Barsalou & Baxter, 2007), and thus are both political and rebellious (Blair & Michel, 2007). As our nation's history is problematic, partial, and partisan, collective and individual memories are reconstructed and disputed and polysemous (Aden, 2012; Bergman, 2013; Blair et al., 1991; Blair & Michel, 2007; Sturken, 1997), and historical knowledge is both culturally hegenomic and resistant to those dominant narratives (Barsalou & Baxter, 2007; Foucault, 1980; Sather-Wagstaff, 2011; Sturken, 1997). Cultural authenticity in historical sites is contested, interpreted, produced, and negotiated (Bruner, 2005; Pollock, 1998) because cultural objectivity is a myth (Pollock, 1998) and historical representation is ideological and "fetishiz[ed]" (p. 11). Cultural memory is entwined with history and is unstable and changeable, says Sturken (1997), which, we suggest, reconciles the canonical and the resistant historical narratives. Thus, historical and commemorative sites such as museums, monuments, and memorials are places not only of memory, but of both education and performance. They are where visitors learn about a nation's history and culture, but they are also spaces in which we perform citizenship and nationalism (Bergman, 2013), identify and empathize with its cultural meaning (Iles, 2006), and create communal connection and participation (Sather-Wagstaff, 2011). The communicative construction of meaning at these spaces of memory and memorial frequently occurs through engagement, performance, consumption, feeling, doing, and embodying, and it is through these experiential actions that meaning and authenticity is constructed (Iles, 2006; Sather-Wagstaff, 2011; Shaffer, 2004). "All history is a production," asserts Wallace (1981, p. 88), one that is culturally and hegemonically created and constructed. Meaning is constructed in spaces such as these through a process of sanctification, designation, rectification, or obliteration, claims Foote (1997), and the tourist experience can be seen as a sort of ritual in which commemorative sites are made sacred ("site sacrilization") through "naming, framing, enshrinement, and reproduction" (Iles, 2006, p. 171).

Commemorative Sites as Cultural Texts

Such commemorative sites can be read as texts – a nation's narrative – of identity construction (Bergman, 2013), or they can be read as iconic signifiers

(Berger, 2013). Certainly, these national narratives range in meaning from the canonical to resistance narratives (Sather-Wagstaff, 2011). The location of these sites in and around our nation's capital makes them "official [and] … authoritative … representations of nationalism, patriotism, and citizenship … [associated] with structures of power" (Bergman, 2013, p. 17); sites of "ideological assertion" (Katriel, 1993, p. 70). Tourists visit them because of their historic and cultural significance (Berger, 2013), because – even though they are bygone remnants, functionally invalid – they are of abundant cultural consequence (Kirshenblatt-Gimblett, 1991). These types of places have multiple layers of meaning – official, public, and vernacular meanings, all of which construct multiple meanings and ideas and which range from the doctrinal to the equivocal (Sather-Wagstaff, 2011). It is important to remember when considering these multi-layered and polysemic meanings, that these spaces were constructed for specific purposes and meanings in specific places and times (Sather-Wagstaff, 2011); however, even when a commemorative site is located in a specific spot for a specific meaning, the constructed and reconstructed meanings of the site transcend space and place (de Certeau et al., 1998; Sather-Wagstaff, 2011). These are sites of what Katriel (1993) calls "consensual and oppositional narrative dialogues" (pp. 71–72); in which nationalist narratives intertwine and compete with other cultural voices in an ongoing process of dialogue and embodiment as canonical and counter narratives compete over a culture's collective memory (Miller, 2005).

Thanatourism

These sites can also be classified and grouped as memorial sites – tourism of death – or what has been called "thanatourism," "traumascapes," "dark tourism," and "morbid tourism" (Sather-Wagstaff, 2011; p. 76). Sather-Wagstaff suggests that because of our fear of death, such places are ones that require and call for transformation and negotiation of space and meaning. Because these are sites of loss, meaning is inserted into the voids through surrogation – alternative narratives that represent and re-present cultural stories and memories (Roach, 1996).

Holocaust Museum

It would be easy to miss the Holocaust Museum if you didn't know where to look for it; from the outside it is an attractive but fairly nondescript brick building along a row of brick and stone buildings on a busy street in downtown Washington, D.C. A sign in front of the museum store next door states "Never Again," the most visible clue of what you are about to enter.

Excited isn't the right word, but I've been waiting with great anticipation to go to the Holocaust Museum on this trip to D.C. My dad's side of the family is Jewish, and although none of my ancestors, as far as I know, were in the Nazi Holocaust, I do have ancestors who fled Russia during the Jewish pogroms there prior to the ones in Germany; and others who were likely killed in Russia when the Nazis briefly invaded there prior to World War II. So this is personal to me. I approach the museum reverently but my anticipation quickly turns to dismay when I see the long line to get into the building. When we finally reach the front of the line, we are behind several large school groups and I'm not sure we will get in before the museum closes.

After we pass through metal detectors, the ticket-taker at the door pauses as he takes our tickets. "Here," he says. "You'll never make it through if you follow these large groups." He motions for us to follow him. "Start at the end. You'll see the whole thing but avoid the long lines." He leads us around a corner and through a back hallway and unlocks a door. "Follow the hallway to the left," he instructs. "And enjoy your tour!"

I feel like I'm in pursuit of a secret, or mystery. I think about how we're starting our tour at the end — looking back, but of course, any historical tour is retrospective, isn't it? We are always making meaning of what we see in light of the fact that we know how the story ends. Or, at least, the canonical version of the story. Ultimately, I discover, this tour is a mixture of horror and sadness, hope and morality, determination and faith.

We start our tour at the end, in a room labeled "Genocide." A sign asks us to "Remember;" "Hall of Remembrance," a sign signifies. "In honor of the liberators who saved our parents and grandparents," I read as I realize it's my grandparents and great-grandparents and other ancestors this could be referring to. I read from the wall a quote from Elie Wiesel, "For the dead and the living, we must bear witness."

I pause. From Genesis 4:10, a sign says, "What have you done? Hark, thy brother's blood cries out to me from the ground!" Giving voice to the dead. Why is this so important, I wonder.

I read: "Only guard yourself and guard your soul carefully, lest you forget the things your eyes saw, and lest these things depart your heart all the days of your life, and you shall make them known to your children, and to your children's children. Deuteronomy 4:9."

There's people's names around the outside of the walls and candles you can light. I read from Deuteronomy 30:19, "I call heaven and earth to witness this day: I have put before you life and death, blessing and curse. Choose life — that you and your offspring shall live."

We are here as witness to life. In the face of the most horrific of death narratives, we are here to choose life.

Clearly, the Holocaust Museum's stated purpose is to be a witness to the horrors and atrocities committed in the Nazi concentration camps (Sather-Wagstaff,

2011). What, specifically, are we here to witness? Cris recalls two memories from the museum:

> *The first is the shoe exhibit. A huge pile of shoes, taken off prisoners as they were led to the gas chambers. I stare at the shoes and imagine them being on a person's feet, imagine those feet leading people to their death, marching to their death. Millions of people killed – Jewish, disabled, homosexual, marginalized, people rendered insignificant because of their different bodies; thousands of shoes representing the most horrific of deaths. A sign next to the exhibit quotes Edward Morrow as saying, "one shoe, two shoes, a dozen shoes. Yes, but how can you describe several thousand shoes?" Shoes, a representation perhaps of forward movement, agency, ability, transformed into symbols of despair, impotence, and hopelessness. But shoes are also incredibly personal. Some Arab cultures throw shoes to signify the gravest of insults. Pope Francis, following Jesus's model, is televised humbling himself by washing people's feet. In the American South, and in parts of Asia, it is considered polite to remove your shoes before entering someone's home. Shoes don't just represent forward movement – they represent the basest and filthiest of our humanity; they also represent the most reverent of services and respect.*
>
> *My next memory from the museum is an exhibit telling the stories from survivors, in their own words. We hear their own voices, resurrected, remembering and telling. One story in particular stands out: This is a story of how the Jews sang songs as they were marched to the gas chambers. Popular knowledge tells us that the Jews thought they were lining up to take showers as they were led to their death. But I learn from this story that the Jews knew what was going on. They saw people going in and bodies being carried out. They smelled the noxious gas, tasted death, felt the horror in their bodies. Yet, they sang. In the face of powerlessness, they resisted through the only agency that remained – through their voices. They sang of their faith, and they sang in defiance. They sang songs of hope and faith. They sang to celebrate God and they sang to affirm the very faith they were dying for. They marched naked and barefoot to their death, in full awareness of their fate, but they sang to hold onto the final aspect of their identities that could not be stripped from them – their voice and their faith.*

The Holocaust Museum's witnessing is tactile and sensory, constructed to be seen, heard, touched, and felt (Sather-Wagstaff, 2011). The Holocaust narrative touches our hearts because it is first embodied through our senses. Certainly, each person walking through the museum projects his/her own standpoints and therefore interpretations into the exhibits (Young 1993), and while each tourist does not have the personal experience of a Jewish heritage, the Holocaust Museum is significant to our country's understanding of ourselves, even though it is a museum of another country's history. It's important to U.S. history because so many of the survivors of the Holocaust came over to this country at the end of World War II, and therefore so many people in the U.S. today are descendants of those who died in the Holocaust. It is also important because, as the exhibit points out, if the U.S. had been willing to enter the war effort earlier, we might have been able to prevent the Nazi atrocities. Finally, it is important to our history because the Holocaust serves as moral justification for our inclusion and enactment in World War II. The Holocaust Museum serves as a counter narrative to hegemony – this is a monument to power and racism gone wrong, and its message is that if people don't understand what it stands for, this will happen again, and again. Culturally, the Holocaust, Nazism, and Hitler, have great meaning in our culture. These are terms frequently evoked politically and carry great meaning and significance for our country. The Holocaust Museum, and the Holocaust narrative, represents this country's collective moral shame and disappointment juxtaposed with our message of victory, salvation, and American exceptionalism. The Holocaust itself has become a meme, and evoking the Holocaust provides justification for entering into any armed conflict around the globe. In fact, when both authors were children, as we participated in atomic bomb drills after viewing old newsreels of World War II, the stories at school of the Cold War and the Holocaust became so intertwined, we expected that any day the Russians would take over the U.S. and put us into concentration death camps.

World War II Veteran's Memorial and the National Mall

You find the World War II Veteran's Memorial fairly easily. It is one of the "official" memorials on the National Mall, a park in downtown Washington, D.C., bordered by the Capitol at one end, the Lincoln Memorial at the other, and the Washington Monument in the middle. A Reflecting Pool in the center stretches from the Lincoln Memorial to the World War II Veteran's Memorial and is flanked by the D.C. War Memorial for World War I, the Korean War Memorial, the Vietnam Veteran's Memorial, and the Declaration of Independence Memorial. The most well-known monuments and memorials in the area of the National Mall also include the Thomas Jefferson Memorial, the Martin Luther King Jr. Memorial, and the Franklin Delano Roosevelt Memorial.

We stroll down Constitution Avenue along the National Mall and look at the Washington Monument in the distance. I notice how the monuments that make up the mall – the Washington Monument, Lincoln Memorial, World War II Memorial, are living monuments, in the middle of a D.C. bustling with traffic, joggers, congestion, and construction. We dodge a tour bus and a group of tourists streaming by.

On this tourist trip, we've been doing a lot of walking and my feet are tired. We take a break and sit on the grassy field. I notice half-dried dandelions in the grass. The mall is a pretty grassy area with sidewalks and traffic and commuters. Bicyclists, joggers, and picnickers surround us.

The Washington Monument is circled by American flags. I read:

The Washington Monument was completed by the U.S. Army Corp. of engineer in 1884. It honors George Washington for his generalship in the Revolutionary War and for his later refusal to serve more than two terms as President of the United States.

We move to the World War II Memorial, a large oval shaped pool surrounded by uniformly sized and positioned granite structures and pillars in a semi-circular pattern. As we approach it, we see a small ceremony taking place at one end: white-haired men in military uniforms, folding chairs, and speeches, too far from us to hear or see details.

Tourists wander through the memorial and I stop to look at the pillars. There is a pillar for every U.S. state and territory. Each pillar has two bronze wreaths; I read one represents agriculture and the other, industry, each symbolizing that the states sacrificed their citizens, resources, and labor to the war effort, and engraved with the name of each state or territory. Gold stars signify the number of Americans dead or wounded from the war. I read there are 4,048 gold stars with each one representing 100 American military deaths, signifying over 400,000 lives lost, or one out of every 40 people enlisted. I read, "Here we mark the price of freedom."

Groups of school children in gold and blue uniforms gather in front of the pool for photo-taking. A fountain shoots up behind them. I move to look closer at a larger pillar and read: "Americans came to liberate not to conquer, to restore freedom, and to end tyranny." Interesting social construction, I think, to justify the juxtaposition of a peaceful nation with military power. We hold military power but use it reluctantly and only to achieve certain national ideals.

Bas-relief of war scenes line the outer ring of the pond. Men rushing into battle, rifles drawn. Men buried, helmets atop their rifle sticking up from the ground. Men looking down sadly at a fallen comrade.

I read a sign in front of the fountains: "Please respect the memorial. No wading. No coins," and my glance moves to the words of Admiral Chester Nimitz: "They fought together as brothers-in-arms. They died together and now they sleep side by side. To them we have a solemn obligation."

All around the mall, there are signs that say, "Please respect your national monuments."

This is a place of reflection, a "rhetoric of reverence" (Dickinson et al., 2006, p. 28). The notion of the reflecting pool and the reflecting memorial seems important. The mall, centered by "the reflecting pool," is bounded by all of these memorials. This is a place where humans come to reflect, where the place quite literally reflects yourself back at you, reflects the memorials back at you, and you are in these images. These places of reflection reflect monuments that reflect the human consumer and the human condition, reflecting multiple identities and ways of being with the reflection of yourself inside them. Quite literally, you can "see yourself" in the memorial. Even off the wall, the presence of water facilitates reflecting.

Balthrop et al., (2010) argue that the World War II Memorial inscribes a reaffirmation of imperialism, "hijacking" (p. 194) the past to make hegemonic arguments for the present. The agenda, contends Behuniak (2012) is to construct the idea of a heroic death to fit in with an American nationalist trope to make a case for a justification of war. This memorial, constructed around the idea of victory and military might rather than individual suffering or loss, valorized war in general and this war specifically (Biesecker, 2009) and "discourage[d] a questioning of war and instead pose[d] an explicit threat of future warfare by showcasing military superiority" (Behuniak, 2012, p. 178).

Korean War Veteran's Memorial

The first thing you see at the Korean War Memorial is the ghostly figures, pewter gray, life-sized and life-like statues of men in various action war poses. It is almost as if you are walking through a combat zone. The faces are almost recognizable, your brother, next-door neighbor, father, everyman. Frozen in their jungle ponchos, packs on their backs, rifles in arms, marching, leaning forward, straining, fighting, frozen in time. Shaded in trees and brush, straining toward an American flag.

I stand there taking this in, imagining myself in the midst, wondering who these men were, who they loved, how they died. Then I move to the wall. Polished black marble covered in chalk-white faces, bodies, ghosts moving toward me, pulling me in, marching, frozen in time, begging for release.

Reflections of reflections, reflecting us, reflecting national identity, reflecting me through the images. Visitors gasp when they enter the memorial, and they don't linger long. This memorial is a place of movement, remembering while passing through, the bodies too haunting to hold you back, too frozen to keep you still. This is a memorial in which the memories are too alive, too ghostly, to do anything but move away. There is no touching or etching; this is a monument to move past, avert one's eyes, stand at a distance. There is one lone wreath, a 1964 gift from the students at Seoul National University, "We remember you forever, with people of the Republic of Korea."

There is no transcendent virtue here; this is a monument to people who died while chasing a flag, marching through the jungle, are still marching, to hunt down an enemy that turned out to be ourselves. Frozen in time and place. This memorial is a testament to a country that is frozen between nationalist grief and love of flag. This is a monument to the ambivalence toward war in a country for whom over half of the budget is war funding, a country that venerates guns but grieves violence.

Martin Luther King, Jr. Memorial

The Martin Luther King, Jr. Memorial is a short walk from the National Mall. It's flanked by Independence Avenue on the north and the Tidal Basin, a picturesque reservoir created from the Potomac River, on the south. Lined with cherry trees, and bordered on its west side by three memorials – the Martin Luther King Jr. Memorial, the Thomas Jefferson Memorial, and the Franklin Delano Roosevelt Memorial – the Tidal Basin itself is a major D.C. attraction. When you approach the King Memorial, the first thing you see is a 30-foot-high granite mountain halved down the middle. As you walk through the opening in the mountain, you see another large stone, as if carved out of this space, and you see imprinted on the stone the words "Out of the mountain of despair, a stone of hope," reference to Dr. King's 1963 "I Have a Dream Speech." (March on Washington for Jobs and Freedom, August 28, 1963). Past the stone of hope, you see the deep blue water of the Tidal Basin, blue sky and white clouds, and, of course, groups of tourists milling about. On a second look across the water, you see the Jefferson Memorial in the distance. Once you've passed through the granite, you see a semi-circle black granite wall engraved with quotations from King's speeches. Before you read them, you turn around and look at the other side of the stone of hope. It is a 30-foot-high statue of King, emerging from the mountain and facing the water. Dressed in a suit and tie, and with no lower limbs or feet (his legs dissolve into the granite base), the granite King has a reflective look on his face and his arms folded in front of him. In one hand he is holding what sculptor Master Lei Yixin says is his "rolled up Dream speech" (O'Toole, 2011, para 7).

Darkness cannot drive out darkness, only light can do that. Hate cannot drive out hate, only love can do that. (March on Washington for Jobs and Freedom, August 28, 1963).

The quotes on the walls, identified by the location and date of the speech quoted, promote "a world perspective," opposition to the Vietnam War (espousing instead that the U.S. be a "moral example of the world"), equal rights, unconditional love, and justice, among others.

We shall overcome because the arc of the moral universe is long but it bends toward justice.

Several impressions stand out in the Martin Luther King Jr. Memorial. There is no mention of his assassination; no mention of his personal life, family, or biography; no mention of his ministry, activism or marches; and no mention of his Nobel Peace Prize, Presidential Medal of Freedom, or Congressional Gold Medal. In the memorial, King emerges not as a normal, mortal man, but as a larger than life figure literally emerging from the mountain of despair into a solid, unyielding, stone of hope. With no feet or legs, this King is not grounded, but superhuman. This King is rock-solid and looming, reflective but strong and unyielding. This is not a man felled by a bullet and the hope inspired by this superman is itself larger than life. The hope emanating from King's stone is ascribed to his words, immortalized around the wall. King looks over the water, toward the Jefferson Memorial, back to the Lincoln Memorial. His hope is grounded in the very history of our country, but it is also forward looking, never despairing, unwavering. King has transcended death – dying as a broken, wounded body, resurrecting unyielding from the stone, his voice forever alive, hope forever on offer.

In this memorial, what's worth dying for are principles of justice, love, hope, and morality. What's reified is vision, grounded in a historical foundation of those very principles; and the principle of free speech that constructs hope for all people.

9/11 Pentagon Memorial

> To get to the 9/11 Pentagon Memorial, you have to get to the Pentagon, either by car or subway. You have to walk across the Pentagon office building parking lot to get to the far side of the Pentagon for the memorial after going through multiple metal detectors and security zones.
>
> The day I go, it is a freezing cold, windy day. I walk across a nondescript parking lot; the same parking lot the Pentagon workers use. The wind whips at me while I walk. After walking what seems like too far, I finally find the memorial, a small plot of land behind a fence on the far side of the Pentagon. I see the two-toned bricks on the multi-storied south wall of the Pentagon, replacement bricks for the ones destroyed in the 9/11 attack; arguably the most tangible reminder here of the reason for the memorial.
>
> Walking across the stone pave way, I spy a plaque.

On September 11th, 2001, acts of terrorism took the lives of thousands at the World Trade Center in New York City, in a grassy field in Shanksville, Pennsylvania, and here at the Pentagon. We will forever remember the loved ones, friends, and colleagues.

> The plaque lists the names and birthdates of the people killed here in this terrorist act, both those working in their offices when the plane hit, as well as those in the plane used for a human bomb.
>
> The setting is a concrete park. There's a stone walkway, a short stone wall, and concrete ground covering. Nothing particularly pretty. Throughout the concrete are trees emerging through holes. I see a short concrete wall with plants, and then a treed area. A sign says, "September 11th 2001, 9:37 a.m.," memorializing the exact time of the attack.
>
> I continue walking and come upon an area covered in gravel. Trees again peek out. Odd-shaped objects are lined in rows, made of marble, with ponds of water

underneath. At first, I think they look like diving boards then I think they are representative of airplane wings. Wings, I think, like the plane that killed them, like angels. Wings to let them fly away.

I later find out they are simply benches. On each bench is carved a name with one date: a year of birth. I remember they all have the same date of death. The benches face multiple directions; I later learn the benches representing the people who were killed inside the Pentagon are facing the Pentagon and the benches representing the people killed in the plane are facing the direction from which the plane came. They remind me of canopies over tiny rectangular ponds of water, engraved with name after name after name.

Kris Romeo Bishundat. Sandra D. Teague. Sergeant Tamara C. Thurman, U.S.A. LCDR David L. Williams, U.S.N.

I realize these are names of military personnel working at the Pentagon who died in the attack. I wonder about the irony of people who returned to a desk job from a combat zone to die at their desks.

I continue walking down a concrete pathway past the memorial benches and I come upon a garden of lush flowers and plants. A concrete wall separates the garden from the benches. On my left side is the highway and between me and the highway is a grapevine. Someday, I think, the grapevine will camouflage the highway. Today, the highway is quite visible. At the end of the five foot concrete wall is a security gate. A sign proclaims:

We claim this ground in remembrance of the events of September 11th, 2001. To honor 184 people whose lives were lost, their families, and all who sacrificed so we may live in freedom. We will never forget.

We note the interesting use of the term "sacrifice." Sacrilization requires sacrifice; does sacrifice require agency? Does being a victim in a terrorist slaughter of innocent people equate with sacrifice? The obvious attempt to reframe a terrorist action into something meaningfully patriotic is striking. We also note the claims of freedom. The people killed here were not killed for their faith or fighting for freedom. They were killed while living their ordinary day-to-day lives, flying on business trips or vacation adventures, sitting at their desks pushing paper and returning emails. They were killed for living ordinary lives. If their deaths were sacrifices, we are all at war.

We also note the injunction to "never forget," and wonder what it is, specifically, we are supposed to not forget. This notion of never forgetting is quite interesting. It's invoked in all the memorials.

There's an American flag flying in the distance. Security here is heavy. There is a metro station next to the Pentagon; it is surrounded by thick bulletproof glass. I read numerous signs proclaiming "Restricted area," "No pictures here," "Do not walk here," Don't go here."

In the face of fear, we are held back. What did they sacrifice for if we are still afraid to walk freely?

Arlington National Cemetery

> To get to Arlington National Cemetery, you have to cross the Memorial Bridge from Washington, D.C. to Arlington, Virginia. You can go by car, metro, or bus. When you approach the cemetery, you see large stone pillars and ornate black iron gates marking the entrance. The pillars are topped by stone eagles who seem to be watching over the cemetery.
>
> I enter the cemetery and walk down the asphalt path. As far as the eye can see – crosses. Small, white crosses against what is often brilliant green grass – grass that speaks of good grooming. I watch the tight, trim Marine stand guard. As far as the eye can see – chairs – small, gray chairs. Sometimes, I see a person – sitting on a bench having lunch, kneeling by a gravesite, touching the white cross, the gray chair. As I watch the dappled sunlight reflect the trees by the pond, I'm not angry, or outraged, or displaced, or proud. I am sad. And I think to myself, this would be a beautiful place to be buried.

At Arlington National Cemetery, there are over 400,000 marked gravesites, nearly 5,000 unknown soldiers, and over 20 specific memorials that tell the story of our nation through wars and death. The cemetery includes memorials and monuments from the Civil War; the remains of the crew of the Space Shuttle Challenger; President John F. Kennedy and his wife Jacqueline and Senators Robert F. and Edward M. Kennedy; and memorials that document most of our nation's military theaters since then – from the Argonne Cross to the Beirut Barracks Memorial.

> "The primary mission of Arlington National Cemetery is to function as the nation's premier military cemetery and shrine honoring those men and women who served in the Armed Forces," I read (http://www.arlingtoncemetery.mil/about). It's an active cemetery; with approximately 30 funeral services conducted each week, it's a cemetery and a shrine; a graveyard and a memorial. "Our nation's most hallowed ground" (http://www.arlingtoncemetery.mil/Funerals/About-Funerals, para 1); it is a long travel narrative of trenches and blood where now one might find fertile fields, preserved parks, and brilliant green grass. It is also, I read, a place to "Honor, Remember, Explore" (http://www.arlingtoncemetery.mil/News/Press-Room/News-Releases/Post/2103/Arlington-National-Cemetery-s-award-winning-app-reaches-30k-downloads, para 3), and each of these purposes are clearly delineated on Arlington's very well-organized website – www.arlingtoncemetery.mil. The appropriateness of its website's. mil handle is evident. These are necessary and justified deaths. It is both a national memorial and a popular tourist site.

John F. Kennedy made his first formal visit to Arlington National Cemetery on Armistice Day, Nov. 11, 1961, to place a wreath at the Tomb of the Unknown Soldier. At the conclusion of the ceremony President Kennedy spoke to more than 5,000 people gathered in the Memorial Amphitheater. President Kennedy's address began:

> *We meet in quiet commemoration of a historic day of peace. In an age that threatens the survival of freedom, we join together to honor those who made our freedom possible …. It is a tragic fact, that war still more destructive and still sanguinary followed [World War II]; that man's capacity to devise new ways of killing his fellow men have far outstripped his capacity to live in peace with his fellow man [sic].*
>
> *"Historic footage of …", para 2*

Spaces for Memory

Sturken (1997) suggests that cultural memory derives its meaning in its consumption; similarly, Behuniak (2012) asserts:

> *The timing, geography, and design of monuments become meaningful only with the interaction of the human beings who view them, walk through them, and use their senses to fully experience them … therefore, any analysis of monuments must include the interplay between these structures and people*
>
> *p. 174*

While these various monuments, memorials, and museums appear disparate, Sturken (1997) reminds us that "memories accumulate" (p. 4) and are constructed collectively. Monuments, memorials, and museums in and around our nation's capital, and in support of our nationalist history, construct a nationalist "ideological agenda" (Biesecker, 2009, p. 403), a justification of "what's worth dying for" in our national conscience – to convince people to continue to fight wars, to tie that rhetorical message tightly to patriotism so that to question "what's worth dying for" becomes treasonous; to enable you to look a victim's family members in the eyes and tell them their loved one's death mattered, even if it is a pretense, even if in the next war our last war's enemies become our allies. We construct memorials to ease our collective guilt for sending our sons and daughters to their deaths for a myriad of reasons. Cloaking sanctioned killing in patriotism justifies it; elevating crime victims – victims of murder, terrorism, hate crimes, and genocide – in heroism soothes the national collective grief and puts a band-aid on national racism, greed, and hatred. National mythologies of sacrifice, if examined too closely, seems more like myths, but that's one of the most effective ways to manufacture consent.

Commemorative sites of national martyrs serve multiple purposes, including honoring the dead through public memorialization, preserving historical memory, and healing the memory of traumatic events (Barsalou & Baxter, 2007; Blair & Michel, 2007). There is something to be said for the solace these places bring the people who lost loved ones, the measure of solace that comes from posting a dream, finding a grave, etching a fallen comrade's name, or placing a crumpled up note into an opening in a chain link fence. As in any cemetery, however, the deceased, and the place, become bigger than the death. Heroic death tropes – tied to successful warfare – intertwine with tropes of tragic death – "without purpose or meaning" (Behuniak, 2012, p. 166) to bridge the personal and the political, and provide a presence to foster a relationship between the living and the dead (Behuniak, 2012).

We note how all of these monuments, museums, and memorials are sensory experiences; all have an interactive nature that call out to be touched, smelled, seen, their materiality cannot be separated from their experiential reality. Their locations are significant – the outdoor spaces of the monuments and memorials open them to the public, to the passer-by, to the casual eye as well as a more intense gaze. It is this visuality of the spaces that adds to their impact, and, we argue, there is a difference between the impact of a monument on the National Mall and one in the parking lot of an office building. The National Mall and Arlington Cemetery open spaces that open a space for memory – a keeping alive of history, a moving of the past into the present, a movement forward. These are places of serenity and remembrance, of a new birth of our nation; commemoration of times, places, and people long gone but yet living places where people still visit. In contrast, the Pentagon memorial in its parking lot freezes a moment of our nation's tragedy and it takes us into our past, a movement backwards. The Holocaust Museum is inside, hidden, and dark. In some ways, it recreates the experience we are asked to remember. It is the juxtaposition of these memories – World War II with Vietnam and 9/11, the Holocaust with the Korean War and Martin Luther King, that take us on a time travel of our national identity, a movement through and past consent and opposition; national narratives and experiences; multi-voiced and polysemic; constructed, reconstructed, and multi-constructed; living monuments to a country alive with potential and possibility. Certainly, the meaning of all of these commemorative sites is symbolic, and, we suggest, it is through a process of sacrilization and enshrinement in which we make our national objects sacred through a tourist ritual. Death makes everything seem more significant, and we sanctify anything that reminds of our dead loved ones. This is true for our country as well. Because these sites commemorate our nation's dead, they symbolize for us our nation's life.

The Martin Luther King Jr. Monument, in contrast, is not a monument to widespread or multiple deaths, but to one person who embodies an ideal. What are the ideals these monuments, memorials, and museums reify? What are the ideals worth dying for? The ideals commemorated at Arlington National Cemetery may seem varied, but everyone buried there is commemorated for giving the ultimate service to our nation in the name of "freedom." Wars are always fought for freedom, but freedom from what? Freedom from enslavement, or freedom to enslave others? All the deaths commemorated in the monuments, memorials, and museums, matter to the national mythology of sacrifice that keeps Americans supporting wars near and far. Empire building, and empire destroying, is a deadly business.

In their entirety, our nation's war memorials necessarily reflect our national ambivalence toward war, nationalism, and national pride. Our earlier wars through World War II were generally perceived to be worthwhile and victorious; subsequent wars and conflicts have different perceptions (Iles, 2006). Our monuments and memorials reflect these changing constructs. These are all places of remembrance, witness, and memory. This is how these sites differ from traditional (non-national) cemeteries in that they call us to witness to sacrifice and tragedy, and they frame our national struggles as juxtapositions against violence, some justifying it, some acquiescing to it, some resisting it.

Spaces that Transcend Death

All of these monuments, memorials, and museums allow us as a nation to transcend death – to discover what's worth dying for, to discover pride in loss, victory in death, a transcendence of hate, an overcoming of fear. Some are monuments to hegemony; others are monuments to resistance, but all these commemorative sites give us as Americans the ability to move beyond death; beyond the ghostly, horrifying, and sad losses of war and violence, and find nationalist meaning in death. Through the deaths of our loved ones, neighbors, and fellow Americans, we find our national identity; we discover what's worth dying for, and, therefore, what's worth living for. Our is an identity of freedom, and in our national ambivalence toward war and violence, this is an identity that frees us from rigid adherence to ideology. It is an identity that seems unfettered and uncontaminated and achievable.

Conclusion

We suggest this array of museums, monuments, and memorials in and around Washington, D.C. commemorating the dead represent the United States' national mythographies of sacrifice. Sacrifice, by definition, implies the willingness to give up something of value (e.g., one's life) in exchange for something of more value: God, country, freedom, faith, equality. This raises the question – are all deaths sacrificial? It's not as if these soldiers, activists, victims, had a choice in dying. Frankly, none of us have a *choice* in dying – we will all die, sometimes randomly, sometimes capriciously, sometimes slowly, sometimes swiftly. What we occasionally are blessed with is the ability to increase the probability of dying in a certain place or time. Our greatest agency is in having a hand in contributing to the meaning that is made of our death by the way we live our lives. For all of these dead, the meaning of their deaths is ultimately beyond their control; their countries, faiths, and cultures have co-opted their deaths to make statements of belonging, believing, and behaving. Nationalist ideologies move us from an individualized view of death – a view tinted by grief, loss, meaninglessness, and lack of agency – into heroic acts that bound the dead and the grieving with the rest of society, which transform a tragedy into something more positive (Seale, 1998). Suggests Seale:

> At the heart of the nationalist mythology is death, represented in the Tomb of the Unknown Soldier …. Ordinary people come to feel that their lives are a part of some greater whole, that will live on after their deaths, and for which it is worthwhile, and indeed heroic under certain circumstances, to die. The paradoxical embrace of death in the interests of the life of the imagined community, character-istic of the martyr, is invoked in nationalist mythologies of sacrifice …. Dying for one's nation can be understood as a type of masochistic surrender … an absorp-tion of the personal trajectory into some far greater and magnificent whole, indeed a transcendence of the basic human problem of being alone. The guarantee of remembrance by those left behind is a further compensation for such a death, and memorials are duly constructed that show the living that this will occur.
>
> Seale, 1998, pp. 55–56.

References

Aden, R. C. (2012). When memories and discourses collide: The president's house and places of public memory. Communication Monographs, 79(1), 72–92.

Balthrop, V. W., Blair, C., & Michel, N. (2010). The presence of the present: Hijacking "The Good War"? Western Journal of Communication, 74(2), 170–207.

Barsalou, J., & Baxter, V. (2007 January). The urge to remember: The role of memorials in social reconstruction and transitional justice. United States Institute of Peace, Stabiliza-tion and Reconstruction Series No. 5.

Behuniak, S. M. (2012). Heroic death and selective memory: The US's WWII Memorial and the USSR's Monument to the Heroic Defenders of Leningrad. At the Interface/ Probing the Boundaries, 82, 165–207.

Berger, A. A. (2013). Theorizing tourism: Analyzing iconic destinations. Walnut Creek, CA: Left Coast Press.

Bergman, T. (2013). Exhibiting patriotism: Creating and contesting interpretations of American historic sites. Walnut Creek, CA: Left Coast Press.

Biesecker, B. A. (2009). Remembering World War II: The rhetoric and politics of national commemoration at the turn of the 21st century. Quarterly Journal of Speech, 88(4), 393–409.

Blair, C., Dickinson, G., & Ott, B. L. (2010). Introduction: Rhetoric/memory/place. In Dickinson, G., Blair, C., Ott, B. L. (Eds.) Places of public memory. pp. 1–54. Tuscaloosa, AL: The University of Alabama Press.

Blair, C., Jeppeson, M. S., & Pucci, E. Jr., (1991). Public memorialization in postmodernity: The Vietnam Veterans Memorial as prototype. Quarterly Journal of Speech, 77, 263–288.

Blair, C., & Michel, N. (2007). The AIDS memorial quilt and the contemporary culture of public commemoration. Rhetoric and Public Affairs, 10(4), 595–626.

Bruner, E. M. (2005), Culture on Tour: Ethnographies of Travel, Chicago, IL: University of Chicago.

de Certeau, M., Giard, L., & Mayol, P. (1998). The practice of everyday life. Volume 2: Living & cooking. Giard, L. (Ed.), Trans. by Tomasik. T. J. Minneapolis, MN: University of Minnesota Press.

Dickinson, G., Ott, B. L. & Aoki, E. (2006). Spaces of remembering and forgetting: The reverent eye/I at the Plains Indian Museum. Communication and Critical/Cultural Studies, 3(1), 27–47.

Foote, K. E. (1997). Shadowed ground: America's landscapes of violence and tragedy. Austin, TX: University of Texas Press.

Foucault, M. (1972). The Archaeology of Knowledge. Trans. by Sheridan Smith, A. M. New York, NY: Harber.

Foucault, M. (1980). Power/Knowledge: Selected interviews and other writings, 1972–1977. Gordon, C. (Ed.), Trans. by Gordon, C., Marshall, L., Mepham, J., & Soper, K. New York, NY: Pantheon.

"Historic footage of JFK's funeral." U.S. Department of Defense. Retrieved from: https://www.defense.gov/News/Special-Reports/Remembering-September-11th-2017/Videos/videoid/374571/?dvpTag=John%20F%20Kennedy#DVIDSVideoPlayer6792

Iles, J. (2006). Recalling the ghosts of war: Performing tourism on the battlefields of the Western Front. Text and Performance Quarterly, 26(2), 162–180. doi: 10.1080/10462930500519374.

Katriel, T. (1993). Our future is where our past is: Studying heritage museums as ideological and performative arenas. Communication Monographs, 60, 69–75.

Kirshenblatt-Gimblett, B. (1991). Objects of ethnography. In Karp, I., & LaVine, S. (Eds.), Exhibiting Cultures: The Poetics and Politics of Museum Display. pp. 386–443, Washington, D.C.: Smithsonian.

Klaassens, M., & Bijlsma, M. J. (2014). New places of remembrance: Individual web memorials in the Netherlands. Death Studies, 38(5), 283–293. doi: 10.1080/07481187.2012.742474.

Miller, J. B. (2005). Coyote's tale on the Old Oregon Trail: Challenging cultural memory through narrative at the Tamastslikt Cultural Institute. Text and Performance Quarterly, 25(3), 220–238. doi: 10.1080/10462930500271786.

Neimeyer, R. A., Prigerson, H. G., & Davies, B. (2002). Mourning and meaning. American Behavioral Scientist, 46(2), 235–251. doi: 10.1177/000276402236676.

O'Toole, M. (2011 August 22). Martin Luther King memorial unveiled on National Mall. Reuters. Retrieved from: https://www.reuters.com/article/us-king-memorial/martin-luther-king-memorial-unveiled-on-national-mall-idUSTRE77L5HJ20110822

Pollock, D. (Ed.) (1998). Exceptional spaces: Essays in performance and history. Chapel Hill, NC: University of North Carolina Press.

Roach, J. (1996). Introduction, history, memory and performance. In Roach, J. (Ed.), Cities of the dead: Circum-Atlantic Performance. pp. 1–31. New York, NY: Columbia University Press.

Sather-Wagstaff, J. (2011). Heritage that hurts: Tourists in the memoryscapes of September 11. Walnut Creek, CA: Left Coast Press.

Seale, C. (1998). Constructing death: The sociology of dying and bereavement. Cambridge, UK: Cambridge University Press.

Shaffer, T. S. (2004), Performing backpacking: Constructing "authenticity" every step of the way. Text and Performance Quarterly, 24(2), 139–160. doi: 10.1080/10462930 4200288362.

Sturken, M. (1991). The wall, the screen, and the image: The Vietnam Veterans Memorial. Representations, 35(summer), 118–142.

Sturken, M. (1997). Tangled memories: The Vietnam War, the AIDS epidemic, and the politics of remembering. Berkeley and Los Angeles, CA: University of California Press.

Taylor, W. (2014). Everyday war memorials to the end of all wars: Building cemeteries and collecting war trophies in a culture of commemoration. Southerly, 74(1), 105–126.

Wallace, M. (1981). Visiting the past: History museums in the United States. Radical History Review, 25, 63–96.

Young, J. E. (1993). The texture of memory: Holocaust memorials and meaning. New Haven, CT: Yale University Press.

EPILOGUE: REVELATION COMMUNICATING TO TRANSCEND DEATH

"Look, Cris!" Deb points to an area near the river that borders Kingston Cemetery. Here, emerald green, perfectly mowed grass is enclosed by a three-inch-tall red brick boundary. At a much lower elevation than the rest of the cemetery, small steps lead down to an area of beautifully carved monuments and memorials shaded by huge live oak trees. Some monuments are still porcelain white; others have mold or rust from wet leaves on them. Some have glassed-in cases; others are all marble. Lambs, angels, and in many cases, infants, are carved into the tops of the glass cases or the bottoms of the marble pedestals. "Oh, I bet this is the Beaty cemetery," Deb murmurs.

Cris, busily snapping photos with her cell phone, puts the cell phone in her bag and says, "What? Who?"

"The Beaty's," Deb replies. "They're one of the oldest Conway families. One of the stories goes that during the 'Northern occupation' of Conway during the Civil War, the union forces were cutting down all of the live oaks in town because they needed the wood. When the union soldiers came to cut the trees in front of the Beaty house down, old Mrs. Beaty, Mary Beaty, one of the matriarchs of the family, came out carrying a shot gun, stood in front of the trees, and said, 'If y'all are going to take this tree down, you're going to have to take me down with it.' The union soldiers weren't sure how to proceed, so they decided to go back to their headquarters, get some advice, and come back the next day. She got all the women in town together – most of the men, including her husband, were on the front lines fighting – and the next day all of the women in town stood in front of the live oak trees with their shot guns. The union soldiers decided they didn't want to risk multiple casualties or a riot, so they left all the trees."

Cris chuckles. "Sounds like a strong woman!"

Deb nods. "One of the versions of the stories says it happened after the war when folks were trying to build the railroad here, but I've always heard the 'standin' up to the soldiers' version, which I think really resonates in this small southern town."

Cris laughs again, then her brow furrows. She looks puzzled. "But why are all these baby tombs here?"

"Oh, that's another great story!" Deb sits down on the brick and begins to tell the story. "Mary Beaty came to the area to teach school in what is now Bucksport in the mid-1800s. She was Mary Brookman then. In 1851 she married Thomas Wilson Beaty, a member of one of Kingston's, now Conway's, original pioneer families. They had five children together, and all of them died young, all horribly. They had four daughters; two of them died as babies from diphtheria. The other two daughters drowned in Kingston Lake behind their home, despite frantic efforts to save them. Their only son, and youngest child, Brookie, died under mysterious circumstances. He had been sick, and Mary was sewing downstairs in their parlor, listening carefully in case he called. All of a sudden, she heard beautiful music, looked up from her needlepoint, and her four dead daughters were standing before her, appearing as angels. Abruptly, the beautiful music soured, and Mary asked the angels why. They replied that they had come for their brother, little Brookie. Mary rushed upstairs to the nursery, and found Brookie dead."

"Oh my God!" Cris exclaims. "That is horrifying! So sad!"

Deb nods. "Yeah, most everyone in town believes it, because Mary Beaty herself told the tale pretty much to anyone who would listen up until the day she died. The whole family's buried here in what's called 'The Beaty Burial Ground.' She even had a famous sculptor, Hiram Powers, carve the girls' tombstone – that's the one encased in glass (Horry County Historical Society, 2014; Langston, 1967; Warwick, 1986)."

"So the cemetery is full of ghost stories!" Cris marvels. "I guess most ghost stories have cemeteries in them, and most cemeteries are full of ghost stories."

"Deaths in the past really do have meaning in the present, don't they?" Deb responds.

Cris and Deb continue walking, and approach an area of the cemetery that is fenced in. Wrought iron and intricately carved, the black fence encloses a yard full of graves, most marked with the Knights Templar cross and/or Confederate flags. Cris reads a plaque in front of the black gate. "Oh!" She turns to Deb and begins rummaging for her camera. "This is the graveyard of the veterans of the Civil War. The Daughters of the Confederacy erected and maintains this section!" She begins to snap pictures. Many of the graves are marked with obelisks. Many of them have the Confederate star on them. Confederate flags wave in the fall breeze.

"These are all graves of men who fought for the Confederacy," Cris comments, picking through the crooked gravestones. Most of the graves have fresh arrangements. The graveyard is spotless, devoid of the fallen brown leaves, magnolia tree cones, and other debris that characterizes Kingston Cemetery. "It's clear that people take care of this section." Cris looks up from her camera. "Just as in life," she says. "Even our deaths are rife with cultural norms, collectivities, absences, presences. Even our deaths are full of life and love, battles and defeats, contests of will and contests of culture." She lays her hand gently on one of the tombstones. "Even in death, we can't escape the choices we make in our lives."

And so it ends. Like all human stories, these stories must also end. Yet, like all human stories, we hope they might also endure. As we have observed throughout this journey, there is both an inevitability and a constancy to death. We will all die, and for all of us, our families, and our loved ones, that death will be our inescapable, penultimate act. However, death is ongoing, and even if we last into old age, our departures from this world will be preceded by many other deaths: the surrender of dreams, the loss of loved ones, the growing realization of the certainty of our demise, the unavoidability of biological changes and endings, the inexorableness of endings. We will suffer. We will grieve. We will experience many losses, and we will pine for people who are gone. Perhaps we will try to cheat death, clinging to the remnants of our lives. Some may try "transcending death through projects that make us immortal" (Chapter 1). We are, indeed, imperfect creatures seeking perfection through life and death; the rhetoric of perfection – alluded to in the first chapter of this book – powerfully and persuasively commands us. However, we argue throughout this book that the more we begin to experience death, the less afraid we are of it.

We echo *Apocalypse Now*'s famous anti-hero Colonel Kurtz, "Horror has a face ... and you must make a friend of horror. Horror and mortal terror are your friends. If they are not, then they are enemies to be feared" (Coppola, 1979). Our experiences throughout our lives are a kind of guidebook to death, helping us understand, accept, and prepare for our own endings. Some of these experiences include creating and/or consuming film, art, and music, which already saturate our daily lives as we watch and stream visual series and go to the movies, glance at graffiti on our commutes to and from work, and listen to and access music. We find ourselves fascinated by ghost stories, and often cheer for the "haunts" who, within their deaths, are trying to correct or avenge the wrongs they suffered in their lives. These all become dress rehearsals for us as we prepare for our deaths without even realizing we're doing it.

Death is a powerful rhetoric, and our fear of it persuades us to live well, to live to the fullest, to "dance like there's nobody watching, love like you'll never be hurt, sing like there's nobody listening, and live like it's heaven on earth" (Purkey, 2001). As we move through our ongoing death and dying, we begin to realize that our deaths – and lives – are not our own. They never were, but we often understand neither the wryness of plot nor the complexities of point of view until the end of a story. Death, like communication, is relational; it never occurs in a vacuum. The Other is as much a part of our deaths as they were during our lives. And death, like life, is a series of dialectical tensions – never solvable, only, we hope, manageable.

These are just a few of the reasons why we seek "a good death." We hope to cheat Death by allowing it the epilogue that we cannot keep it from writing on our behalf, but we want to deny Death its most defining characteristics other than its irrevocable finality: pain, suffering, horror. Similar to the longing of a patient who's been diagnosed with a terminal illness, we want the truth but we need hope. We want an end to the pain and suffering, but we often still do not want that end to be our death. There are all kinds of pain: physical, emotional, psychological, biological, professional, familial, phantom; the promise of hospice offers us some respite and refuge from pain, but like us, hospice is not immortal; it too will end, for us and like us, when we're gone. Like the good death so many of us want, we seek something we cannot have. It really is an oxymoron – a good death. Like so many aspects of death and dying, a series of dialectical tensions both constrain and enable us (Giddens, 1984). While the experience of death is indeed relational, it lacks the humanity of life. We can't accompany others all the way to the end. We can't die with them. It is relational, but not reciprocal, unlike the relationships that protect us through life. Those relationships cannot protect us from death, but they can ease its horror just a bit. We suggest that our quest for a good death is bound up in our active lives. We seek good lives; we hope those choices will bring good deaths.

Some of us will outlive most of our loved ones. The authors of this book are beginning to discover that, as, perhaps, you are. As we write these final words, it is fall in the southeast. Once green trees are shedding their leaves, and those leaves become orange and brown and yellow and red piles of organic matter, thick and matted, grouped on the ground like tombstones in a cemetery. Verdant forests are now bare trunks and stems. Stripped of all life, they are immersed in death, betting on spring, much like the Greek goddess Demeter, who is said to await her kidnapped daughter's release from death so that flora can bud, re-birth, and become alive again, even though those trees were never really dead to begin with. Demeter's hope is like our own; beliefs in an afterlife, or lives, infuse many of the social, cultural, spiritual, and religious rituals that surround our lives and inform our deaths. Hope runs laps with us as we rehearse our deaths. We are always living, and we are always dying.

Death casts a pall on life, but like the palls used in many death rituals, it too is dialectical. It covers, and it uncovers. It hides death and reveals life simultaneously. It is opaque; while it is not clear, we can squint our eyes and see through it. It is hazy. It is ephemeral. It is like our lives and our deaths. It is a bride, a redeemer, and a reckoning. Death and life both constrain us, but they both enable us as well. And those constraints, and that freedom, are situated within and yet also span race, gender, religion, class, social status, and familial origin. We will all live and die, but we will all live and die within and under the pall of standpoint, the cards that we've been dealt. And one of the strongest of those cards, in Tarot and in real life, is Death.

Our lives and deaths are also constrained by our nation. Death, like nationalism, is mythological. The sacrifices we make for our country are like the sacrifices we make to preserve our ways of life – beautiful, endearing, metaphorical – and yet often revocable. They are often revised through the years. Death, like war, will continue, will return, and will undoubtedly allow us to see the futility of our final battle – Death. Like St. Paul, we hope we "have fought the good fight … finished the race … [and] kept the faith" (Holy Bible, 2 Timothy 4:7). And that's really all we can hope for.

Death is our final social construction. It is our final meaning making activity as communicators within this world. It is the tally and the score. It is the last time we will see all that we loved, all that we made, all that we are. Like a bad novel, it will move us from present to past tense. But our social constructions of death allow it to be more than that. It is an ending, but it is also, perhaps, a beginning.

> This is the end, beautiful friend
> This is the end, my only friend, the end
> Of our elaborate plans, the end
> Of everything that stands, the end
> I'll never look into your eyes again.
> Can you picture what will be?
> So limitless and free
> Desperately in need of some stranger's hand
> In a desperate land …
> It hurts to set you free
> But you'll never follow me
> The end of laughter and soft lies
> The end of nights we tried to die
> This is the end
>
> *Densmore et al., 1967*

References

Coppola, F. (Producer). (1979). Apocalypse Now. [Motion Picture]. Available at https://www.youtube.com/watch?v=FAlARcNhQ3A

Densmore, J., Manzarek, R., Krieger, R., & Morrison, J. (1967). The End. [Recorded by The Doors]. On The Doors. Record. Los Angeles: Elektra.

Giddens, A. (1984). The constitution of society. Oakland, CA: University of California Press.

Holy Bible. (1973, 1978, 1984, 2011). 2 Timothy 4:7. (New International Version®). Biblica, Inc.®. Available at https://www.biblica.com/niv-bible/

Horry County Historical Society. (2014). Mary Elizabeth Brookman Beaty. Downloaded December 16, 2017 from http://www.hchsonline.org/bio/mebb.html.

Langston, M. Q. (1967, April). Mary Elizabeth Brookman Beaty. Independent Republic Quarterly, 3(2).

Purkey, W. W. (2001). "Dance like there's nobody watching …" Available at http://www.quoteland.com/author/William-W-Purkey-Quotes/1591/

Warwick, E. C. (1986, Fall). Mary Elizabeth Brookman Beaty. The Independent Republic Quarterly, 20(4), p. 13.

INDEX OF NAMES

INDEX OF TOPICS